PARTIAL MAGIC

PARTIAL MAGIC

The Novel as a Self-Conscious Genre

ROBERT ALTER

UNIVERSITY OF CALIFORNIA PRESS
Berkeley • Los Angeles • London

University of California Press
Berkeley and Los Angeles, California

University of California Press, Ltd.
London, England

Copyright © 1975, by
The Regents of the University of California

ISBN 0-520-02755-8
Library of Congress Catalog Card Number: 74-77725
Printed in the United States of America

FOR CAROL
*"in a green
airy space."*

Contents

All novels are self-conscious,
from *Don Quixote* to the newest
nouveau roman.

> Harry Levin, "From *Gusle*
> to Tape-Recorder"

That novels should be made of
words, and merely words, is
shocking, really. It's as if
you had discovered that your
wife were made of rubber: the
bliss of all those years, the
fears ... from sponge.

> William Gass, *Fiction and
> the Figures of Life*

Preface

A friend with whom I have shared gratifying exchanges on the central idea of this book since its first conception once teasingly suggested that I call it *The Other Great Tradition*. At this point, of course, such a polemic invocation of F. R. Leavis's *The Great Tradition* is hardly necessary, and in any case I would have been guilty of self-parody, my last published book having used the word "tradition" prominently in its title. Nevertheless, Leavis's one-track notion of a line of great English novelists in which only four writers are confidently included is worth pointing to here as an extreme, occasionally still detectable, symptom of more widespread assumptions about the novel that this study seeks to balance.

Especially within the sphere of English criticism of the novel, there has been a recurrent expectation that "serious" fiction be an intent, verisimilar representation of moral situations in their social contexts; and, with few exceptions, there has been a lamentable lack of critical appreciation for the kind of novel that expresses its seriousness through playfulness, that is acutely aware of itself as a mere structure of words even as it tries to discover ways of going beyond words to the experiences words seek to indicate. The fact that at least three of the supreme masterpieces of English fiction are supremely playful novels has not deterred the critical proponents of seriousness, as Leavis himself so clearly demonstrated when he casually dismissed Fielding, Sterne, and Joyce from his canon of the English novel. An analogous kind of monocular vision, moreover, has operated well beyond the realm of Anglo-American moral criticism. To cite a central instance: on the Continent, where explicitly Marxist and Marxist-influenced notions of the novel have continued to enjoy great currency, one still often encounters an insistence on the idea of the novel as "the epic of bourgeois life," its prime achievement conceived as the minutely circumstantial representation of changing social realities and how they impinge on individual existences. One could scarcely deny that both moral and social realism have been at the heart of many major manifestations of the novel in its checkered history of more than three and a half centuries. What I shall try to show through the chapters that follow is that in many important novelists from Renaissance Spain to contemporary France and America the realistic enterprise has been enormously complicated and qualified by the writer's awareness that fictions are never real things, that literary realism is a tantalizing contradiction in terms. If modern philosophy can be said to begin with Descartes's methodological skepticism, his making ontology essentially problematic, a whole tradition of the novel, as the paradigmatically modern narrative genre, is informed by that same critical-philosophical awareness, beginning almost half a century before Descartes with Cervantes. Ontological critique in the novel, moreover, is carried on typically not as discursive exposition but as a critical exploration through the technical manipulation of the very form that purports to represent reality. The discussions here of specific novels, therefore, will devote considerable space to the purposeful experiments with form undertaken by the novelists, experiments intended in various ways to draw our attention to fictional form as a consciously articulated entity rather than a transparent container of "real" contents.

A self-conscious novel, briefly, is a novel that systematically flaunts its own condition of artifice and that by so doing probes into the problematic relationship between real-seeming artifice and reality. I would lay equal stress on the ostentatious nature of the artifice and on the systematic operation of the flaunting. It is possible, of course, to have isolated pockets or fits and starts of fictional self-consciousness in a novel that is for the most part conventionally realistic, as I shall try to illustrate in some detail when I come to discuss the nineteenth-century novel. A fully self-conscious novel, however, is one in which from beginning to end, through the style, the handling of narrative viewpoint, the names and words imposed on the characters, the patterning of the narration, the nature of the characters and what befalls them, there is a consistent effort to convey to us a sense of the fictional world as an authorial construct set up against a background of literary tradition and convention.

The phenomenon of an artwork mirroring itself as it mirrors reality is of course by no means restricted to the novel; and in literature it could be traced back as far as the bard within the epic in the *Odyssey* and Euripides' parody of the conventions of Greek tragedy. Renaissance theater, to cite a central instance, offers many striking examples of such artistic self-consciousness: two of the most memorable for English readers are the Induction to *The Taming of the Shrew* and Ben Jonson's stage-keeper in *Bartholomew Fair*. Pirandello's self-conscious theater had abundant predecessors, including, by the way, the plays of a novelist represented in this study, Denis Diderot. And it goes without saying that the poem that explores and exposes itself as a structure of words has had a recurrent fascination for modern poets, from Mallarmé and Valéry in France, to Wallace Stevens in America, to Osip Mandelstam in Russia.

Nevertheless, it seems to me that there were strong elements in the historical setting of the novel, the conditions of its formal production, its relationship to earlier genres and even to the other arts, which made it uniquely congenial to this kind of self-consciousness, and which raised fictional self-consciousness to a distinctive generic trend. To be sure, there are visible lines of affinity between the operation of the self-reflexive mode in the novel and in other genres or in other media, but the manifestations of the mode are also in part determined by the formal limits of the genre and the medium. Artistic self-consciousness is bound to take on certain distinctive features in a form where the artist is free to manipulate, say, typography, narrative tempo, point of view, in an extended narrative structure in prose designed to be read silently by single readers in the privacy of their own armchairs. The case would be quite different for a self-conscious lyric poem or a self-conscious play.

Since the general subject is endless, it seemed reasonable to keep the focus strictly on the novel. What a novel may be is of course always open to some debate. In the discussions that follow, I mean to assume a pluralistic view of this bewilderingly capacious genre. To legislate a rigid set of defining terms would be precisely to deny the continuously and necessarily innovative nature of what Gide once described as the "lawless" genre. Some limiting guidelines of conventional usage, however, are obvious and seem sensible to adopt. Swift's ostentatious artifice, for example in *The Tale of a Tub* is not a direct concern of this study because in the bold schematism of Swift's satiric-allegoric overview of religious history and modern European civilization, there is very little of that concern with consecutive individual character and quotidian experience that we usually associate with the novel. Sterne, of course, learned many of his tricks directly from Swift, as one art form will frequently draw from another of a different category, but unlike *The Tale of a Tub*, the ostentatious artifice of *Tristram Shandy* continually serves characteristically novelistic concerns, as I shall try to show when I consider Sterne.

In order to avoid any initial confusion, I should like

to make clear that a self-conscious novel, where the artifice is deliberately exposed, is by no means identical with an elaborately artful novel, where the artifice may perhaps be prominent. The first-person narrators, for example, of Conrad's *Lord Jim* and Ford Madox Ford's *The Good Soldier*, on some level make us aware of the intricate artifice of their narrations as they circle round and round the same central events, gradually divulging more information, leading us to experience through the narrative pattern itself the complexity and elusiveness of morally judging people and their actions. Nevertheless, in both those novels the conspicuous elaboration of narrative artifice is performed in the service of a moral and psychological realism, operating even in its occasional improbabilities as a technique of versimilitude, not as a testing of the ontological status of the fiction. Conrad and Ford give us the world through a labyrinthine narrative because that seems to them the most faithful way of representing a labyrinthine world.

When, on the other hand, John Fowles, disguised in a Victorian beard, causes himself to sit down in the same railway compartment with his protagonist in *The French Lieutenant's Woman*, then contemplates his character, wonders how he should dispose of the poor fellow as he weighs the conventions of the Victorian novel which he is recreating against the critical strictures of the French New Novelists, and, finally, in order to decide what to do in the remaining six chapters, flips a coin he has extracted from the frock coat donned as part of his Victorian costume—in such a case, we are indubitably in the presence of a self-conscious narrator. This novelist, in other words, pointedly asks us to watch how he makes his novel, what is involved technically and theoretically in the making, as the novel unfolds.

Clearly, the utilization of such a device says nothing about the relative artistic strength or weakness of the novel in which it may occur. For a novelist, in the midst of the evoked fictional life of his novel, to devise a way of saying, "Look, I'm writing a novel," could conceivably be no more than a mannerism, a self-indulgent game. When such devices are integrated into a large critical vision of the dialectic interplay between fiction and reality, they may produce one of the most illuminating dimensions of the experience we undergo in reading a novel, and that is what I shall try to demonstrate by considering in detail a chronological sequence of major self-conscious novels from the seventeenth century to the present.

Many of the notions about this mode of fiction were ones I first formulated for myself in *Fielding and the Nature of the Novel* (Harvard University Press, 1968), and in retrospect, I can see that the present book is in a sense a large extension of issues I tried to take up briefly in the last chapter of my study of Fielding. I am obliged to mention the Fielding book in introducing this one because it explains one apparent gap in the historical argument here. The four major self-conscious novelists of the first great age of the novel (from the beginning of the seventeenth century to the end of the eighteenth) are Cervantes, Fielding, Sterne, and Diderot. There is no chapter devoted to Fielding because I was unwilling merely to recapitulate what I had written at length about him elsewhere. I have tried to compensate in part for this omission by a number of analytic comparisons with *Tom Jones* in my discussions of other novels: Fielding clearly remains in my view a principal model for the self-conscious novel, a writer who realized its possibilities with a superbly confident artistic poise that has not been surpassed.

In general, the deployment of these chapters is an attempt to combine close scrutiny of some of the strategically important self-conscious novels with several overviews of the larger literary and historical contexts in which this mode of fiction developed, for a time grew peripheral, then returned to prominence. Such a plan obviously does injustice to writers and novels only briefly alluded to in the sketching out of broad patterns, but the tactic seemed to me necessary in order to be able to join an insight into central works with a clearer perception of the role played by the self-conscious tradition in the unfolding of the genre. No attempt is made at an encyclopedic coverage of the subject because of the limits of my own knowledge—for example, my spotty acquaintance with German things led me to omit the German Romantic imitators of Sterne—and also because I wanted to avoid the tedium of merely illustrating the same ideas with many different books. The ultimate intent of this critical argument is not to tell readers that novels have been doing something other than what they thought all along, only to suggest that novels have been doing rather more than prevalent critical assumptions would allow for. In this perspective, the novel as a genre may seem somewhat less closely linked with the solid assurances and material views of bourgeois society than some observers have imagined, and more an intimate expression in innovative form of the restless self-questioning that has characterized so much of modern intellectual culture.

Most of this book was written with the support of a Senior Fellowship from the National Endowment for the Humanities, and I would like to express my gratitude for that generous grant. Typing costs and minor research expenses were covered by a grant-in-aid from the Committee on Research of the University of California at Berkeley. One or more chapters were examined in draft versions by Alfred Appel, Carol Cosman, Luis Murillo, and Richard Terdiman, all of whom I thank for their attentive reading and their helpful suggestions, even those I have chosen to ignore. Chapters One, Two, Seven, and part of Four appeared, respectively, with appropriate geographical distribution, in the *Southern Review*, the *Far-Western*

Forum, Northwestern's *Triquarterly*, and the *Georgia Review*; and I would like to express my appreciation to the editors for their receptiveness. Finally, many of the ideas about specific novels were first tried out on my students in various courses in the Berkeley Department of Comparative Literature over the past few years, and I could not have asked for a more congenial and critically alert trial audience.

Berkeley

November 1973

Chapter 1

The Mirror of Knighthood and the World of Mirrors

Why does it disturb us that Don
Quixote be a reader of the *Quixote*
and Hamlet a spectator of *Hamlet*?
These inversions suggest that if the
characters of a fictional work can be
readers or spectators, we, its readers
or spectators, can be fictitious.

J. L. Borges, "Partial
Magic in the *Quixote*"

One of the most essential and unsettling qualities of
modern culture is the geometric rate of increase in its
dissemination. Ever since Gutenberg, when technology
first intervened decisively in the reproduction of artifacts,
the rapid expansion and development of Western culture
have progressively sharpened a basic ambiguity. The artist,
with new means of dissemination and new media of imple-
mentation at his disposal, could imagine enormous new
possibilities of power in the exercise of his art. At the same
time, the conditions of mechanical reproduction made it
necessary for the individual artist to swim against a vast
floodtide of trash out of all proportion to anything that
had existed before in cultural history; and the reproduced
art object itself, in its universal accessibility, could be
cheapened, trivialized, deprived of its uniqueness, stripped
of any claims it might have to be a model of value or

a source of truth.[1] The transmission of artfully ordered words moves chronologically down a pyramid toward a broad numerical base, from the oral recitation of the traditional bard, who imparted an immemorial, or inspired, wisdom to a small circle of listeners actually gathered around him; to the handwritten word inscribed on scroll or tablet, still often thought of as magical or sacred, promulgated among a literate elite; to the printed text, made easily available in thousands upon thousands of copies, which at best preserves from its literary antecedents a flickering, intermittent aftersense that what it says *ought* to be true because it is written down in a book. The development, moreover, of still easier means of proliferation further dissipates even that vestigial sense of the authority of the written word: anyone now, with a walk to the nearest photocopy service and an investment often far smaller than the publisher's price, can "make" his own book from a borrowed copy, and with this convenience the qualitative distance in many people's minds between book and typescript or mimeographed text dwindles to a matter of clearer print and justified margins.

The novel as a genre provides a specially instructive measure of a culture caught up in the dynamics of its own technological instruments because it is the only major genre that comes into being after the invention of printing, and its own development—structural or thematic as well as economic—is intimately tied up with printing. I do not mean to fall into the error of certain voguish theorizers who assume that *all* important cultural changes are the result of modifications in the media of communication. On the contrary, I would take it as self-evident that the enormous social, political, and economic upheavals from

[1] For a brilliant discussion of this process, see Walter Benjamin, "The Work of Art in the Age of Its Mechanical Reproduction," *Illuminations* (New York: Harcourt, Brace and World, 1968).

the turn of the seventeenth century to the present, with the concomitant transformations in belief and world view, are not only reflected in the novel but also have very significantly determined the nature of the novel. All the good criticism, Marxist and non-Marxist, that connects the rise of the novel with the growth of the bourgeoisie, is surely not beside the point—it is only that it approaches the point from a bias, insisting that "realism" is the inherent goal of the novel and thus passing by much that deserves careful consideration.

The novel begins out of an erosion of belief in the authority of the written word and it begins with Cervantes. It fittingly takes as the initial target of its literary critique the first genre to have enjoyed popular success because of the printing press—the Renaissance chivalric romance. Although novelists were by no means the first writers to recognize clearly the fictional status of fictions, I think they were the first—and Cervantes of course the first among them—to see in the mere fictionality of fictions the key to the predicament of a whole culture, and to use this awareness centrally in creating new fictions of their own. For many novelists, to be sure, the crisis of belief in the written word of which I speak has been no more than an unregarded common cultural substratum for their work, while nowhere do they consciously exploit it in the solid-seeming fictional realities they create. Numerically, the novelists who write deliberately out of an undisguised skepticism about the status of fictions undoubtedly constitute a lesser tradition than that of the realists, but it is a brilliant tradition nevertheless, and one that throws a good deal of light on the nature of the novel as a genre. One measure of Cervantes' genius is the fact that he is the initiator of both traditions of the novel; his juxtaposition of high-flown literary fantasies with grubby actuality pointing the way to the realists, his

zestfully ostentatious manipulation of the artifice he constructs setting a precedent for all the self-conscious novelists to come.[2]

Especially because so many generations of readers have
rhapsodized over Don Quixote as a timeless image of
humanity, it may be worth stressing that he exists simultaneously on two very different planes of being. On the
one hand, the gaunt knight on his emaciated hack rides
in the mind's eye across the plains of a very real La
Mancha, appearing as a possible if bizarre figure of his
time and place who in fact succeeds in becoming a general
image of mankind in all the stubbornness of its idealism
and the hopeless futility of its blind misdirections. Cervantes takes pains, on the other hand, to make us aware
also that the knight is merely a lifelike model of papier-
maché, a design in words, images, invented gestures and
actions, which exists between the covers of a book by
Miguel de Cervantes.[3] There is a perfect appropriateness
in the fact that, toward the end of Don Quixote's adventures, when he comes to Barcelona, he should stumble
into a printing shop where he witnesses the processes of
proof-drawing, type-setting, revision, and is treated to a
disquisition on the economics of publishing and bookselling
(2:62). The effect is not very different from the cinematic
device that has recently been put to such abundant and
various use in which cameras, klieg lights, costumes, and
props obtrude into the filmed scene. At such a moment
we can hardly forget that Don Quixote himself is no more
than the product of the very processes he observes, a

[2] The seminal essay on Cervantes as the paradigmatic novelist is Harry Levin's
"The Example of Cervantes" in his *Contexts of Criticism* (Cambridge: Harvard
University Press, 1957).

[3] Shortly after writing this, I discovered the same point, though made from
a different orientation and elaborated in Freudian terms, in Marthe Robert's
"Toujours Don Quichotte" in her *Sur le papier* (Paris: Grasset, 1967). Mme
Robert interestingly sees the tension between manifest fictionality and apparent
reality as a generic dilemma of the novel on into the nineteenth and twentieth
centuries.

congeries of words set up in type, run off as proof, corrected
and rerun, bound in pages, and sold at so many reales
a copy. Cervantes, moreover, repeatedly reminds us that
without the rapid activity of presses like these churning
out the first part of his hero's adventures, most of the
adventures of the second part could never have taken
place.

It is not only in the mind of the unhinged hidalgo that
the reality of books and the reality of daily experience
are hopelessly scrambled. Don Quixote's adventures, of
course, begin in a library and frequently circle back to
the contents of that library in thought or in speech, and
more than once in action; but it is equally remarkable
that the world into which he sallies is flooded with manu-
scripts and printed matter. Sancho's ever-engaging presence reminds us that there is still a solid class of illiterates
whose verbal culture is entirely—and pungently—oral;
nevertheless, at times it begins to look as though all mankind were composed of two overlapping classes: readers
and writers. It seems as if from behind every roadside bush
and every wooded hill another author is waiting to spring
out, clutching a sheaf of verses; even a dangerous convict
is busy planning the second part of his autobiography as
he marches off to the galleys; and the unlooked-for pleasures a traveler may find in the attic of his inn are as
likely to be a trunk full of books as the embraces of a
hospitable serving girl.

This novel, like so many others after it, presents us a
world of role-playing, where the dividing lines between
role and identity are often blurred, and almost everyone
picks up the cues for his role from the literature he has
read. Don Quixote could not be so successful in infecting
the human world around him with quixotism if the chivalric romances did not enjoy such a large readership
(again, the printing press would seem a precondition for
his adventures): he repeatedly falls in with people who

can play answering roles to his because they are almost
as adept as he in the language, conventions, and actions
of chivalric literature. Even so unlikely a person as the
blanket-tossing innkeeper turns out to be such an enthusi-
astic reader of the chivalric romances that the shrewd
Dorothea is moved to remark, "Our host could almost play
a second to Don Quixote" (1:32).⁴ If we begin to wonder
where literature stops and "reality" starts in a world so
profuse in its mimickry of the printed page, Cervantes
himself makes a point of compounding our confusion. Don
Quixote at the printing shop may give us pause, but, still
later in the novel, Don Quixote conversing with Don
Alvaro Tarfe, a character from the spurious continuation
of *Don Quixote* by Alonso de Avellaneda, is almost enough
to induce ontological vertigo—a fictional character from
a "true" fictional chronicle confronting a fictional character from a false one in order to establish beyond doubt
his own exclusive authenticity.

Fictional characters, properly speaking, have no dimensions, since dimensions pertain to spatial existence and
fiction exists in thought, not in the world of extension,
but we are in the habit of applying the term "three-dimen-
sional" metaphorically to characters that seem convinc-
ingly lifelike, a usage that may reflect something of the
ambiguity with which we usually think about fictional
characters. Cervantes, even before the currency of the
metaphor, was finely aware of the ambiguity, and he
illuminates it quite early in his novel when he pointedly
reduces—or perhaps one should say raises—his protagonists
to a two-dimensional plane. At the end of the eighth
chapter, at the peak of a climactic adventure, when Don
Quixote is encountering his first armed adversary hand-to-
hand—the formidable Biscayan astride his she-mule, sword

---

⁴ All quotations from *Don Quixote* are from the Samuel Putnam translation
(New York: Viking, 1949).

aloft, cushion extended as shield—Cervantes suddenly
freezes the action, leaving the bloody-minded antagonists
with their swords hanging in mid-air, while he explains
that the "author of this history" was unable to find any
further documents pertaining to the exploits of Don Quixote. The chapter ends in this state of suspension, and a
new one begins with the narrator ("the second author of
this work") suddenly switching to the first-person singular
to report in a relaxed anecdotal manner how one day in
the marketplace of Toledo he ran across a series of notebooks written in Arabic characters which turned out to
be none other than the *History of Don Quixote de la
Mancha, Written by Cid Hamete Benengeli, Arabic Historian.* (The mediation of Cid Hamete is itself a complicated and intriguing matter to which we shall return later.)
The first notebook, conveniently enough, contains a carefully drawn illustration of the very moment when the
preceding narrative broke off. The coincidence is clearly
to be marveled at; only the artificer who conceived both
the first and the second authors of this history as well
as the industrious Arabic historian could be responsible
for such perfect synchronization of two discrete narratives
and two different media. This is the way the illustration
is described:

> There was a very lifelike picture of the battle between
> Don Quixote and the Biscayan, the two being in precisely
> the same posture as described in the history, their swords
> upraised, the one covered by his buckler, the other with
> his cushion. As for the Biscayan's mule, you could see at
> the distance of a crossbow shot that it was one for hire.
> Beneath the Biscayan there was a rubric which read: "Don
> Sancho de Azpeitia," which must undoubtedly have been
> his name; while beneath the feet of Rocinante was another
> inscription: "Don Quixote." Rocinante was marvelously
> portrayed: so long and lank, so lean and flabby, so extremely
> consumptive-looking that one could well understand the

justness and propriety with which the name of "hack" had
been bestowed upon him.

Alongside Rocinante stood Sancho Panza, holding the
halter of his ass, and below was the legend: "Sancho
Zancas." The picture showed him with a big belly, a short
body, and long shanks, and that must have been where
he got the names of Panza y Zancas by which he is a number
of times called in the course of the history. There are other
small details that might be mentioned, but they are of little
importance and have nothing to do with the truth of the
story—and no story is bad so long as it is true.

The poised ambiguity with which Cervantes conceives the
representation of reality here suggests why he stands at
the beginning of a Copernican revolution in the practice
and theory of mimesis. The whole passage, of course, is
a representation within a representation within a representation of what one finally hesitates to call reality—a
picture within a book within a narration by "the second
author of this work." Its effect is like that of a mirror
within a painting reflecting the subject of the painting,
or the deployment of still photographs within a film:
through a sudden glimpse of multiple possibilities of representation we are brought up short and thus moved to
ponder the nature of representation and the presence of
the artful representer.

Don Quixote, I would suggest, is impelled to his adventures by a nagging sense of the irreality of his own dull
existence in the Iron Age. At any rate, he clearly draws
an equation between being real and being recorded in
literature. In the first part of the novel, he prepares for
every action with an acute consciousness of "the sage who
is to write the history" of his exploits, for it is only through
the writing down that he can be sure he has become as
real as Amadís, Don Belianís, Felixmarte, and all the rest.
The traditional epic hero, of course, also desires his glory
to be sung after him by the sons of men, but Don Quixote,

a bookish man, actually wants to become a book. Instructively, in Part Two, when Don Quixote's ambition has precipitously caught up with him and he is pursued everywhere by the knowledge that he is already in a book, he begins to suspect that his chronicler may not be a sage after all but rather one of those willful sorcerers who are persecuting him. At this early point in the novel, however, we are offered a literally graphic image of the knight with his ambition already achieved, but the reality he has attained is a wavering fabric of contradictions.

The details of the illustration are brought forward to confirm the authenticity of the preceding narrative: if two independent sources, the unnamed first "author of this history" and Cid Hamete Benengeli, give us identical portraits, then this must be the "true" Don Quixote. Yet the authentication is really a transparent sleight-of-hand trick, for when the picture is described as "very lifelike," what this means in effect is that it is very like the picture at the end of the narrative that concluded with the previous chapter: internal consistency is quietly substituted for verisimilitude, though not so quietly that we do not reflect for a moment on the substitution. (Peculiarly, there is one small detail here that fails to jibe with the subsequent narrative. Sancho is not called "Panza y Zancas," or "paunch and shanks," a number of times in Cid Hamete's chronicle. Is this one of Cervantes' careless strokes, or a strategem for casting a faint shadow of doubt on the reliability of the Arabic notebooks, or of their translator?) In any case, by the time we are told at the end of the passage that only those details bearing on the truth of the story have been reported, we are likely to suspect that we no longer know what the truth of the story means, and the raising of such doubt may well be one purpose of the passage.

As for Don Quixote, with his aspirations to be translated into the sphere of literary reality, where does this whole graphic representation leave him? Fixed forever in a text, made the subject of a new iconography, he has achieved everything and almost nothing. He and Sancho have scarcely set out; all the "exploits" we are as yet aware of as readers are a handful of hilarious misconceptions of the knight's, and so the content of his immortality would seem to be the mere fact of being recorded on a printed page. Indeed, at this particular juncture, the page is not yet a printed one, since Cid Hamete's chronicle is set down in notebooks. The accompanying illustration, then, which seems so much like an engraving, would have to be a pen-and-ink drawing. Thus a notebook with sketches is imperceptibly metamorphosed into an illuminated volume, and we become aware of how tentative an affair the knight's immortality is, how much all reality in the novel is the product of the artist's *trompe l'oeil*.

The new novelistic reality that Cervantes created is real-seeming in many important respects yet avowedly arbitrary, and a central device for communicating an awareness of that double nature here and throughout the novel is the game played with the naming of names. Inventing and assigning names is the ruling passion of Don Quixote. As a corollary to the belief that to be real means to be recorded in literature, he is convinced that no identity can have reality until it is assigned an appropriate name. Yet, as several critics have observed, he knowingly chooses names that while euphonically appropriate to the new Golden-Age roles, are transparent revelations of Iron-Age identities, like Rocinante, who was a hack (*rocín*) before (*ante*), and is now supposed the first of all hacks.[5] A related doubleness of perspective is suggested in a different way here in the illustration, where each of the three human figures in the picture is carefully labeled with a rubric beneath it, and comment is devoted to the graphically

[5] See Leo Spitzer, "Perspectivism in the *Quijote*," in *Linguistics and Literary History* (Princeton: Princeton University Press, 1948).

demonstrated aptness of the name coinages "Rocinante" and "Panza y Zancas." Such rubrics, of course, were often used in Renaissance illustrations, and they serve here, at least ostensibly, as evidence of the narrative's veracity, each character scrupulously assigned his proper name. (Cid Hamete evidently has more documentary material at his disposal than the First Author, since he is able to give us the full name of the hitherto anonymous Biscayan.) At the same time, nothing could be more clearly a formal artifice, a contrivance of convention, than to represent personages with their identities neatly labeled below their feet, and this in turn may lead us to reflect on the sheer arbitrariness of the literary naming of names, on the purely verbal processes of authorial fiat through which characters come into being. In primitive culture, the word is magical, exerting power over the physical world; in the biblical tradition it is sacred, instinct with unfathomable divine meaning. For Cervantes, the word simultaneously resonates with its old magical quality and turns back on itself, exposing its own emptiness as an arbitrary or conventional construct. The French critic, Marthe Robert, in her brilliant essay on *Don Quixote*, offers an elegant and precise formulation: "The quixotic Word [*la verbe donquichottesque*]... is invocation and critique, conjuration and radical probing, both one and the other with their risks and perils. [6]

This ontological doubleness of language in Cervantes is mirrored in the new kind of narrative structure he devised: the fictional world is repeatedly converted into a multiple regress of imitations that call attention in various ways to their own status as imitations. The paradigm for this structure is clearest in the episode of Master Pedro and his puppets (2:26). Master Pedro's assistant stands out in front of the stage, narrating the action while

---

[6] *L'Ancien et le nouveau: de Don Quichotte à Kafka* (Paris: Petite Bibliothèque Payot, 1963), p. 25, note.

ERRATUM

On page 12 the second complete sentence should begin as follows: "Don Quixote, as the principal member of the audience, repeatedly interrupts the boy's narrative to point out inadequacies in the management of its artifice. . .."

and punishment of one of the characters by a reference to Moorish legal practice, Don Quixote chides him, "Child, child, keep to the straight line of your story and do not go off on curves and tangents," and Master Pedro chimes in, shifting the metaphor, "Boy ... do as this gentleman says ... stick to your plain song and don't try any counterpoint melodies, for they are likely to break down from being overfine." The transparently fictional illusion, in other words, of the puppet-show narration, is again and again broken into by literary criticism from the "real" world. The critics, moreover, are themselves both masqueraders, though for very different reasons—Alonso Quijano the Good tricked out in armor as a medieval knight; the escaped convict of literary bent, Ginés de Pasamonte, disguised as an itinerant puppeteer.

Literary criticism, it should be noted, is intrinsic to the fictional world of the *Quixote* and of all the self-conscious novels that follow it. Such criticism is present not only in the parodistic exposure of the absurdities of chivalric romances and in the lengthy discussions of literary matters that take place among the protagonists several times in the novel, but it is also, to borrow Master Pedro's figure, a repeated counterpoint to the narrative plain song throughout the book, as the interruption of the puppet show illustrates with schematic clarity. In this self-conscious mode of fiction, literary criticism is not, as it may sometimes seem, interpolated, but is an essential moment in the act of imagination, an act that is at once "conjuration and radical probing."

Thus, Cid Hamete's chronicle is accompanied by the judgments of three commentators. The most prominent of these is of course the unnamed Second Author, who has much to say about the veracity of Cid Hamete, his dedication as a historian, the "hackled, twisting, winding thread of Benengeli's plot" (1:28), and so forth. Then the Arabic historian himself intervenes, either directly or through the report of the Spanish author, to marvel over the events he chronicles, to question the authenticity of Don Quixote's experience in the Cave of Montesinos, to complain of the monotony of Don Quixote's adventures with Sancho, and thus defend the practice of interpolated tales against the critics of Part One. Even the distinctly subordinate Moorish translator gets into the act, making occasional comments about Cid Hamete and pronoucing one chapter to be apocryphal because Sancho's speech in it seems to him inconsistent with what we know of Sancho. Finally, various characters criticize tales told within the main narrative, questioning their probability, the motivation of their characters, the appropriateness of the language used in them. One of the most striking instances of this sort, again one in which role-playing and literary criticism are intertwined, is the romance within a play within the novel as told and commented on by the duke's major-domo masquerading as the Countess Trifaldi (2:38). In the course of the romance which she invents about herself, the countess quotes some verses sung by a lover, and then sharply observes on their style: "I should not have allowed myself to be moved by such labored conceits, nor should I have believed that the poet was speaking the truth when he declared, 'I live dying, burn in ice, tremble in the fire, hope without hope, go and stay,' along with other contradictory conceptions of this sort with which their writing is filled."

But let us return briefly to Master Pedro's puppet show, for we have not yet considered what is surely the most remarkable thing about that episode—the way Don Quixote brings it to an abrupt end by suddenly leaping up to the stage and hacking the puppets to pieces with his sword while the puppet master cries in dismay, "Those are not real Moors that your Grace is knocking over, maiming, and killing, but pasteboard figures." On the level of farcical satire, the point of this dénouement is obvious enough: the infallible button connecting directly to the mad gentleman's *idée fixe* has again been pressed, and he responds like a comic doll, once again raising his valorous right arm to succor the distressed of an imaginary world of adventures. It is noteworthy, however, that this outburst of chivalric madness is immediately preceded by one of his most lucid moments in the critical discussion of mimesis. When bells ring from the towers of the mosques in the play, Don Quixote interrupts to object that this is utter nonsense because the Moors do not use bells. Master Pedro retorts that it is a picayune objection, since countless plays—such as Lope's, one gathers—are filled with much more glaring inaccuracies, and Don Quixote concedes the point, apparently willing to allow that in some sorts of imitations of reality, strictly consistent verisimilitude is not necessary. In the next moment, then, the knight leaps sword in hand from the clearest recognition of the puppet show as an artifice to a total acceptance of it as reality. Perhaps the best way to define the "lucid madness" attributed to him several times by the narrator is to say that he repeatedly polarizes within himself opposing attitudes toward fictions which most of us hold together in some sort of suspension. The moment when the impulse of consciousness darts from pole to pole is an illuminating one, for Cervantes understands that there is an ultimately serious tension between the recognition of fictions as fictions and the acceptance of them as reality, however easy it may seem to maintain these two awarenesses simultaneously. Knowing that a fiction is, after all, only a fiction, is potentially subversive of any meaningful reality that might be attributed to the fiction, while assenting imaginatively to the reality of a represented action is a step in a process that could undermine or bewilder what one ordinarily thinks of as his sense of reality. Cervantes' novel could be described as a comic acting-out of the ultimate implications, both moral and ontological, of this tension of attitudes.

If the *Quixote* calls into question the status of fictions and of itself as a fiction, it also affirms a new sense of the autonomy of the artist who has conceived it. I proposed the term *trompe l'oeil* in connection with the picture of Don Quixote and the Biscayan, and it may be helpful to imagine the whole novel for a moment as a series of *trompe l'oeil* panels that slide open consecutively to reveal the author peeping out at the end of the series. The Tale of the Captive, which occupies so many pages in Part One, provides a clear example of how this tricky structuring works. The Captive introduces his story, at the very end of Chapter 38, by announcing to his listeners that they will "hear a true tale which possibly cannot be matched by those fictitious ones that are composed with such cunning craftsmanship." He immediately proceeds, however, to begin his narrative with the most patently conventional of folktale beginnings—the father who divides his estate in three among his three sons, sending one to the Church, one to the sea, and one to a career of arms. By the end of the story (1:42), Cervantes is prepared to point out this conventionality to the reader. Thus, the curate remarks, "He told me a story about his father and his brothers which, if I had not known him to be so truthful a man, I should have taken to be one of those tales that old women tell by the fireside in wintertime," and the captive's brother, himself one of the protagonists of the beginning of the story, admits that it must seem "to be a fairy tale."

It is in the midst of this story, purportedly real in content, recalling a fairy tale in its form, that the narrator mentions another Spanish soldier who was imprisoned with him in North Africa, a certain Saavedra (1:40). Saavedra is, of course, Miguel de Cervantes Saavedra, the inventor of the captive and his story and of all the other obvious and devious narrators of this novel. The captive makes a few brief statements about the actual captivity of Cervantes, and then, with pointed coyness, Cervantes has him conclude, "If time permitted, which unfortunately it does not, I could tell you here and now something of that soldier's exploits which would interest and amaze you much more than my own story."

Many influential theories of fiction, like that of Ortega y Gasset in his *Notes on the Novel*, have contended that the "world" of a novel has to be hermetically sealed, for any penetration of untransformed materials from the world outside it would only shatter its compelling but fragile illusion of reality. The theory, I think, does not give the novel enough credit for its ability to confront *formally* the radical skepticism of the troubled historical period in which the genre has developed. It is, indeed, ironic that Ortega should have become one of the promulgators of such a theory; for a decade earlier, in his *Meditations on Quixote*, he shows a fine sense of the ontological duality of the genre, and in particular his comments on Master Pedro's puppet show in the Ninth and Tenth Meditation remain enormously suggestive.

Cervantes himself, as we see in this instance, did not hesitate to open up a loophole in the fictional reality looking out to the frankly autobiographical reality of the

writer. (Elsewhere, of course, he introduces himself
through references to his other works, and at one point,
1:47, the curate conjectures that the anonymous *Story
of the One Who Was Too Curious for His Own Good*—a
"fictitious" story because it is discovered within the narrative frame of the novel—might be by the same hand as
Riconete and Cortadillo, one of Cervantes' *Exemplary
Novels*, not yet published when Part One of the *Quixote*
appeared.) That Saavedra should appear in the narrative
of a fictional character invented by Saavedra is the author's way of affirming his absolute proprietorship over
the fictional world he has created. If he chose, he could
relate his own adventures as a soldier and prisoner instead
of the captive's, for the act of fiction is purely a matter
of the choice of the artist; it may resemble actual experience in a variety of ways, but it is not compelled in an
Aristotelian sense to imitate, is not the slave of what
common sense rather confusedly calls "reality."

It is perfectly appropriate, then, that the relationship
of the writer to the reader at many junctures should be
a teasing one. Cervantes' walk-on appearance as captive
soldier anticipates the strategem of that archest of novelists, Vladimir Nabokov, who at the end of *Pale Fire* has
his deranged homosexual hero affirm that he will continue
to exist in some other form: "I may turn up yet, on another
campus, as an old, happy, healthy, heterosexual Russian,
a writer in exile, sans fame, sans future, sans audience,
sans anything but his art." This is, of course, a portrait
of Nabokov, though self-ironic in its echo of the Ages of
Man speech from *As You Like It*. In any case, the momentary appearance of the author in his own work has the
same basic implication as in Cervantes: these fictional
materials, we are told in effect, however lifelike, however
absorbing, have been assembled in the imagination of the
writer, who is free to reassemble them in any number of

ways, or to put them aside and tell his own story directly, and the fictional materials have no existence without the writer.

The intuition of life that, beginning with Cervantes, crystallized in the novel is profoundly paradoxical: the novelist lucidly recognizes the ways man may be painfully frustrated and victimized in a world with no fixed values or ideals, without even a secure sense of what is real and what is not, yet through the exercise of an autonomous art the writer boldly asserts the freedom of consciousness itself. The imagination, then, is alternately, or even simultaneously, the supreme instrument of human realization and the eternal snare of delusion of a creature doomed to futility.

The extraordinary complexity with which Cervantes sustains a full awareness of both sides of the paradox is worth considering further. It is most easily perceptible in the way he relates as the artist responsible for the novel to his protagonist, Don Quixote, and to his surrogate author, Cid Hamete. Many readers have regarded the device of the Arabic historian as gratuitous, and perhaps something of a nuisance, though I suspect that the perfect rightness of Cid Hamete as intermediary has recently come to be better understood. Benengeli is the demiurge of the world Cervantes has created, and, like the demiurge of gnostic theology, he is a somewhat ambiguous intermediary. The Second Author repeatedly extols his virtues as a faithful historian and at one point (2:40) addresses a rhapsodic tribute to him in a formal apostrophe. Yet Cid Hamete is first identified for us as the member of a nation of liars; he himself admits to having introduced the interpolated tales of Part One out of boredom with his main subject and in order to give his pen full scope to write what it chooses, and he occasionally expresses contradictory judgments or makes rather puzzling observations. If he begins one chapter (2:8) in proper Moorish fashion by exclaiming "Blessed be the mighty Allah!" three times, he is not averse from starting another chapter (2:27) with "I swear as a Catholic Christian." The Second Author makes no comment on this anomaly, but the translator offers a bizarre explanation which is, in its peculiar way, instructive: "the author merely meant that, just as a Catholic Christian when he takes an oath swears, or is supposed to swear, to tell the truth in all that he says, so in what he himself has to set down about Don Quixote he will adhere to the truth as if he were taking such a Christian oath." Whether all this actually confirms Cid Hamete's truthfulness or throws it into question is a matter over which the reader may puzzle. In any case, the translator's explanation illustrates a tendency shared with the protagonist of the novel by several of its narrators, which is to take metaphorical comparisons as literal equations. This odd practice is merely the reduction to the microscopic level—individual words and objects instead of actions and ideas—of the quixotic confusion between fiction and fact. In the same fashion, Don Quixote can transmute a meager codfish into veal and kid by juggling a series of similes (1:2), and the First Author can casually substitute dromedaries for she-mules by giving a comparison free reign (1:8). Who, one begins to wonder, is a reliable narrator here, or is language itself, with its constant need to extend its expressive scope through metaphor, intrinsically unreliable?

If figurative comparisons assume their own independent life, so, of course, do fictions, again for the dedicated historian as well as for the mad protagonist. When the mock-countess Trifaldi is first introduced (2:38), two observations are made on her name: "She was known as the Countess Trifaldi, as one might say, the Countess of the Three Skirts, an opinion that is supported by Benengeli, who asserts that the lady's right name was the Countess Lobuna and that she was so called on account of the many wolves in her country." This obviously parodies the devotion to precise nomenclature of a true epic chronicler, but it is nevertheless peculiar. By this point in the narrative, almost any reader would see, even here at the beginning of the episode, that the countess and her bizarrely costumed entourage are bogus, merely staging another in the series of elaborate practical jokes conceived by the duke and duchess. Cid Hamete inevitably knows this, in fact knows the countess's part is being played by a man, for he is the chronicler of the rest of the chapter, yet here he is reported gravely ascertaining her "right" name through his familiarity with the fauna of her non-existent country! Cid Hamete, the historian who both follows and controls his material, can also become its captive, slipping inside the frame of the world of masks and deceptions that he describes. The effect when the fiction begins thus to assume autonomy is the complementary opposite of *trompe l'oeil*, resembling the kind of transition between planes of reality recorded in the Chinese tale where the imperial architect, turning from the wrath of his emperor, opens the door in the drawing of the palace he has made and disappears inside.

It has recently been suggested by the Hispanist Ruth El Saffar that Cid Hamete is the artful means through which Cervantes interposes a necessary distance between himself and his work. This seems to me just, though one might add that Cid Hamete at the same time serves as a parodistic reflection of Cervantes' ambiguous relationship to his work. In any case, Mrs. El Saffar is apt in observing the effect on us of the paradoxical presence of the Arabic historian: as Benengeli's narrative point of view vacillates between following the protagonists and pulling back to an overview of retrospective omniscience, "the reader is successively drawn into the suspense and interest that the characters themselves provide and is wrenched away from them to an awareness of the pen which controls them."[7] This contradictory effect is precisely the one produced by virtually all self-conscious novels, from Cervantes onward. It is worth noting that Cervantes' principal means for achieving the effect is to split himself off into a fictional alter ego, the Moorish chronicler who is supposedly the true author of the history; Don Quixote himself is another kind of surrogate for the novelist, being prominent among the characters of the novel as an author manqué, who is impelled to act out the literary impulse in the world of deeds, to be at once the creator and protagonist of his own fictions.

Doubles, as we shall see, recur again in later developments of novelistic self-consciousness. This is hardly surprising in a kind of fiction repeatedly concerned with both the instructiveness and the deceptiveness of similitudes, with the ambiguity of identity and fictional character, and, above all, with the relation of the author to his work. A propos of the last of these concerns, Marthe Robert makes a shrewd observation about the *Quixote*: "Since the multiple oppositions embodied in the pair hero-author are far from being always superimposable, the play of antitheses is repeated through all the personages of the narrative, which, on the same account, is literally peopled with doubles."[8] This is immensely suggestive, though a little cryptic. What it means, I think, is that the novel is, both structurally and thematically, an unstable dialectic, working with a series of partly overlapping oppositions that might be conceptualized through such terms as art and nature, fiction and reality, ideal and actuality, role

---

[7] "The Function of the Fictional Narrator in *Don Quijote*," *Modern Language Notes*, March 1968, p. 167. A more fully persuasive account of the various uses of Cid Hamete is offered by Mia I. Gerhardt in her finely intelligent *Don Quijote: La vie et les livres* (Amsterdam: Hollandsche Uita. Mig., 1953). She sees the Moorish historian as Cervantes' principal means for making it clear that the author "is not the dupe of his own fiction" and for creating between the writer and the perceptive reader "a delectable complicity over this subtle fraud which is the novel" (p. 16).

[8] *L'Ancien et le nouveau*, p. 22.

and identity, past and present, timelessness and tempora-
lity, belief and skepticism. Because the dialectic is inherently unstable, no opposition can produce the resolution of a synthesis, and so each set of antitheses, whether
embodied in the characters of the novel or in its narrative
structure, tends toward the invention of further antitheses.
In the course of time, this dialectic within the novel-form
produces in experimental modern writers like Alain
Robbe-Grillet and Raymond Queneau fictional worlds
where every event is represented as sheer hypothesis, to
be dismantled and reassembled in new ways, the element
of instability dominating all.

We have already noted how Cervantes projects segments
of himself as a writer into two very different doubles, Cid
Hamete and Don Quixote, the former acting as an intermediary between himself and the latter. Don Quixote, of
course, proceeds to pair up with his opposite, Sancho, and
the two enter into the most famous dialectic of the novel,
in which the knight quixotizes the squire as the squire
sanchifies the knight. At the same time, Don Quixote tends
to convert those he encounters into amusingly distorted
and opposing doubles of himself, beginning, in an external
way, with the gallant Biscayan, culminating in the bachelor Sansón Carrasco, who as a reflection of Don Quixote
appropriately assumes the sobriquet, Knight of the Mirrors. The interpolated stories, moreover, exhibit a fondness
for antithetical pairings of characters—friends, rivals,
lovers—many of whom stand in interesting relations of
opposition and parallel to figures in the main narrative.
As always, Cervantes has a sure instinct for parodying
his own procedures, and at one point (2:12) he goes out
of his way to remind us that he has even continued the
principle of *dédoublement* from mankind to the animal
kingdom. Rocinante and the gray ass are, of course, a
doubling of the Quixote-Sancho pair, and Cervantes calls
our attention to the fact here by devoting a page to the

lofty friendship of the two beasts, comparing them to Nisus and Euryalus, Orestes and Pylades.

The proliferation of doubles in this first model of the novel as self-conscious genre can also be explained in another way. A double, of course, is a reflection or imitation, and often a covertly parodistic imitation that exposes hidden aspects of the original. (Thus, in the most familiar folkloristic use of the double motif, an ostensibly respectable person is confronted with the image of his demonic other self.) A mode of fiction, therefore, focused on the nature of imitation and its aesthetic or ontological implications may well find doubles to be of great utility. It should be emphasized, moreover, that the self-conscious novelist utilizes the double with a conscious quality of intellectual playfulness, in sharp contrast to writers like Poe, Dostoevski, and Conrad, who try to give the double its full mythic resonance as an embodiment of the dark Other Side of the self.

In *Don Quixote*, this utility of doubles as an experiment in imitation and a critique of fictions may be easier to see in doublings of plot than in those of character. Thus, Don Quixote's descent into the Cave of Montesinos is, to begin with, a parody of the portentous descent into the underworld of the traditional epic hero at a crucial midpoint of his journey, and both Sancho and Cid Hamete express considerable skepticism about the whole experience, while even the knight is led to wonder whether it may all have been a dream. This questionable adventure is in turn parodistically doubled in Sancho's fantastic aerial visions astride the wooden horse, Clavileño, an imaginary ascent matching the earlier imaginary descent, as Don Quixote himself makes clear in his final words to Sancho on the subject: "Sancho, if you want us to believe what you saw in Heaven, then you must believe me when I tell you what I saw in the Cave of Montesinos. I need say no more" (2:41). Not content with this parody of a parody of a descent into the underworld, Cervantes later makes Sancho go through another, more realistic, doubling of the same experience, when the squire stumbles into a pit and finds himself trapped in an underground cavern (2:55). Again, the writer draws our attention to the parallel between the episodes by causing Sancho, who can imagine nothing but treacherous holes in this underworld, to cry out: "This may be hard luck for me, but it would make a good adventure for my master Don Quixote. He would take these depths and dungeons for flowery gardens and Galiana's palace." (In the Spanish here there is a pointed pun: *Esta que para mí es desventura, mejor fuera para aventura de mi amo don Quijote.* That is, it needs only a turn of the screw of imagination, as small but crucial as the change of a prefix, to convert *desventura* to *aventura*, to transform the whole nature of what seems to impinge on one as reality. Yet, bumping against the hard rocks of a very palpable underground prison, Sancho must also suspect that such transformations are mere fictions, as arbitrary and inefficacious as the changing of a word to its opposite in the abstract realm of language through the shift of a letter or two.) Finally, close to the end of the novel, we are given a *third* parodistic repetition of the initial dubious descent into the underworld, when the maid Altisidora, who has been play-acting at being dead, manufactures a report of her experience in hell that is in effect a flamboyant spoof of both Sancho's concocted vision of his voyage on Clavileño and the knight's synthetic romance in the Cave of Montesinos (2:70). Altisidora's hell, in which planes of literary reality intersect, is a literary underworld in a different sense from Don Quixote's: in it, demons in fashionable dress play tennis using books "filled with wind and rubbish," among which the most swollen and empty turns out to be the spurious continuation of *Don Quixote.*

The world, in this multiplication of internal parodies,

becomes an assemblage of mirrors—the armor of Sansón Carrasco, covered with small mirrors, could serve as its emblem—but since parody is precisely the literary mode that fuses creation with critique, the mirrors are in varying degrees distortive, so that the characters parade through a vast fun-house hall where even the most arresting figures can suddenly swell into monstrosities or shrink to absurdities. (The juncture of sharply etched verisimilitude and fantasy is one that will be characteristic of the whole self-conscious tradition of the novel.) Virtually everything, then, is composite, made up of fragmented images, refractions, and reflections of other things, which is to say that virtually everything is mediated by literature, whether the body of literary works and conventions outside this novel or the various literary inventions generated within the book itself. The novel creates a world at once marvelous and credible, but the most splendid evocations of character or action bear within them the visible explosive freight of their own parodistic negation.

This instability of fictional realities is most evident in Don Quixote's supreme fiction, Dulcinea. As many commentators have observed, Don Quixote is utterly clear about the fact that Dulcinea is his own invention yet deadly serious about his unswerving devotion to the ideal fiction he has made for himself. One of his early evocations of her aptly illustrates the new kind of relationship between literature and reality at work in this novel:

> Her name is Dulcinea, her place of residence El Toboso, a village of La Mancha. As to her rank, she should be at the very least a princess, seeing that she is my lady and my queen. Her beauty is superhuman, for in it are realized all the impossible and chimerical attributes that poets are accustomed to give their fair ones. Her locks are golden, her brow the Elysian Fields, her eyebrows rainbows, her eyes suns, her cheeks roses, her lips coral, her teeth pearls, her neck alabaster, her bosom marble, her hands ivory, her

complexion snow-white. As for those parts which modesty keeps covered from the human sight, it is my opinion that, discreetly considered, they are only to be extolled and not compared to any other. [1:13]

Don Quixote begins from a town in La Mancha where, of course, there are no princesses, but he immediately proceeds to affirm Dulcinea's royal rank, for the necessities of the literary convention from which she is drawn dictate absolutely what he understands to be the facts about her. What follows is essentially a catalogue of poetic clichés, virtually announced as such, which makes clear that Dulcinea is entirely a composite creature, assembled from the much-used materials of timeworn literary traditions. The effect of the passage, however, is strangely not that of a tired rehearsal of exhausted conventions. On the contrary, one senses that Don Quixote is making a fervent poem, however synthetic the poetry, out of Dulcinea, and the fact that she is composed of purely literary materials is precisely what endows her with prestige for him. (In the Spanish the passage has greater lyrical *élan*, reads a little less like a catalogue, because of the controlled rhythmic emphases and the variation of the long series with elegant poetic inversions.) If Dulcinea is too much a composite to be immediately present for us, the aura of her presence in the knight's imagination shines through the passage, and so we see how a manifest fiction can become a reality in the imagination of its beholder, even as he recognizes the materials from which the fiction has been composed.

The amusing pratfall of the final sentence—in the original, the final clause of a single long sentence and thus syntactically continuous with the string of poetic clichés— is instructive in another way. This most chaste of lovers slips, though decorously, from rosy cheeks and coral lips to incomparable genitalia, objects of amorous adulation that are decidedly outside the courtly literary conventions he has adopted. His violation of his own conventional framework in order to depict the "whole" Dulcinea suggests contradictory implications that push against one another in a precarious opposition. On the one hand, Dulcinea is so real for Don Quixote that she extends beyond the frame of literary convention in which he has created her. This incongruous physiological completeness, on the other hand, of his portrait of her hints that he himself exists in a flesh-and-blood world against which the divine Dulcinea, distilled as she is from familiar poetic hyperboles, must begin to seem purely a verbal concoction.

Perhaps it may help us see in perspective Cervantes' bold innovation in the management of fictions if we set this passage alongside another seventeenth-century composite of literary images of the ideal, Milton's evocation of Eden in *Paradise Lost* (4:235-287). Like so many Renaissance writers, Milton is also conscious of a tension between art and nature. The first paradise is the ultimate natural state, where "not nice Art . . . but Nature boon" pours forth a profusion of beauties. The poet, then, must struggle with the paradox of representing in art what transcends the merely human scope of art—he aspires to "tell how, if Art could tell," implying that it really cannot. Milton's solution to this difficulty is to flaunt the paradox, emphasizing the means of art he employs as he transforms prelapsarian nature into a brilliant artifact with sapphire fountains, golden sands and burnished fruit with golden rind, pebbles of orient pearl, crystal-mirror streams. Then he invokes a whole series of wondrous pleasure-gardens from the literature of antiquity only to suggest that all of them are no more than wavering, imperfect shadow images of the true Garden. Like Don Quixote, he represents the ideal by a grand synthesis of the imagery of a literary tradition—in this case, the pastoral tradition—though of course he brilliantly orchestrates the expressive possibilities of the tradition instead of simply stringing together traditional formulas. When Don Quixote, praising Dulcinea's beauty, says that "in it are realized all the impossible and chimerical attributes that poets are accustomed to give their fair ones," his words call our attention to her status as a fiction, to the fact that she is woven out of those impossible and chimerical attributes by a bookish mind that has come to believe in the possibility of their literal existence. When Milton writes, "*Hesperian* Fabtrue,/ If true, here only," the effect is quite the opposite. The truth of art may be doubted not because art is mere invention, but because art (or the human imagination) by its inherent limitations can offer only an intimation of the resplendent truth of divinely created nature.

Milton is perhaps the last great moment in a tradition of mimesis that begins for Western literature with Homer and the Bible. His poem memorably represents that aspect of the Renaissance which is the conscious culmination of a continuous cultural development through two and a half millennia. Cervantes' novel, on the other hand, is one of the supreme achievements of that impulse in the Renaissance which was already moving toward the troubled horizon of modernity. Cervantes cannot share Milton's Christian-humanist confidence in the power of language and the literary tradition to adumbrate the glory of God's nature. Revelation, after all, remains the bedrock of Milton's vision; and because revelation takes place through language—precisely in Scripture, by shadowy types in classical literature—it guarantees the possibility of some real correspondence between literary art and divinely wrought nature. For Cervantes, on the other hand, as a fundamentally secular skeptic (his hero's deathbed conversion notwithstanding), art is obviously questionable because it is understood to be ultimately arbitrary, while nature is still more problematic because it is so entrammeled with art, so universally mediated by art, shaped by art's peculiar habits of vision, that it becomes difficult to know what, if anything, nature in and of itself may be. From this point on, cultural creativity would proceed more and more through a recapitulative critique of its own past, and a major line of fiction would be avowedly duplicitous, making the paradox of its magically real duplicity one of its principal subjects. In these respects, Cervantes does not merely anticipate a later mode of imagination but fully realizes its possibilities; subsequent writers would only explore from different angles the imaginative potentialities of a kind of fiction that he authoritatively conceived. In this, as in other ways, *Don Quixote* is the archetypal novel that seems to encompass the range of what would be written afterward. Ironically reaching for the dream of a medieval world through Renaissance literary productions, it remains one of the most profoundly modern of all novels.

Chapter 2

Sterne and the Nostalgia for Reality

Tristram Shandy is the most typical
novel of world literature.
Viktor Shklovsky,
The Theory of Prose

But *Tristram Shandy*, my friend, was
made and formed to baffle all criticism.
Laurence Sterne, *Letters*

One of the characteristic reflexes of the self-conscious
novel is to flaunt "naive" narrative devices, rescuing their
usability by exposing their contrivance, working them into
a highly patterned narration which reminds us that all
representations of reality are, necessarily, stylizations.
Perhaps the most obvious example is the ostentatious
narrator, beginning with Cervates' mitotic multiplication
of narrators and commentators, through to Fielding's
urbanely ironic contriver, to the zany jugglers of narrative
convention in Sterne and Diderot, and on, most recently,
to the composite self-observing narrator of Nabokov's *Ada*
and the ventriloquistic "Victorian" voice that reports the
action in John Fowles's *The French Lieutenant's Woman*.
Another central case in point is the interpolated tale. In
Don Quixote the device is sometimes used to present
fractured or distorted mirror-images of the main action,
and more pervasively, to provide a series of contrasts in
narrative texture, placing against the comic realism of the
mock-chivalric novel insets of pastoral, picaresque, exotic

romance and adventure, cautionary tales. In mid-eight-
eenth-century England, where the explicit imitation of
Cervantes is most abundantly evident, Fielding puts interpolation to similar use though in a far more symmetrically
fashioned narrative design, while Smollett, brilliant back-
slider in the art of the novel, uses the naive device with
untroubled naiveté. Beyond them (in every sense of the
preposition), Sterne insists on the ultimate implications,
aesthetic, psychological, and epistemological, of telling
stories within stories, being in this as in most other respects
the great *jusqu'auboutiste* of the self-conscious novel.

The very notion, of course, of interpolation tends to
break down in a book where virtually all progression is
digression. The story of Le Fever's death, Slawkenbergius's
Tale, Trim's amours, even Tristram's extended flight
across Europe, can be felt only minimally as "insets" in
a novel where at every turn of a phrase, at every turn
of the stairs in Shandy Hall, the mind goes skittering off
in self-delighting demonstration of its own essential
waywardness. The general effect of all this is a highly
polarized version of the paradox of evident artifice as
seeming reality. The zigzag movement of narration is an
authentic rendering of the mind's own resistance to the
neatness of pattern and schematization, and at the same
time it is a continuous declaration by the author of the
artful arbitrariness of all authorial decisions—as his graphic introduction of actual zigzags and convoluted lines
(6:40) suggests. But to see how radical Sterne is in the
practice of fictional self-consciousness, it is worth looking
closely at one of his interpolations within a digression.
In Volume 7, as Tristram leaves the much-interrupted
account of his conception, birth, and upbringing to tell
the story of his pursuit of health through France and Italy,
he pauses over one of the tourist attractions of Lyons,
the Tomb of the Two Lovers. This gives him occasion to

recount what is purportedly the Tale of the Two Lovers
(Chapter 31):

> O! There is a sweet aera in the life of man, when, (the
> brain being tender and fibrillous, and more like pap than
> any thing else)—a story read of two fond lovers, separated
> from each other by cruel parents, and by still more cruel
> destiny—
>
> > *Amandus*—He
> > *Amanda*—She—
>
> each ignorant of the other's course,
>
> > He—east
> > She—west
>
> *Amandus* taken captive by the *Turks*, and carried to the
> emperor of *Morocco's* court, where the princess of *Morocco*
> falling in love with him, keeps him twenty years in prison,
> for the love of his *Amanda*.—
>
> She—(*Amanda*) all the time wandering barefoot, and with
> dishevell'd hair, o'er rocks and mountains enquiring for
> *Amandus*—*Amandus*! *Amandus*!—making every hill and
> vally to echo back his name—
>
> > *Amandus*! *Amandus*!
>
> at every town and city sitting down forlorn at the gate—Has
> *Amandus*!—has my *Amandus* enter'd?—till, going round,
> and round, and round the world—chance unexpected bring-
> ing them at the same moment of the night, though by
> different ways, to the gate of *Lyons* their native city, and
> each in well known accents calling out aloud,
>
> > Is *Amandus* ⎫
> > Is my *Amanda* ⎬ still alive?
>
> they fly into each others arms, and both drop down dead
> for joy.
>
> There is a soft aera in every gentle mortal's life, where
> such a story affords more *pabulum* to the brain, than all
> the *Frusts*, and *Crusts*, and *Rusts* of antiquity, which
> travellers can cook up for it.[1]

---

[1] Quotations from *Tristram Shandy* follow the text of the edition by James
A. Work (New York: Odyssey Press, 1940).

We have had occasion to observe how Cervantes' hero weaves a reflexive, ambiguously luminous poetry out of literary clichés. This passage from Sterne is, like many of Don Quixote's speeches, a tissue of patent clichés, but a different principle of parody is at work here, the effect of which is much more severely reductionist. In regard to details of plot, such as they are, the story of the two lovers could easily serve as one of the interpolated tales in *Don Quixote*, including as it does a separation of fond lovers by cruel parents, a captivity in Morocco, a Moorish princess in love with her Christian slave, and a final tragically ecstatic reunion. What Sterne does, however, with these elements is to distill from them a quintessential scheme of all such tales of romance, the conspicuousness of the scheme precluding any illusion of reality. In all his cap-and-bells antics, Sterne is one of the shrewdest literary critics of his century, and a central insight of his novel is that any literary convention means a schematiza- tion—and thus a misrepresentation—of reality. *Tristram Shandy* abundantly illustrates, moreover, that a new "au- thentic" literature liberated from conventions is a sheer impossibility. The act of literary communication can take place only by virtue of certain tacit contractual agree- ments between writer and reader—about the meaning and nature of words, about typography and pagination, about chapter divisions, about characterization and motivation, about cause and effect in narration, and much more. Whatever Stern's commitment to spontaneity, he knows that the attempt to transcend these conventional agree- ments would reduce the literary feast (Fielding's favored metaphor) to mere word-salad, and so instead he makes us continually conscious of the conventions, exploring their limits, their implicit falsity, their paradoxical power to transmit fractional truths of experience. Sterne treats each literary convention much as the inquisitive lady in Slawkenbergius's second tale (9:21) treats a certain unmentioned something—"looks at it—considers it—samples it—measures it—stretches it—wets it—dries it—then takes ... teeth both to the warp and weft of it."

Imaginative play with the duplicity of literary conventions is by no means the invention of the novel—one has only to think of the toying with supposed source-manuscripts in medieval romance and the use of inductions and plays-within-plays in Renaissance theater. There is considerable justice in Roland Barthes's lapidary formulation of the issue, though the attractions of aphoristic neatness may lead him to a degree of overstatement: "To give the imaginary the formal guarantee of the real, while leaving this sign the ambiguity of a double object, at once verisimilar and false, is a constant operation in all Western art."[2] What the novel, specifically, has been able to do, as the post-Gutenberg genre generally designed to be enjoyed by each reader in privacy at his own tempo with leisure to reread and freedom to skip, is to explore the ambiguity of its imaginary "signs" in slow motion, microscopically, from multiple angles, and, if the writer chooses, quite relentlessly. *Tristram Shandy* is in fact "the most typical novel of world literature" in this one peculiar sense, that it represents an extreme realization of an underlying direction implicit in the novel-form and followed out elsewhere less rigorously or less spectacularly by other novelists. If Barthes, taking his metaphor from the theater, can assert that "in the West ... there is no art that does not point a finger to its own mask," one must say that the distinctive situation of the novel enables the performer (for every narrator is that, none more conspicuously than Tristram) to step down from the stage, walk among the audience, invite the individual spectators to examine his mask, consider its substance, design, texture, weight, col-

[2] Barthes, *Le Degré zéro de l'écriture* (Paris: Editions de Seuil, 1953), p. 51.

oring, even guess about the reality of the face behind the mask.

The Tale of the Two Lovers illustrates how merciless this examination can become. It is, quite deliberately, the reduction of a tale of romance to an embarrassingly bare outline. The outline quality of the narration is felt not only in the succinct catalogue of formulaic phrases—"separated ... by cruel parents, and by still more cruel destiny," "wandering barefoot, and with dishevell'd hair," "each in well known accents calling," *et cetera*—but in the typography as well. First we have the exposition of the story in four words, two lines, set at the center of the page, the lovers in perfect symmetrical parallel, separated from each other by a line space and distinguished from one another by a Latin gender-ending (*"Amandus*—He/ *Amanda*—She—"). The designation of the lovers merely by the gerundive forms that mean "he who is to be loved" and "she who is to be loved" is an ultimate reduction of Cervantes' ambiguous play with the magic of naming names. If the coinage "Rocinante" points a finger to the mask, the names "Amandus" and "Amanda" turn the mask into a perfect transparency. (Significantly, the one central attempt at name-magic made by a character in the novel is deflected by circumstance, Walter's wished-for "Trismegistus"—thrice-powerful—truncated to "Tristram," a sorry creature indeed.) After the exposition, in another indentation, we are given the complication of the plot, again in a strictly schematic parallelism of four words ("He—east / She—west"). Finally, once more at the center of the page, we get the requisite recognition scene, the ever-parallel lovers, though still a line space apart, now at last united by the gently curving embrace of a typographical bracket. This is followed by a dénouement of thirteen swift words (fifteen syllables) which conclude in an iambic cadence on "joy." To cap the story, Tristram, adhering to the niceties of a rondo form, offers at the end an incremental repetition of his initial sentence, calling our attention to the purely verbal medium of the storytelling by the italicized, capitalized rhyme-words, *Frusts* (apparently Sterne's own coinage from the Latin *frustum*), *Crusts*, and *Rusts*.

The entire "reality" of the tale, then, is a compound of rigidly formulaic devices conveyed to us on the printed page through the mechanics of typography. The final turn, however, of the reductionist screw is made here not through the schematizing parody itself but through the parenthetical commentary at the beginning together with its concluding echo at the end. The era in a man's life when he relishes such stories is "sweet" and "soft"—like pabulum—which is just the consistency of the story itself or of any brain that would take a liking to it. Sterne's rapid movement from the realm of feeling to the realm of material processes is especially worth noting because it reflects an impelling problematic consciousness in *Tristram Shandy*. The tale begins with "sweet," a sensory word used figuratively. From there we proceed at once to a "tender" brain and are misled for a brief instant to read the adjective as an item in the vocabulary of sentimentalism before we see that it is followed by a medical term, "fibrillous," which in turn leads into the slap-in-the-face comparison, "like pap." Tenderness, then, is a purely physical condition of semiliquid gray matter, and we are invited to infer that all such fine structures of sentiment issue from some physical substratum which may be less than edifying to contemplate.

In the world of *Tristram Shandy*, as at least two of Sterne's more perceptive critics have recently noted, there is a constant dynamic tension between the mental and the material spheres. Extravagant attention is devoted to the minute rendering of each—to Corporal Trim's desolation over his brother's plight, on the one hand, and to the elaborate series of movements that produce the puffing of a pipe, on the other hand. The contiguity of the two realms is evident, their interconnection and causal relation a continual enigma, a continual source of frustration, comedy, and surprise. If one wonders why Sterne should be so much more ruthless as a critic of literary artifice than Cervantes, a chief reason would have to be that he writes at a point in intellectual history—for his novel is eminently a document of intellectual history—when there was manifest cause for worry that the tender feelings evoked by the refinements of literature might be finally just a question of mushy gray matter.

Tristram Shandy was created toward the end of the great century of confident mechanistic science that began with the publication of Newton's *Principia* in 1687. Descartes' metaphysical analysis had introduced an ontological cleavage between mental and material existence that would remain a crux of philosophical debate for generations to come. In the realm of physics pure and simple, Newton founded an explanation of the physical world on what seemed to be an entirely adequate basis of measurement, with quantification in terms of mass held as the key. Conscious of the new Newtonian physics, Locke transferred the mechanistic mode of explanation to the realm of psychology. Existence was split into "primary qualities," which were wholly quantifiable, and "secondary qualities," projected onto objects by the mind. The world of value and sensuous opulence was reduced to a mental construct; nature in and of itself was colorless, tasteless, odorless, and, finally, senseless. Lockean psychology, with its mechanistic model of the *tabula rasa* and the association of ideas, is a preeminent instance of what Whitehead has characterized as the Fallacy of Misplaced Concreteness.

It is no wonder that Sterne begins his novel by throwing a machine into the Lockean system, that regularly wound clock linked in poor Mrs. Shandy's mind with her husband's monthly conjugal performances "from an unhappy association of ideas which have no connection in nature" (1:4). If Locke, as the regnant figure of philosophical psychology for Sterne's century, provided a basis for the associative method of *Tristram Shandy,* the novel treats him even more as a teacher to be taunted, a hobgoblin to be exorcised, because his ontological devaluation of the imagination and its products cuts the ground from under the whole enterprise of literature. *Tristram Shandy* is a continuous demonstration and celebration of the irrepressible power and ubiquity of the imagination,[3] but at the same time Sterne must repeatedly concede the possibility, so palpable in the thought of his age, that the imagination is a cheat, a purveyor of substanceless flimflam in a mechanistically determined physical universe. Martin Price, with the problem of philosophical dualism particularly in mind, has aptly caught the tenor of this tension in Sterne's novel between two opposed but somehow contiguous realms:

> Sterne carries the duality of man to its ultimate expression. He comically exaggerates the outside view of man as a physically determined creature, the sport of chance or mechanical causation, the lonely product of a valueless material world. He exaggerates no less the inside view of man as a creature of feeling, convinced phenomonologically that he has a soul, creating the world in which he chiefly lives by the energy of his own imagination. The disjunction is as violent as Pascal's.[4]

What sharpens the paradoxicality of Sterne's fiction is the fact that the recent development of the novel as a genre has made available striking techniques of comic and

---

[3] I have tried to trace the process of demonstration elsewhere in "*Tristram Shandy* and the Game of Love," *The American Scholar,* Spring 1968.

[4] Price, *To the Palace of Wisdom* (Garden City, N. Y.: Doubleday, 1964), p. 324.

serious realism at the very moment when the new science and philosophy were raising questions about the inherent connection between imaginative literature and reality. Parody, together with direct imitation and plain borrowing, is pervasive in *Tristram Shandy*, Sterne's models including Rabelais, Montaigne, Burton, Descartes, Locke, Swift, and a host of lesser writers, scholastic, scientific, historical, and satirical. It is worth noting in particular, however, the way he parodies all the principal models of novel-writing available to him by pushing the method of each to its logical extreme. Written scarcely twenty years after the form had got fully under way in England, *Tristram Shandy* is the first novel about the crisis of the novel.

"Cervantick" realism, Sterne perceived, operates by a repeated juxtaposition of soaring fantasy with earthbound, coarse-grained actuality, the quixotic principle colliding with the sanchesque. *Tristram Shandy* comically and philosophically expands this central strategy of *Don Quixote* by making it the ubiquitous pattern of every man's relation to every other and to the world of physical existence. The obvious Quixote-Sancho pairings in the novel, Toby and Trim, Walter and Mrs. Shandy, in fact suggest an infinite *dédoublement*, for everyone is quixotic in putting some private construction of the mind—some personal lexicon—upon reality, and any other is a potential Sancho to one's own quixotry: Walter to Toby and Toby to Walter, Jenny to Tristram, Obadiah (and his horse) to Dr. Slop, the scullion to Trim, the bull to all the Shandys. One functional justification for the pervasiveness of *double entente* in the novel is that sexuality is conceived as every person's Sancho Panza—the hot chestnut in the codpiece, "that one thing which *Dolly's* hand is in search of" (2:2), the universal human preoccupation that binds us while systems sizzle, hypotheses hatch, and ratiocination goes its merry solipsistic way.

From Fielding, himself the author of a novel "Written,"

as its title page proclaimed, "in Imitation of the *Manner* of Cervantes," Sterne adopted the self-conscious, self-advertising narrator who reflects discursively on the innovative nature of his fiction as he makes it. Here, again, it is Sterne's peculiar brilliance as a borrower to push so far what he has taken that it is no longer a device or a technique but a fundamental problematic, both literary and philosophical. The narrators of *Joseph Andrews* and *Tom Jones* call attention to themselves as artificers in a variety of ingenious and elegantly ironic ways. The narrator of *Tristram Shandy* draws us so intimately and inventively into the present tense of his writing that all the other elaborately indicated times of narrated events ultimately dissolve into it, and the stumbling chase of a self trying to catch its own or any experience through an act of written communication becomes the true plot of the novel.

The contradictory fusion of conjuration and critique is at its most spectacular in this novel, typicality attained over and over through extremeness. We know, on the one hand, that the clowning narrator is less a personage than a pretext, a mask for the Laurence Sterne who, to pick up one of several such notations he offers us, pens the eighteenth chapter of the first volume in his Yorkshire study on March 9, 1759. All the talk in *Tristram* about critics and different kinds of readers, about time, duration, and narrative conventions, the black and blank and marbled pages that force us to see the process of semantic integration through which each reader assembles the world of a novel in his head—all these make us aware of novel-writing as a highly complicated activity of construction with the materials of convention. Yet Tristram, precisely because the distance between him and Sterne flickers and fades, also seems very real without novelistic realization, humanly poignant in his urgency to get something of himself across to us through the labyrinth of literary and linguistic conventions that surrounds him, that surrounds all of us. At one remove of creation from Tristram, we are intermittently moved to assent to the reality of the personages—Sterne's inventions—that populate his story because we identify with him in his effort to make his experience real through writing. Fielding's Squire Western remains a manifest fabrication, brilliantly lifelike, wonderfully memorable, but clearly a device in an invented narrative manipulated by the novelist's narrating persona. Sterne's Uncle Toby we know is a fabrication as well, but at times, by virtue of this peculiar novel's mirror-game of mimesis, he seems to be something more: because Tristram is his own elusive subject, we want Tristram's tale of his uncle to be real so that Tristram can be real, we want to accept as facts of experience the minute rendering of Toby's sorrow over the death of the fly, Toby's childlike joy over his model fortifications, his terror of Woman on the sofa next to the Widow Wadman. It is not really so surprising that generations of readers unattuned to Sterne's sophistication as a self-conscious novelist and out of sympathy with the slippery play of his sexual wit were nevertheless able to enjoy the novel sentimentally for the touching lifelike eccentricities of its characters.

Sterne's radical transformation of the self-conscious narrator, which he picked up from Fielding, is perhaps most suggestively revealed in the role death comes to play in *Tristram Shandy*. Fielding's self-conscious narrator by his very nature implies comedy of a particularly pure kind: the narrated action, we are continually reminded, is part of a cunning design where one assumes the creator will protect the deserving among his creatures from any real disaster. Death is a narrative convenience through which characters like Captain Blifil and Tom's father can be eliminated for the purposes of the plot, but the gallows that cast their shadow over Tom we recognize as an elaborate authorial joke, the novelist toying with mock-tragedy before he reveals his comic dénouement. In the end, the hero must return to the sunlit sphere of Paradise Hall where, in the last unfolding vista of married bliss and propagation, one finds it hard to imagine there has been any First Disobedience that could bring death or woe into this world.

The comedy of *Tristram Shandy* is clearly of another order—not the affirmation of artifice as a means of constructing models of harmonious integration but the use of laughter as the defense-action of an embattled psyche, its chief means of confronting the terrors of loneliness, frustration, pain, of its own inevitable extinction. There is nothing of Fielding's comic confidence in the language Sterne chooses to describe his enterprise in his dedicatory epistle to Pitt: "... I live in a constant endeavour to fence against the infirmities of ill health, and other evils of life, by mirth; being firmly persuaded that every time a man smiles,—but much more so, when he laughs, that it adds something to this Fragment of Life." Sterne's novel begins with the act of conception that is supposed to lead to the birth of the hero, but a death—Yorick's—is the most prominent event of the first volume. The famous black page, prefaced by the double quotation of "Alas, poor YORICK!" reduces death to a literary and typographical joke, yet paradoxically confronts us with death as an ultimate, irreducible fact, the final opaqueness beyond the scope of language and narrative invention, beyond even the tracery of significant black lines on the white ground of a printed page. Similarly ambiguous attention is lavished on the deaths of Le Fever and Bobby, the element of pathos being stressed in the former, the hilarious comic discrepancy between event and response emphasized in the latter case. By the time Death himself knocks at the door at the beginning of Volume 7, mortality is no fictional plaything but the real motor force that drives Tristram-Sterne on his wild scramble to write, and write still more.

The "vile cough" that wracks Tristram is autobiographically Sterne's, and death now can no longer be conjured with but must be eluded—physically, by the flight across Europe, narratively, by devoting digressive attention to anything else the mind can play with, especially anything like codpieces and slit petticoats, because they speak of life. Sterne's nervous yet exuberant bandying with real and imagined death is the clearest illustration of how his extravagantly artificial comic novel opens into an existential realism beyond the purview of comedy, where artifice and artificer collapse into a vulnerable man trying to add something to his Fragment of Life.

This ultimacy of parodistic extrapolation that we have observed in Sterne's relation to Cervantes and Fielding is also detectable in the use to which he puts the other two novelists who were immediate models for him, Smollett and Richardson. In regard to Smollett, of course, the borrowing is more obvious and direct, the humorist's fascination with outrageous eccentricity that links Sterne with the Scottish novelist even leading him to take Commodore Hawser Trunnion's nautical household in *Peregrine Pickle* as a model for Uncle Toby's garden fortifications. Nevertheless, Sterne's imagination of eccentricity and its implications differs profoundly from Smollett's. The Hawser Trunnions and Tom Bowlings and Matthew Brambles that vivify Smollett's fiction are all seen from the safe vantage point of a reasonable, "normal" observer, and so are held at a distance as endearing objects of amusement that entertain through their bizarreness, their wild deviation from an implicit rational norm. In *Tristram Shandy* there are no straight men and there is no norm. The world is entirely peopled with Smollettian eccentrics, rendered, however, in most instances with gentle sympathy. Bizarreness is grasped as an essential condition of every human being living inside his own peculiar skin and peering out on the world through the weirdly refracting

medium of his own conceptions and predispositions. Comic
eccentricity, then, implies for Sterne the problem of the
dysfunction of language that is at the heart of *Tristram
Shandy*. Smollett had happily conceived the idea of a series
of eccentrics each insisting on his own special vocabulary.
Sterne's genius leads him to transmute the phenomenon
of private vocabularies into a whole world of mutual
misapprehensions and slapstick intersections where communication can take place only (and occasionally) through
gesture and intuition, or through the sexuality common
to all.

As for Richardson, Sterne may have drawn some inspiration from him for his own interest in the novelistic
rendering of sentiment, as some of the literary handbooks
claim, but I think what arrested his imagination more
decisively in Richardson was the attempt at an exhaustive
presentation of reality with the concomitant slowing down
of narrative tempo. In Richardson's novels, one feels the
palpable weight of minute-by-minute experience conveyed
with a particularity of social, psychological, at times even
physical detail that is quite new in European fiction. The
idea of exhaustive presentation through slow-motion narration intrigued Sterne: the possibilities of its comic exaggeration titillated him; but above all it suggested to him
a fundamental problematic bearing on the inherent limitations of literary mimesis. Walter Shandy's advancing foot,
hovering over the first step from the landing for the whole
length of a chapter in which Sterne reflects upon chapters
(4:10-12), is surely, among other things, a comic blow-up
of Richardsonian narrative pace. Here, as elsewhere in the
treatment of his novelistic predecessors, the effect of
Sterne's parody is not reduction but fantastic expansion,
raising over and over the question whether language, with
its serial nature and its drastically selective bias, can ever
yield an exhaustive account either of a narrated event
or of the contents at a particular moment of the narrator's

mind. The fantastic character of this expansion is worth stressing because Sterne's ingenious procedures act, like the slow-motion camera, close-ups, odd camera angles, and rapid cutting of different shots in film, to uncover a world of fantastic proportions and connections in the most familiar and prosaic scenes. One sees the aptness of Jean-Jacques Mayoux's characterization of this strange mode of fiction, in his brilliant essay on Sterne, as an "absurd and alienating realism."[5] But the role of fantasy in Sterne's artifice of exaggerated realism is a subject to which we shall return.

We began with a reductionist parody of a tale of romance, the method illustrating how literary convention can be a schematic betrayal of experience, which is multifaceted, quirky, entrammeled in physical existence. The counterpoint of such parody is the affirmation of an antithetical realism, and what Sterne concentrates on in the last two volumes of *Tristram Shandy*, following upon the parodistic outline of the Tale of Two Lovers in Volume 7, is a Shandean transmogrification of the tale of romance that offers one of his many asymptotic approaches to reality. The model here is Trim's amour with the fair Beguine (8:23), the episode that arrested Diderot's attention enough for him to translate it whole into the ending of *Jacques the Fatalist and His Master*. Like so many of the stories within stories in *Tristram Shandy*, this is a tale told to a misapprehending audience, demonstrating still again how most of us fail to get straight even straightforward accounts of lived experience because we interpose our own preconceptions and psychological reticences, our own expectations of narrative convention. Trim's tale, quite clearly, is of skilled female fingers on a slow march to an erogenous objective, but the tender-hearted, pap-

---

[5] Mayoux, "Laurence Sterne," tr. John Traugott, in *Laurence Sterne: A Collection of Critical Essays*, ed. Traugott (Englewood Cliffs, N. J.: Prentice-Hall, Inc., 1968), p. 116.

brained Toby can extract from it only fine literary sentiments:

> The more she rubb'd, and the longer strokes she took—the
> more the fire kindled in my veins—till at length, by two
> or three strokes longer than the rest—my passion rose to
> the highest pitch—I seized her hand—
> —And then, thou clapped'st it to thy lips, *Trim*, said
> my uncle *Toby*—and madest a speech.
> Whether the corporal's amour terminated precisely in the
> way my uncle *Toby* described it, is not material; it is enough
> that it contain'd in it the essence of all the love-romances
> which ever have been wrote since the beginning of the world.

One major impulse of Sterne's realism is to bring eth-
erealizing fancy and abstracting reason solidly down into
the physical realm where, necessarily, they have their
origins. His sexual puns effect this linguistically by constantly reminding us how metaphorical usage develops
from a base of physical experience, whether consciously
or not. Thus, in Trim's story, the conventional figure of
rising to a high pitch of passion becomes an allusion to
the functioning of erectile tissue, and "passion" has a plain
physiological meaning. Trim's dalliance with the Beguine
contains the essence of all love-romances ever written
because it leads our attention back to the sexual interaction that is always present in a love story, however the
pretensions of the story and its conventions may try to
avoid, disguise, or cosmetize the underlying sexual facts.
Sterne underscores the paradigmatic role of Trim's
amour by providing three different doublings of it in the
final volume of the novel. The story of the romance
between Trim's brother Tom and the Jew's widow in the
Lisbon sausage shop is, in the transparent *double entente*
that runs through the whole chapter (9:7), another
tale of a deft woman's hand stroking "forced meat," with
the good widow finally capitulating when she sees that
Tom's sausage "had more gristle on it." Less messily,

Trim's courtship of Bridget (9:28) is again a matter of a strategic laying on of hands: "It was somewhat unfortunate for Mrs. *Bridget,* that she had begun the attack with her manual exercise, for the Corporal instantly—" at which point the narrative explodes into three and a half lines of asterisks, leaving us with another variation on the essence of all love-romances. Bridget's manual attack, in turn, mirrors in accomplished fact the blushing, hesitant intention of her mistress, the Widow Wadman, to place her finger over the very place where poor Toby was wounded at Namur (9:20).

Now, with this insistence on Trim's tactile affair with the Beguine as paradigm, it may seem that what passes for realism in Sterne is sexually reductionist. This is not strictly true, however, because Sterne, probably more than any other writer before Freud, had a conscious awareness of repression and its manifold implications, the keenness of his comic realism often largely generated by his shrewd rendering of those implications. The essence of all love-romances is not just a male member and female touch but the psychological strategies of coping with those two basic facts by the potential lovers and by the audience. Depending on their various habits of sublimation, avoidance, ambivalent vacillation, impulses to gratification, Shandean lovers are likely to stand under an overarching question mark of misunderstanding, and the reader's personal familiarity with the same sort of habits makes *double entente* the most appropriate vehicle for the Shandean love-romance.

The culminating misunderstanding between Uncle Toby and the Widow Wadman is a vivid case in point. Significantly, Sterne concludes the slow preparation to this climax that has been winding through a volume and a half by one of his most ostentatious overturnings of the conventions of reading and printing. After Tristram has at last invited us to follow Toby and Trim across the

Wadman threshold, he introduces two blank pages, labeled "CHAP. XVIII" and "CHAP. XIX" (we will get the chapters out of order ten pages later), and then the twentieth chapter, which begins with two whole paragraphs of asterisks, followed by Toby's mistaken offer to let the widow see the very place where he was wounded. The missing chapters and the asterisks of course heighten comic suspense while reminding us how arbitrary all narrative selections and divisions are. More to our present point, though, this strategic abandoning of language for blank space and printer's symbols is Sterne's visible means of "halving" things, as he says elsewhere, with the reader, "do[ing] all that lies in my power to keep his imagination as busy as my own" (2:11). Art here points not only to its mask but to its inherent limits, inviting the reader to conjure up for himself the details of a narrative event that in its excitements and emotional complications, its psychological multiplicity, must remain beyond the highly selective reach of language and narration.

After this eloquent use of typographical silences, Sterne returns to language with virtuoso skill. First, Toby makes his generous offer, impervious through his habitual sublimation in seige-works to what is obviously uppermost in the mind of this widow who has been waiting so long to be wadded by a man. Her own response to what she misconceives as an offer to get to the naked essence of love-romance is brilliantly rendered by Sterne:

> Mrs. *Wadman* blush'd—look'd towards the door—turn'd pàle—blush'd slightly again—recovered her natural colour—blushed worse than ever; which for the sake of the unlearned reader, I translate thus—
> *"L—d! I cannot look at it—*
> *What would the world say if I look'd at it?*
> *I should drop down, if I look'd at it—*
> *I wish I could look at it—*
> *There can be no sin in looking at it.*
> *—I will look at it."*

Sterne's use of stacatto pauses and dashes achieves the precision of a quasi-musical notation of minute gesture—here, the quick ebb and flow of color in a woman's cheeks. The darting interplay of conscience and desire, first indicated through six external movements, is then "translated" into six verbal statements, the pairs bracketed with hilarious appropriateness ("look'd toward the door"—"*What would the world say?*"; "turn'd pale"—"*I should drop down, if I look'd at it*"; "recovered her natural colour"—"*There can be no sin in looking at it*"; "blushed worse than ever"—"*I will look at it*"). The teasing game of correspondences between inner and outer, mental and material, that we have already noted in *Tristram Shandy* is delightfully evident here. Long before Faulkner, Sterne adopts italics for a new convention of designating interior speech, but his very characterization of the six lines as a "translation" of gestural language suggests that the verbal formulation, however meticulous, is not quite the thing itself. We come closer here to the subtle movements of consciousness than the novel will bring us until Joyce and Proust, yet the strategy of presentation also reminds us that mercurial consciousness, which can express itself involuntarily in the contraction and dilation of the fine capillaries in the skin, is not necessarily or entirely verbal.

No critic has grasped the paradoxicality of Sterne's self-mocking realism so firmly as Jean-Jacques Mayoux. "If every representation," Mayoux writes, "is in some degree parody, is not every parody in danger of becoming in some degree representative?" This ingenious formula suggests why the enterprise of mimesis is intrinsically comic, playful, and—in the philosophic sense—absurd for Sterne, and why, therefore, there is an ultimate difference in kind between his ostentatiously coy rendering of gesture and thought and the modern attempt to provide a "transcription" of consciousness in the various techniques of interior monologue. The effect of Sterne's method is of course enormously amusing but also disorienting, for while

the purported realism of previous literature is repeatedly
exposed as absurd, what is patently absurd at times strangely conforms to the lineaments of reality. Mayoux continues: "We never quite touch absolute reality. We come
close to it only by signs more or less inadequate, of which
the most immediate, the most powerful, correspond to our
intuitions, and the most hackneyed are frozen in the code
we call culture. Culture masks what would perhaps be
reality; and the nostalgia for reality is one of the liveliest
of Sterne's sentiments."[6]

This is beautifully observed, though the notion of intuition needs to be extended beyond its usual sense. It is
true that *Tristram Shandy* repeatedly creates channels
for the flow of intuition, ranging from the imagination
of fleshly desire to the impulse of creaturely sympathy.
Perhaps the simplest illustration is Trim's kitchen lecture
on mortality (5:7), where a stark gesture, the dropping of
a hat, puts the corporal's listeners in touch for a fleeting
moment, immediately qualified by irony, with the actual
meaning of Bobby's death. Gesture makes a connection
with feelings masked or deflected by culture, but even the
intuition triggered by gesture is not immediate, for a
gesture is itself a mediation, caught up only a little less
than spoken language in the fine mesh of culture. (Hats,
after all, are made by hatters and worn in certain cultural-
ly determined circumstances; falling as an image of death
is an agreed-upon sign; and the casting down of the
top-piece in any case merely punctuates the rhythmic
rhetoric of Trim's speech.) I think Mayoux is right in
claiming that Sterne associates intuition with our closest
approximations of reality, but since Sterne equally recognizes that all experience is mediated by mental processes,
themselves conditioned by culture, he also frequently
evokes the restless dynamic of the mind interacting with

[6] Mayoux, p. 113.

itself as the indisputable reality we inhabit, and thus his extreme consciousness of artifice and reader-response becomes an instrument of realism. Here culture is a "mask" because it numbs the mind's awareness of its own liveliness, cripples the creativity of the imagination by accustoming it to work perfunctorily with fixed stereotypes.

The ultimate approximation of reality in *Tristram Shandy*, I would argue, is in the zany and unpredictable engendering of associations that springs the mind loose from its conventional set, enables it to experience its own athletic vitality. Sterne's method reminds us that the irrepressible world of fantasy is, at least from one point of view, our most humanly familiar reality. Many moments in *Tristram Shandy* are neither narration nor commentary nor expository digression but odd invitations for the mind to move in the most unexpected ways, the materials of fantasy being delicately coaxed into the light of consciousness.

Thus, the fifth chapter of Volume 8 begins with a brief, enigmatic reflection on why women are attracted to weavers, gardeners, and gladiators (because they work with beams, sticks, and swords?), or to a man with a shriveled leg (the impotence theme once more). Sterne then proceeds, by the obscurest of connections, to a disquisition on water-drinkers:

> A water-drinker, provided he is a profess'd one, and does it without fraud or covin, is precisely in the same predicament: not that, at first sight, there is any consequence, or shew of logic in it, "That a rill of water dribbling through my inward parts, should light up a torch in my *Jenny's—*"
>
> —The proposition does not strike one; on the contrary, it seems to run opposite to the natural workings of causes and effects—
>
> But it shews the weakness and imbecility of human reason.
>
> —"And in perfect good health with it?"

—The most perfect—Madam, that friendship herself could
wish me—

—"And drink nothing!—nothing but water?"

—Impetuous fluid! the moment thou pressest against the
flood-gates of the brain—see how they give way!—

In swims CURIOSITY, beckoning to her damsels to follow—
they dive into the centre of the current—

FANCY sits musing upon the bank, and with her eyes
following the stream, turns straws and bulrushes into masts
and bowsprits—And DESIRE, with vest held up to the knee
in one hand, snatches at them, as they swim by her, with
the other—

O ye water-drinkers! is it then by this delusive fountain,
that ye have so often governed and turn'd this world about
like a mill-wheel—grinding the faces of the impotent—
bepowdering their ribs—be-peppering their noses, and
changing sometimes even the very frame and face of nature—

The initial assertion about water-drinkers, like the
statement about weavers, gardeners, and gladiators that
precedes it, is momentarily reminiscent in tone of the
so-called essayistic passages in Fielding. With Fielding,
however, logic and consequence are the constant under-
pinning both of the narrator's discourses and of the larger
structure of the novel. Here, by contrast, we are immediately put on notice that what seems to follow logically
as cause and effect may have very little to do with what
actually goes on in the world of physical existence—thus
a cold rill of water works aphrodisiacally in Tristram to
light up a torch in his Jenny's—. Reason (what Locke calls
"judgment") is imbecile when it assumes that its neat
structures correspond to a reality infinitely inventive in
its perverse variety. The faculty that does answer to the
erratic and paradoxical nature of reality is not reason but
imagination, as Sterne's method brilliantly illustrates here
by breaking down the Fieldingesque disquisition into a
fantasia of consciousness, graphically forcing "the flood-
gates of the brain" to give way.

Starting with water-drinkers (while we still puzzle over the weavers, and others before them), Sterne takes us through a series of quick shifts in focus and method of presentation that is analogous in effect to a rapid series of cinematic dissolves. What we experience before all else in the passage is the kinetic energy of the imagination itself, an energy confined and thwarted by conventional literary modes and logical methods of thought. From the instance of the consequences of water-drinking and the reflection on their illogicality, we are tumbled pell-mell into a dialogue between Tristram and Madam. Sterne's ubiquitous "eavesdropped effect" is acutely felt here. On a second reading we can begin to make out what Tristram and Madam are really saying to each other, but the fragmentariness of communication persists, the teasing sense that, as in ordinary life, we simply cannot get full enough information to draw conclusions with the certainty we would like. Tristram has hardly got his dialogue with Madam under way before he shifts—for a moment, as in a film dissolve, we do not realize it is a shift—into a formal apostrophe to water.

The apostrophe, in turn, with the metaphor of flood-gates acting as a trigger, immediately flips into a weird allegorical landscape in which capitalized female figures of FANCY and DESIRE sit on a riverbank while CURIOSITY and her entourage of water-nymphs go diving into the stream. All this began, one recalls, with an interior rivulet coursing toward Tristram's virile member, and so the bucolic scene appropriately is a sexual fantasy in which FANCY—a term used by Sterne in approximate synonymity with fantasy, wit, and imagination—follows the illogical metamorphosis of sexual physiology itself by turning fragile straws and bulrushes into phallicly swollen masts and bowsprits. DESIRE, in a suitable state of undress, shows herself a true sister to Bridget and the fair Beguine by snatching at these passing beams born of motes.

Just as the allegory is approaching the climactic essence
of all true love-romances, the narrator breaks off with a
dash, as in the amours of Bridget and the Beguine, and
again he leaps to new ground—an apostrophe to water-
drinkers. This final apostrophe sweeps through a field of
reference so wide and wild that the effect is of a comic
phantasmagoria. The stream that has already been turned
into an image of male potency here becomes a global and
historical source of power, of aggressive energy, turning
the world around like a mill-wheel, "changing sometimes
even the very frame and face of nature" (Sterne's "Freudian" intuition could hardly be better illustrated). Equally
noteworthy is the way this last paragraph literally defies
ordinary logic—already explicitly abused—by suddenly
crashing the fantasy of virility that has informed the whole
passage against the author's recurrent preoccupation with
impotence, the impotent emerging from the collision here
with faces ground and noses be-peppered, like poor Tristram himself.

The narrator's erratic progress is amusing, titillating,
and by this point we no longer know quite what to make
of it, perhaps are no longer intended to know. The zigzag
movement of the passage, one might observe, is unsteadily
but perceptibly outward toward an expanding horizon of
imagination—from a trickle of water in inward parts to
a generalization and expostulation, to a stream bearing
straws turned to bowsprits, to the great world spun round
like a mill-wheel. One of the general aims of Sterne's
method, I would suggest, is to make us repeatedly aware
of the infinite horizon of the imagination. Since infinity
can hardly be contained in a finite narrative form, what
Sterne must do is constantly cut back sharply from the
expansive associative movement of his prose through the
sudden disjuncture of a dash—and return us to the small
world of his comic actors. Here, we cut from the "frame
and face of nature" to a very brief exchange between

Yorick and Eugenius, and then, as a fitting conclusion to the chapter, Tristram's resolution "never to read any book but my own, as long as I live." The horizon evoked, however, does not entirely fade: its constant presence in the novel is one major reason why this elaborately rendered world of trivialities and frustrations nevertheless imparts to the reader a peculiar sense of comic liberation. Shandean man is everywhere in the fetters of circumstance but everywhere the imagination is free; the blind forceps of reality may crush one's nose, or whatever, to a pulp, but the mind can still spin Slawkenbergian fantasies of a man with a proboscis so enormous that it mesmerizes an entire city.

What I should like to stress about this whole bizarre procedure of Sterne's, here and elsewhere, is how far it takes us from anything like novelistic narration without ever really abandoning the enterprise of the novelist. Sterne is in fact fascinated by the challenge of rendering nuanced interaction of characters in intimate social settings, of conveying the complex feel of quotidian experience, and his own response to that challenge of mimesis is in several ways more subtle and convincing than any previous representation of reality in a novel. He is keenly aware, however, that mimesis is a task of Sysiphus, and he surrounds the "reality" of the little Shandy world with the constant swirl and eddy of another reality—his mind's and ours. This latter reality, he knows, is in some of its essential aspects either preverbal or metalinguistic, but he is able to implicate us in its internal dynamism through the ingenious ways by which he manipulates language and the typographical appurtenances of the printed word. *Tristram Shandy* is as much an act of pure play as any novel ever written, but as with other kinds of games, it is play that makes us strenuously rehearse some of the vital processes by which we must live in reality. In this early but ultimate instance of self-reflexive fiction, the many mirrors of the novel set to catch its own operations also give us back the image of the mind in action; and at a moment when dominant intellectual assumptions had seemed to subvert philosophically the realistic aspiration of literature, literary self-consciousness paradoxically proves to be a technique of realism as well.

One could hardly conceive a more explicit illustration of the notion that books are made up out of other books than Diderot's ostentatious use of Sterne in *Jacques the Fatalist and His Master*. From the beginning, we are alerted to the fact that the final point toward which the zigzags of Diderot's digressive narrative are headed is the amours of Jacques with the fair Denise—which are of course but a Gallic transposition of the amours of Trim and the fair Beguine. Diderot is careful to call our attention to the borrrowing in the extended editorial note with which he concludes his novel and invites our complicity in the making of it. The manuscript of *Jacques*, claims the fictitious editor, ends with three paragraphs, the second of which seems to him a spurious interpolation, for it is "copied from the life of Tristram Shandy."[1] The editor

---

[1] *Jacques le fataliste et son maître*, in Diderot, *Oeuvres romanesques*, ed. Henri Benác (Paris: Garnier, 1962), p. 778. All subsequent references are to this edition. The translations are my own.

and the active implication of the reader in the narration for rather different purposes than Sterne, and therefore in a perceptibly different manner.

With such narratives that make us conscious of the arbitrariness of all beginnings and endings—Diderot's does this even more pointedly than Sterne's—one might as well begin with the end, the penultimate moment in the amours of Trim-Jacques. Although the supposed editor of *Jacques* asserts that a paragraph has been "copied" from *Tristram Shandy*, what Diderot in fact has done is not at all a translation of Sterne but a condensed paraphrase, shifting the point of view and, as we shall see, transposing the whole fictional event into a different narrative key. Let us first recall in detail the relevant passage from *Tristram Shandy* (8:22), minute detail of course being the essence of Sterne's distinctive technique, the method in his madness. Trim, one remembers, has been describing to Toby that intolerable itch of his healing wound long ago, which the fair Beguine offered to relieve through the most exquisite of massages.

Let me see it, said she, kneeling down upon the ground parallel to my knee, and laying her hand upon the part below it—It only wants rubbing a little, said the *Beguine*; so covering it with the bed cloaths, she began with the forefinger of her right-hand to rub under my knee, guiding her fore-finger backwards and forwards by the edge of the flannel which kept on the dressing.

In five or six minutes I felt slightly the end of her second finger—and presently it was laid flat with the other, and she continued rubbing in that way round and round for a good while; it then came into my head that I should fall in love—I blush'd when I saw how white a hand she had—I shall never, an' please your honour, behold another hand so white whilst I live—

—Not in that place: said my uncle *Toby*—

Though it was the most serious despair in nature to the corporal—he could not forbear smiling.

The young *Beguine*, continued the corporal, perceiving it was of great service to me—from rubbing, for some time, with two fingers—proceeded to rub at length, with three—till by little and little she brought down the fourth, and then rubb'd with her whole hand: I will never say another word, an' please your honour, upon hands again—but it was softer than satin—

—Prithee, *Trim*, commend it as much as thou wilt, said my uncle *Toby*; I shall hear thy story with the more delight—The corporal thank'd his master most unfeignedly; but having nothing to say upon the *Beguine*'s hand, but the same over again—he proceeded to the effects of it.

The fair *Beguine*, said the corporal, continued rubbing with her whole hand under my knee—till I fear'd her zeal would weary her—"I would do a thousand times more," said she, "for the love of Christ"—In saying which she pass'd her hand across the flannel, to the part above the knee, which I had equally complained of, and rubb'd it also.

I perceived, then, I was beginning to be in love—

As she continued rub-rub-rubbing—I felt it spread from under her hand, an' please your honour, to every part of my frame—

> The more she rubb'd, and the longer strokes she took—the
> more the fire kindled in my veins—till at length, by two
> or three strokes longer than the rest—my passion rose to
> the highest pitch—I seiz'd her hand—

We have already noted, in another connection, the
shrewdly reductionist effect of the allusion here by *double
entente* to physiological facts, the rising passion archly
equated with the rising of something else. The rhythm
of the passage as a whole imitates the slow-building
rhythm of the physical arousal that is being described,
moving ever so patiently from one finger to two, to three,
and so forth. As Sterne has long since conditioned us to
expect, that rhythm is in turn broken into by comic
comment and expostulation from another time-scheme,
the present tense of the teller of the tale and his auditor.
In any case, what should be particularly observed at the
outset is the microscopic niceness of detail through which
Sterne renders the gradual crescendo of teased desire—a
forefinger guided backwards and forwards along the edge
of the flannel, then the end of a second finger, then both
fingers laid flat on the flesh, then still another, *et cetera*.
All this appropriately elicits in the subject, Trim, a delicate
fluctuation of fine sensations—a slight tactile feeling, a
sudden thought, a blush, a perception of satiny softness,
a suffusion of physical euphoria. The verbal account comes
so close to the lived rhythm of the experience that a
nursery-rhyme mimickry of action by language—"she continued rub-rub-rubbing"—can provide a perfectly appropriate preclimax to those last long strokes. There is more
to be said about the implications of these procedures, but
let us first see how Diderot has transformed them.

> Denise volunteered to relieve him; she took a little piece
> of flannel; Jacques set his leg out of the bed, and Denise
> began to rub with the flannel below the wound, first with
> one finger, then with two, then with three, with four, with

her whole hand. Jacques watched her perform and was
intoxicated with love. Then Denise began to rub with the
flannel on the wound itself, the scar of which was still red,
first with one finger, after with two, with three, with four,
with her whole hand. But it was not enough to have eased
the itching below the knee, on the knee; it still had to be
eased above where it was making itself felt all the more
sharply. Denise placed the flannel above the knee, and began
to rub there quite firmly, first with one finger, then two,
with three, with four, with her whole hand. The passion
of Jacques, who had not ceased watching her, grew to such
a point that, no longer able to resist, he pounced upon
Denise's hand . . . and embraced. [pp. 778-779]

The conspicuous fact that Diderot's rendering of these
narrative data is a little more than one-third the length
of Sterne's reflects the essential difference between the
two. Though Diderot is quite as aware as Sterne that this
manner of caress by incremental repetition has erotic
piquancy, his interest lies in transmitting it deftly and
elegantly as a narrated event, not in recreating it as an
experience to be felt on our pulses. All the minute speci-
fication of forefingers lightly touching and whole fingers
laid flat is eliminated; and the hypnotic to-and-fro rhythm
of the caress, punctuated by the gently suggestive words
of the caresser, disappears in the brisk forward rush of
Diderot's prose. In Sterne, the introduction of each addi-
tional finger requires the slow suspension of a clause or
an elongated phrase—"till by little and little she brought
down the fourth, and then rubb'd with her whole hand."
Diderot trips through the whole series in an accelerating
rhythm that races to the little climax—"*d'abord avec un
doigt, puis avec deux, avec trois, avec quatre, avec toute
la main.*" The double repetition of this compressed series
is not a rhythmic conjuration of the experience but a nice
symmetry of narration: one to five fingers below, on, above
the knee, moving to the equivocal resolution of "*la baisa*"

which could mean he kissed either the hand or the girl.[2]
Here the concluding confusion of the *double entente* is
not a misunderstanding between characters or even an
archly titillating contrivance of the narrator in the manner
of Sterne, but rather a carefully engineered narrative ploy
to turn the reader back to the indeterminacy of fictional
events and fictional endings. The Shandean *double entente*
always hovers teasingly, with a suspicion of sensualist
relish, over a half-perceived erotic meaning. Here, by
contrast, the clearcut difference between the two possible
antecedents of *la* (and perhaps between the two meanings
of *baiser*) amounts to a difference in plot—is Jacques'
amour consummated or isn't it?—and this in turn implies
a difference in views as to the plausible motivation of
character. Jacques, we have learned from several of his
anecdotes, is no man to postpone pleasure, but then the
"editor" surprises us here by going on to argue that Denise
was *sage*, a nice girl, and that Jacques would hardly want
to abuse his future wife. In any case, the reader cannot
escape participation in the processes of fabulation: "If you
are not satisfied with what I reveal to you of Jacques'
amours, reader, do better yourself, I consent to it. Whatever manner you adopt, I am sure that you will end up
as I do."

The ultimate difference between these two passages is
generated by two markedly different conceptions of literary form. For Sterne, the phantasmagoric flow of consciousness, the minute pulsations of kinesthesia, dictate
literary form; it is fidelity to these that leads him to
overthrow traditional narrative conventions, chronological sequence, lexical decorum, grammatical coherence.
Characteristically, in his version of the ascending massage,

---

[2] J. Robert Loy argues plausibly for an incipient instance here of *baiser* in
its later sense as a vulgar term for sexual intercourse. See *Jacques the Fatalist
and His Master*, ed. tr. J. Robert Loy (New York: New York University Press,
1959), note, pp. 287-288.

normative syntax dissolves into disjunct members floating
between dashes in order to approximate the stacatto
excitements of the experience rendered. One should note
that Diderot, in general, plays with narrative convention
and therefore chronological sequence without however
transforming time into subjective duration and without
any major violation of lexical decorum or grammatical
coherence. I have already observed how he converts the
incremental series of fingers laid on into a triple symmetry
of narration, and what one senses throughout the passage,
as elsewhere in the novel, is the presence of a lucid orderer
of the narrated materials. On the level of syntax, Diderot,
in sharp contrast to Sterne, is meticulous in the use of
subordinate clauses, participial phrases, distinctions between past perfect and simple past verbs, to keep actions,
motives, and persons in clear and intelligible relation to
one another. (My translation above deliberately surren-
ders some of Diderot's stylistic elegance in order to reproduce in English the ordered clarity of his syntax.)
In all this, the French writer remains faithful to the logic
of his language, for the predominant tense of his narration
is the historical past, or *passé simple*, a form not in
colloquial use but primarily reserved for histories and
fictions. "Its role," Roland Barthes has suggested, "is to
reduce reality to a point, to abstract from the multiplicity
of lived and superimposed times a pure verbal act cut loose
from the existential roots of experience and oriented
toward a logical connection with other actions . . .; it
announces a development, that is, a narrative intelligence
[*une intelligence du Récit*]."[3]
If the ultimate subject of *Tristram Shandy* is a mind
in harum-scarum pursuit of its own experience, the ultimate subject of *Jacques the Fatalist* is an *intelligence
du Récit* experimenting with means of ordering narrative

[3] Barthes, *Le Degré zéro de l'écriture* (Paris: Editions de Seuil, 1953), pp.
46-47.

materials which will not do excessive violence to the essential disorderliness of ordinary discourse, of human psychology, of the chain of events and circumstances in most lives. If Sterne slows down time to the fluttering suspension of felt duration, Diderot, when he is narrating and not reporting dialogue, tends to negate duration by reducing the intricate laminations of experienced times to a pure verbal act, symmetrically shaped and attitudinally defined. The breathless rapidity which so often characterizes his narrative tempo makes us perceive the points of the narration as members of a series guided by a controlling intelligence to a determined end. In what is virtually an internal parody of this technique, Jacques answers his master's question about the purpose of his brother Jean and Père Ange in going to Lisbon with twenty-one rapid-fire words: "To seek an earthquake, which could not take place without them, be crushed, swallowed up, burnt; as it was written Above" (p. 734). The device surely owes something to Voltaire's *Candide*, as the very mention of the Lisbon earthquake might remind us. Jacques is less explicitly a satiric target in his espousal of his captain's fatalism than Candide in his espousal of Pangloss's optimism, but as in Voltaire, the drastic schematization of the accelerated narration makes us see how a distinctly debatable viewpoint has interpreted and thus emphatically structured the events it reports. What comes across to us, in any case, is hardly Jean's and Père Ange's experience in Lisbon but rather Jacques' wry view of what befell them, which selects, arranges, and thus converts the occurrence into a miniature *récit*.

The informing insight of *Jacques the Fatalist*, I would contend, is that language can never give us experience itself but must always transmute experience into *récit*, that is, into narration, or, if you will, fiction. This entrapment in narration, however, does not necessarily imply inauthenticity for Diderot because man as the language-using animal is quintessentially a teller of tales, and narration is his way of *making* experience, or, from another point of view, of making nonverbal experience distinctively human. Nine years before the composition of *Jacques*, Diderot had celebrated in his ecstatic *Eloge de Richardson* the power of fiction to impose itself on the reader as reality with the absoluteness of immediate experience. If, after a tentative effort at a modified version of the Richardsonian mode in *La Réligieuse* Diderot moved to the opposite extreme, flaunting artifice and eschewing the minute circumstantiality he had extolled in Richardson, it was not only because of his progressive disenchantment with "sensibility" during the later 1760s and early 1770s but also, I believe, because he came to see more clearly that no fiction could really escape from its conspicuous condition as an arbitrary ordering. Having come out of Richardson on the other side of Sterne, as it were, he would abandon all thought of that "multitude of little things" which had struck him with wonder in *Clarissa* and go on to report fictional events in as ostentatiously distanced a manner as this:

> And so here they were, launched on an interminable quarrel about women; one claiming they were good, the other wicked: and they were both right; one, that they were stupid, the other—witty: and they were both right; one—false, the other—true: and they were both right; one—beautiful, the other—ugly: and they were both right; one—blabbermouths, the other—discreet; one—frank, the other—devious; one—ignorant, the other—enlightened; one—chaste, the other—libertine; one—mad, the other—sensible; one-big, the other—small: and they were both right. [p. 513]

Sterne might have taken us into the actual details of such a debate for half a volume, commenting with great circumstantiality on the postures and gestures of the debaters, cramming their exchanges with mutual misapprehensions, interrupting them by an untimely visit from the doctor, a kitchen mishap, a discourse on tailors and fashion, a long complaint about logic-choppers and debaters, an equivocal anecdote about large and small women from the narrator's recent experience. What Diderot does is to abstract from the concrete interchange of the argument between Jacques and his master a verbal act that calls attention to itself as such through the outrageous excess of its symmetry and its identically repeated structures. The drastic selectivity, of course, conveys a satiric viewpoint, that all possible contradictory assertions can be made on the subject, and given the variety and contradictions of women themselves, that all the assertions are equally valid. (Diderot pursues this very symmetry on a larger scale in *Ceci n'est pas un conte* by telling back-to-back a story illustrating the maxim that there are very good men and very bad women, then one to illustrate precisely the converse.) There is manifestly no sense here of the duration of the debate, the only real time being the time taken by the narration of the event. Throughout the novel, in fact, other times fade before the actual duration of narration, which is one reason why the logic of the method leads to extended dramatic dialogue, where the time of speaking is completely equal to the time of the event. Yet, paradoxically, the enormous speed of Diderot's report as he runs through this catalogue of opposites does communicate something of the animated energy and see-saw tempo of the debate, not by following its actual contours but rather by boldly schematizing its underlying principle, offering us a verbal design of its dynamic.

As Diderot's aesthetic writings make clear, he maintained a traditional mimetic theory of art, but by the time he came to *Jacques*, he had arrived at a much more shrewdly skeptical, essentially modern notion of what was involved in the imitation of life by art. He repeatedly built his novels and tales out of actual anecdotes about contemporary personages he knew or had heard of, and partly for this reason he felt he could announce in a title that "This Is Not a Story," just as in *Jacques* he affirms again and again that it is no novel he is writing but that he merely means to adhere at any cost—even the reader's boredom, he claims—to the "truth of the story" (*la vérité de l'histoire*). The eighteenth-century French *roman*, which often enough was a potpourri of exotic adventures and fantastic contrivances, led Diderot to view the very term as a pejorative, so that he takes repeated pains to remind his reader that he has strenuously resisted more extravagant narrative options to avoid the dire fate of writing a mere novel: "I see that with just a little imagination and style, nothing is easier than to spin out a novel. Let us stick to the truth (*Demeurons dans le vrai*)" (p. 731). This assertion comes late in the book, as part of a larger claim that the author has followed throughout the single purpose of adherence to the facts. Near the beginning of the novel, virtually the same affirmation is made with a finely equivocal qualification: "It is quite clear that I am not making a novel, for I pass over that which a novelist would not fail to use. He who would take what I write for the truth would perhaps be less in error than he who would take it for a fable" (p. 503). The triple hedging of bets—the conditional verbs, the modifier "perhaps," and the negative backhand comparison, "would be less in error"—expresses a philosophically precise perception about the relativity of truth as it is conveyed through language. That is exactly the point of *Jacques'* peculiar method and of the sundry tales we are asked to consider in the course of the novel.

Diderot recognizes no less than Cervantes what a problematic notion the "truth of the story" is, and it is quite to the point that he adopts from *Don Quixote* the errant master-servant pairing as the scheme of his novel, once actually noting the parallel to Cervantes for us, since he, too, sees truth as the unstable product of a constant dialectic, a mutually modifying interchange of opposite viewpoints. Interestingly, the servant Jacques, with his faith in the Great Scroll of Fate on high, is generally the more quixotic of the two protagonists, he being the narrator's surrogate and his master the reader's. Yet Jacques' role as a keen and witty observer suggests that there is a marked tension of contradictions within him between creed and character and that the dialectic here is therefore less sharply polarized between the two protagonists than in Cervantes. In any case, the picaresque journey of Jacques and his master is more deeply recessed into a world of pure fabulation than that of Sancho and Don Quixote, for little of importance happens on the journey (even a stolen horse is eventually restored, things put back where they started); and the journey is really only an occasion for telling stories along the way. When Jacques, like the baffled Don Quixote, complains of a persistent "enchantment" that he yearns to break (p. 536), it is a spell that prevents him from reaching the conclusion of his story, not of some knightly adventure; for the sphere of frustrated achievement in this novel is not action but narration itself. The ill-fated charge of heroic aspiration into unheroic reality, that element of the quixotic paradigm that would exercise such fascination over the nineteenth-century novelist, is ignored by an advanced analytic spirit like Diderot, for whom even the illusion of heroism is something of a bore, deflecting our attention from what seems to him truly interesting about people living in society. Extremely modern in this respect but in another very much an Enlightenment mind, Diderot conceives the novel less as an ironically exemplary quest for authenticity, like that of the Don and his nineteenth-century heirs, than as an occasion for understanding; and so the urge to completion is removed to the plane of storytelling, where the delusory giants and castles are the properties and conventions of a bogus literary tradition to be eschewed, and the obstacles to progress are the quirky associative habits of the mind and the impatience and misdirections of human discourse.

What meaning, then, can be attached to a concept like the "truth of the story" on the basis of Diderot's own novelistic practice? The celebrated beginning of *Jacques* both brilliantly illustrates his method and immediately introduces us to the nature of the tension between fiction and reality as he conceives it. For a boldly uncompromising laying-bare of the schematic premises of fiction as a fiction is being put to use, there is probably nothing quite like it again until Beckett:

> How did they meet? By chance, like everyone. What were their names? What difference does it make to you? Where were they coming from? The nearest place. Where were they going? Does one know where one is going? What were they saying? The Master said nothing; and Jacques was saying his captain said that everything either good or bad that befell us down here was written up there. [p. 493]

Diderot, like Sterne, at once enters into contention with an impatiently curious reader. Sterne's method, however, engages the reader not only at the point where his bad reading habits show but in the tangle of his total psychology, while Diderot directs himself more exclusively to the reader as reader. The tartness of the narrator's first retort to his reader, "*Que vous importe*?," "What's it to you?" makes it clear that he will have no truck with vicious literary practices, however addicted to them his audience may be. In other words, he will simply not be bothered by all the circumstantial machinery that creaks and groans in conventional fiction in an effort to make it seem like reality. All fictions are, after all, implicitly paradigmatic, so why not, without fuss about circumstance, frankly *assume* Jacques and his master, who happen to encounter each other "like everyone" and are obviously like most of us going from one place to another? Thus in half a dozen swift lines Diderot has completed his exposition, stated his major philosophical theme, and is about to launch the dialogue of Jacques and his master in which Jacques momentarily will begin that account of his amours doomed to so many interruptions.

Now, the effect of all this is sharply paradoxical. On the one hand, we are immediately confronted with the fictional world as pure *récit*, as a completely arbitrary verbal construct. Over and over in the novel, Diderot will assert teasingly or downright provokingly his authorial freedom to do whatever he pleases with his characters, or, alternatively, he will from time to time offer the reader the possibility of making his own decision about the physical circumstances of the narrative, giving him multiple choices from which to select. Yet, somewhat surprisingly, the repeated affirmation that this fiction is sheer invention does not preclude a strong sense that in fact it reflects a greater fidelity to reality than other kinds of fiction. The narrator immediately discards everything that is secondary, everything that could be construed as embellishment or mere illusionistic trickery, to get to the recognizable human center of his tale, two people talking, avid, as we all are, for pleasure and piqued like most people by the idea of love, eager to recount their own experiences and to hear the experiences of others, insistently curious about motives and the variety of humanity and its acts yet impatient to pronounce their own opinions on what ever may occur.

Diderot is also acutely aware from the very start that narration cannot be consecutive and neatly unified without distorting a fundamental aspect of reality, where it is by chance that encounters take place and one never fully knows where one is going. Traditional narrative is teleological, every beginning implying continuous development and a realized conclusion, every once-upon-a-time already pregnant with its happily-ever-after. For Diderot,

however, reality is fundamentally random, its course un-
chartable, despite Jacques' simplistic fatalism and his
metaphor of the Great Scroll. The flaunted authorial
arbitrariness, then, is a formal analogue to the unfathomable arbitrariness of what would traditionally have been
called "fate," and the veering interruptions of the many
storied narrative, in which each of the component tales
is in fact essentially continuous and formally coherent
within itself, is a way of producing the realistic appearance
of randomness in what is, after all, a well-conceived series
of skillfully shaped tales. Jean-Jacques Mayoux sums up
this whole aspect of *Jacques*, as it stands in contrast to
Tristram Shandy, with great incisiveness: "The
waywardness of narrative and caprice of digression which
is with Sterne a portrait of the mind as it runs, is with
Diderot a portrait of life, of reality, as it appears."[4] The
author of *Jacques* perforce knows what will become of
the personages he has invented, for his novel is hardly
an exercise in automatic writing. By continually display-
ing, however, alternative possibilities of plot as though he
scarcely knew which to choose, he creates the illusion that
his characters are marked by the same ontological indeterminacy that characterizes our own unforseeable lives.
Thus, in one exchange with the reader, the narrator
resumes and expands a note announced in the opening
paragraphs of the novel: "But for God's sake, author, you
say to me, where were they going? . . . But for God's sake,
reader, I shall answer you, does one know where one is
going? And you, where are you going?" (p. 537).

Yet the randomness of reality explains only part of
Diderot's narrative caprice, which is equally a function
of the unpredictable nature of communication, implying
as it must a giver and a receiver of information, each with
his own peculiar preferences and concerns. One part of

---

[4] Mayoux, "Diderot and the Technique of Modern Literature," *Modern Language Review* 31 (1936): 524.

Sterne's problematic is thus Diderot's as well. But in this regard it is noteworthy that what goes on in *Jacques* is for the most part conceived as though it were oral communication—on one level, between Jacques and his master (hence the prominence of straight dramatic dialogue), on another, between the narrator and the reader. It is for this reason that Diderot, while adopting a whole range of Sterne's self-conscious strategies, uses none of his typographical devices, nothing that calls attention to the novel as material conveyed in print. He makes clear his own conception of the tale as "spoken" words to be read, together with the chief implication of that condition, in the short prefatory paragraph of *Ceci n'est pas un conte*: "When one tells a story, it is to someone who listens; and however briefly the story lasts, it is rare that the teller is not sometimes interrupted by his listener. That is why I have introduced into the narrative about to be read, which is not a story, or which is a bad story, if you have any doubts about it, a figure who will play approximately the role of the reader" (*Oeuvres romanesques*, p. 793).

Sterne's narrator is basically an isolate, sitting with pen and ink in his provincial study conjuring up a remembered familial community long vanished, which itself breaks down into the stubborn and bizarre subjectivity of its individual members. In this, he is more radically modern than Diderot, whose as-if spoken presentation implies a society where mutual interchange takes place, and whose novel comfortably settles down for a long central section at an inn where weatherbound travelers, in a manner that harks back to Boccaccio and Chaucer as well as to Cervantes, entertain one another and affirm their community by the telling of tales. In *Tristram Shandy*, the digressive narrative is built on erotic concerns because the author uses his own erotic obsessions to explore the psychological connections and disparities between imagination and reality, *verba* and *res*. With Diderot, on the other hand, one

senses that the recurrent erotic subjects of the tales told
are the result of a coolly calculated decision to give the
reader, in a variety of unexpected ways, what he has come
to expect from his reading. In part, this is a simple
expedient for maintaining interest in a book that repeatedly resists the ordinary sort of narrative continuity.
Since you insist, the narrator tells his impertinently
curious reader more than once, on tales of love, I shall
give you as many as you like, one after the other. "Writing
for you, one must either dispense with your approval or
serve your taste, and you have clearly decided for tales
of love" (p. 671). Diderot follows this with a long list of
literary genres, to which he adds opera, painting, and
sculpture, all of them, he claims, amounting to little more
than tales of love. This is the sort of stuff audiences have
been accustomed to from time immemorial, and this is
what the author, however serious his intentions, is compelled to provide them.

The concessive quality of such statements is at least
partly ironic, for Diderot recognizes the erotic imagination
as a great energizing force of art, the power that actually
interinvolves people in the most complex, bizarre, and
amusing ways, and that fixes our attention upon the
artistic renderings of those interinvolvements. Eros makes
societies and it also makes literature about society. *Jacques* can function effectively and efficiently as a fiction
combining conjuration with critique because in the
amorous materials of its tales, ranging from a Shandean
parable of a sheathe and a knife to a fabliau-like anecdote
of two concupiscent housewives and a more-than-willing
lad, it invokes a whole variegated tradition of Renaissance
and late-medieval storytelling. To speak more precisely,
part of a whole tradition is invoked, since any idealized
and idealizing varieties of literary love are firmly excluded
from the novel. The erotic impulse, in other words, is a
fascinating subject for Diderot because it sets into action

the complex play of realistic motives and contradictions, deceptions of self and of others, which is the "truth" he wants his story to realize. The reality Sterne reaches for is experiential; for Diderot it is analytic and intellectual, even as it bears on the emotional nature of man as a moral animal. Thus *Tristram Shandy* stands at the beginning of a current in the novel that will issue in the great stream of consciousness of *Ulysses*, while *Jacques the Fatalist*, very much part of a French tradition of the novel, has its logical heir in Proust, who joins the evocation of felt passion with the analysis of the nuances of motive and character. If Diderot could assert of Richardson that he translated into action everything that had been put in maxims by Montaigne, Charron, La Rochefoucauld, and Nicole, the statement throws less light on the author of *Clarissa* than on his own program for the novel. The open digressive structure of *Jacques* fits it perfectly for use as a series of narrative experiments in moral behavior, focusing multiple perspectives on the kinds of principles that the masters of the French aphorism tried to state in their lapidary formulas. Indeed, there are moments when Jacques, the engaging spokesman for his author, sounds quite like a Montaigne or a La Rochefoucauld as he comments tartly on his own experience: "I don't know what principles are except rules one prescribes to others for one's own benefit" (p. 579).

The remark is cynical enough, but *Jacques* does not expound a doctrine of cynicism; it only forces us to see the inadequacy of simplistic moral preconceptions about motives and cause and effect in human lives. The narrative, then, does not have the polemic tendentiousness of, say, the novels of De Sade, but it continually veers off in unexpected directions to shake us loose from the illusions of convention. Thus, Jacques describes to his master how he gave most of the contents of his purse to a young woman in distress. His master, ever the naive audience, immediately acclaims it as a beautiful action. No, Jacques corrects him, it was rather a stupid thing to do, since he was immediately attacked by thieves who had concluded that so generous a benefactor must be well provided for, and when the thieves discovered he had nothing for them, they gave him a sound beating. Diderot does not assume that all actions are motivated by selfish calculation; Jacques' benevolence flows from a genuine altruistic impulse, in contrast, for example, to Valmont's public act of charity in *Les Liaisons dangereuses* which in the cynical perspective of that novel can only be a strategem in a scheme of seduction. The surprise reversal here of the little tale of philanthropy makes a point of literary criticism on the basis of a moral realism: it is only in the frozen conventions of edifying tales that virtue invariably confers its awards, while in reality the consequences of any act are unpredictable and on occasion may be quite perverse.

The amorous complications of most of the tales in *Jacques* are of particular interest to Diderot because they involve intrigue, masking, and deception, thus vividly exposing the extreme dispositions of gullibility and cunning, sometimes in the same character, constantly reminding us that the judgment of human actions is an endlessly challenging task. The erotic impulse, or its frustrated deflection, is the driving power in most of the schemes laid, as well as the force that blinds the dupes to the snares being set for them. Through it, characters not only give pleasure to one another but also inflict pain; so that its operation opens up vistas of psychological contradiction and moral ambiguity. The broad rule-of-thumb about the tales in *Jacques* is that the longer and more ambitious they are as narrative structures, the more elaborate are the mechanisms of deception on which their plots hinge. Thus, on the simplest level of seeking immediate physical gratification, Jacques deceives Suzanne and Marguerite about his supposed virginity in order to enjoy their sexual tutelage, just as he deceives both his friend Bigre and Bigre's father in order to secure a morning in bed with Justine, Bigre's girlfriend. By contrast, the two longest consecutive narrative pieces in the novel, the story of Mme de la Pommeraye's revenge and the tale of the Master, Agathe, and the Chevalier de Saint-Ouin, are built upon the most intricate strategies of deception that require months of patient preparation for their execution. In both instances, an extremely elaborate masquerade is used to gull a doting lover, Mme de la Pommeraye marrying off to a whore the man who had failed her, the chevalier staging a scene in which the master is caught in bed with the chevalier's pregnant mistress and blackmailed into supporting the child that is indubitably Saint-Ouin's.

Things are rarely what they seem in the world of *Jacques the Fatalist*—a paragon of piety turns out to be a whore; a man's best friend, a treacherous villain; two dueling enemies, bosom friends; the person who seems to Jacques one of the most decent he has met, none other than the hangman. If deceptive appearances confuse characters in their actions, they equally confuse us as readers in our effort to make moral judgments on the characters. Diderot's technique of interruptions is especially useful in this regard, for it enables him as narrator, or the personages of the frame-story, to walk around the characters of the sundry tales, contending about their motives as they act, praising or censuring them. The most extended instance of this procedure occurs at the end of the story of Mme de la Pommeraye, where the narrator intervenes for two pages to argue persuasively that we cannot facilely condemn any of the principal actors, for if we try to imagine the viewpoint of each, each had his or her own anguish and justification. The overarching paradox of *Jacques the Fatalist* is that art itself is a mode of deception, a manifest fabrication passing itself off as the truth; and what the writer does technically in this novel is to turn the trickery of fictional art inside out in order to bring us closer through a literary form to the elusive truth behind deceptive moral appearances.

Robert Loy, in what remains the standard critical study of *Jacques*, has suggested that the novel is woven around three major themes—the artistic problem of realism in the novel, the philosophical problem of fatalism, and the moral problem of judging virtue and vice.[5] The observation seems accurate enough, though it may help us see the interconnection among the three terms to note that only the concern with fatalism is, strictly speaking, thematic. The ontological question, that is, dictates the peculiar anticonventional "realism" of *Jacques* and this technique in turn generates a special amplitude and tentativeness of moral perception in the way it presents characters and events.

Let me try to spell this out briefly. Jacques' fatalism, that diluted and popularized version of Spinoza he has carried away from his captain, is finally seen as an inadequte definition of existence, which for Diderot is constant unpredictable flux, equally resistant to predetermined moral categories and prefabricated literary forms. The caprice of the narrative is meant to reflect the caprice of reality, but then the expository passages on realism and the novel are not so much thematic disquisitions as a principal manifestation of the anticonventional technique, caprice, or the arbitrariness of art, asserting itself by the repeated obtrusion of the artificer into his artifice. If, moreover, any version of an event is so patently a "construction" of it, positing an artful decision that has imposed temporary order on the flux of experience, the moral judgment of persons and actions will have to be a good deal more tentative and self-questioning than it is wont to be.

In this regard, the beautiful utility of the dialogue form

[5] Loy, *Diderot's Determined Fatalist* (New York: Columbia University Press, 1950).

for Diderot should be particularly noted. Dramatic exchange, substituted extensively for more conventional narration, is, from one point of view, an unembellished, "unmediated" presentation of interchange among characters. As spectators, we listen, conjure up our own images, draw our own conclusions, the verbal medium operating no differently than when we observe people talking in real life. From another standpoint, however, the theater within the novel is a conspicuous vehicle of fictional self-consciousness, beginning with Master Pedro's puppet show in *Don Quixote*; and I think we cannot escape, nor are we entirely meant to escape, from the awareness that in abandoning the artifice of narration Diderot has adopted the artifice of the theater. We preserve, at any rate, at least a peripheral consciousness that Jacques and his master discourse and gesticulate like actors on a stage, and that recessed within their dialogues, in contravention of any formal verisimilitude, are extended dialogues between other characters, far removed from them in time and space. The dialogue form thus produces a distinctly equivocal illusion of immediacy, doing away with authorial intervention, while all around the dialogues the author constantly intervenes, flaunting his proprietorship, asserting his privilege to do what he pleases with the characters.

This central contradiction points up the intrinsic connection between the philosophic theme of the novel and its innovative form. The novel becomes for Diderot an experiment in provisional freedom against a metaphysical background where free will, if not a mere illusion as Jacques' fatalism would have it, is at least called into question by the infinite concatenation of material causes through which all events take place. Jacques' metaphor of the Great Scroll is, after all, a literary metaphor, and it is hardly accidental that he refers to its inscriber as *auteur*. The author of *Jacques* is constantly pretending that he can only report what the characters have done and constantly affirming his freedom as the designer of his own scroll to make of them what he will. If, like most self-conscious novels, this one turns out to be an elaborate game, it is a game in which the author uses the limits of a fiction to test out the tensions between freedom and determinism, and thus his novel is formally an interplay between randomness and controlled pattern.[6] The author is very much like the little boy of Jacques' anecdote, who cries when he is asked to say A because he knows that what will immediately follow is the request to say B. Refusing to be determined by the received signs of a gratuitous formal system, the narrator ostentatiously rejects ordinary narrative conventions, beginning his story at D and jumping to Q, doubling back to C, and concluding, as his proposal of alternative endings may suggest, more on an X than a Z.

This account runs the risk of making *Jacques* sound like a lecture in geometry (and, indeed, at one point the narrator boasts of speaking in the precise language of geometry), but of course the delightful and delighted bantering tone of the novel is inseparable from whatever "meaning" the book may have. Diderot affirms that as long as one tells tales one is gay not only because man the storyteller relishes stories for their entertainment but also because he experiences through them a kind of freedom, pattern produced in the tale not by blind events but by an ordering consciousness that creates its own time and consequence. In Sterne, somewhere at the back of all the mirth and warmth is an awareness of the black hole that swallows everything up, so the merriment has a little edge of urgency, of existential unease. In Diderot, one senses an exquisite poise in the humor because the humor celebrates the mind's ability to control, however

---

[6] On the play between order and chaos in Diderot, as it stands in contrast to Sterne's pervasive disorder, see Alice G. Fredman, *Diderot and Sterne* (New York: Columbia University Press, 1955), pp. 208-209.

provisionally, the rush of events in a world of contingency. Thus Diderot toys playfully with his characters and with his reader on a note of gay assurance, knowing that human foibles and limitations held at an intellectual distance for narrative manipulation become the proper subject of amused and bemused contemplation. The final paragraph of the novel perfectly illustrates this delicate control of tone that fixes the perspective of the whole book. Jacques, one recalls, is supposed to have settled down to a happy ending, married to Denise and living with his master in the chateau of Desglands.

> People have tried to persuade me that his master and Desglands fell in love with his wife. I don't know anything about it, but I am sure that evenings he would say to himself: "If it is written up there that you are to be a cuckold, Jacques, there's nothing you can do about it, you will be one; if it is written, on the other hand, that you will not be one, there's nothing they can do about it, you will not; so sleep my friend ..." and he went to sleep. [p. 780]

This last tongue-in-cheek touch is, one should note, a double parody, invoking with an ironic twist the convention of happy endings as it recalls the ironic conclusion of *Lazarillo de Tormes*, where the hero resigns himself to cuckoldry, or chooses not to know about it, in his own better interests. The gaiety of the narrator's parting glance at Jacques coyly expresses the superiority of his vantage point, his authority as Jacques' inventor. Even at the end, he can make of Jacques what he will, despite his pretended dependence on what "people" (*on*) report to him. Jacques, consistent to the principles on which he has been conceived, will continue to insist that his fate has already been prescribed in the Great Scroll though, as throughout, there is a piquant contradiction between his worldly knowingness and the simplicity of his fatalistic faith. The restless mobility that has characterized the whole world of *Jacques* is not suspended at the end, as it would be in a more conventional conclusion. Human appetites and the fragility of social institutions being what they are, the long-delayed dénouement of Jacques' *conte d'amour* implies the beginning of a new tale in which Denise will have someone else for a lover, but this is a story the narrator chooses not to tell, and so he gently puts his hero to sleep and ends his book.

Now, in the self-conscious novel the act of fiction always implies an act of literary criticism, but, broadly speaking, it may move either outward, to the society that supplies the materials for literary representation and that tries to dictate literary convention, or inward, to the experiencing mind that gives the literary artifact whatever life it can have. *Jacques the Fatalist* and *Tristram Shandy* obviously move respectively in the two opposite directions, and one is tempted to see in the difference between them a contrast between the French literary tradition, with its centripetal pull to a great capital and its focus on men and women in society, and English literature, with its frequent dispersals into the provinces, its settings in country houses, its fondness for queer or even cranky isolation. In both the geographical and the characterological sense of the word, Sterne is an eccentric, writing about a world of eccentrics. Crouched—fetally, one assumes—in a phantasmagoric cavern of the mind, he is ultimately concerned with epistemological questions: how do we ever know anything or communicate anything to one another? Diderot, sauntering along the roadside with his protagonists, addresses himself to a consideration of the ontological frame in which they exist and how it impinges on the issues of moral psychology raised by their sundry tales.

This contrast between the two writers suggests a final paradox. Sterne, imagining so vividly the entrapment of each individual in his own private lexicon, his own system of references, was avid for immediate response from the reading public. The reception of the early volumes of *Tristram* is one of the spectacular literary success stories of the eighteenth century, and the Yorkshire parson thrived in every sense on the acclamation he received. His explorations of the psychology of reading and writing were sustained, spurred on, by real readers who could applaud the originality and ingenuity by which he had engaged them. The edge of anxiety in an imagination flourishing under the shadow of solipsism seemed almost to require the reassurance of success, the confirmation by others that its inventions had touched them as hoped.

Jacques the Fatalist, on the other hand, is a novel written for the author's drawer; in fact, it was not published till 1796, twelve years after Diderot's death and more than twenty years after its probable date of composition. Diderot's lack of concern for a public response to the novel in his lifetime may have had a little to do with his caution about censorship, but to judge by his statements elsewhere on the kind of readers he wanted, he would appear to have been more centrally motivated by a desire for an ideally appreciative audience, which, like Stendhal, he was content to defer to posterity.[7] What this refusal of a contemporary readership expresses is not wavering reticence but a supreme confidence. Diderot, sure of having worked out a new technique that yields a less falsifying representation of men in society, was willing to let the work wait for a society less enslaved to philosophical prejudice and to stultifying literary and social convention. Before our own century, *Tristram Shandy* could continue to enjoy a popular following over half a dozen generations, though frequently for the "wrong" reasons. *Jacques*, more sharply intellectual in conception and more basically engaged in a process of literary criticism, is much more a manifestation of the elitist impulse in the self-conscious

[7] See Herbert Dieckmann, "Diderot et son lecteur," in *Cinq leçons sur Diderot* (Geneva: E. Droz, 1959).

novel, and it would not elicit any general enthusiasm until there had been a radical shaking-up of preconceptions about literary form and the nature of fiction. Diderot's prognosis about posterity, then, proved correct, though on a longer time-scale than he had imagined: despite scattered approbation from various of the German Romantics, it was not until the twentieth-century revolution in the technique of fiction that *Jacques* came to be appreciated as a brilliant experiment with the possibilities of the novel. Why the nineteenth century should have been so 'out of phase with Diderot's achievement is a question that bears on the whole course of the novel in the era of its greatest expansion, and this large subject is one that deserves separate consideration.

Chapter 4

The Self-Conscious Novel in Eclipse

He neither hates nor loves; for
him no one exists but himself.
> Mme de Staël on Napoleon,
> *Considérations sur la
> révolution française*

Who does not keep a carriage these
days? What a society! Everybody
is determined to bankrupt himself.
Never have *appearances* been so
despotic, so imperious, and so
demoralizing.
> *The Goncourt Journals*,
> 1851-1870

1. Paris, Capital of the Nineteenth Century

The introduction of politics into a novel, Stendhal affirmed
more than once in his own fiction, "could have the effect
of a pistol-shot in the middle of a concert."[1] There is, as
critics have often observed, an amusing contradiction in
this assertion on the part of Stendhal, each of whose three
major novels is deeply and intricately rooted in the political life of the post-Napoleonic era. The contradiction is
instructive as well as amusing because it points up the
transition in Stendhal's own person from the first great
age of the novel between the turn of the seventeenth

---

[1] Stendhal's earliest use of this cherished aphorism of his is in *Armance* (1827),
at the end of Ch. 14.

century and the end of the eighteenth to that unique flowering of the novel in the nineteenth century which he himself contributed to so impressively. The political particulars of the real world could in fact be a jarring intrusion in the kind of novels he had read and passionately admired during his formative years—like *Don Quixote, Tom Jones, Tristram Shandy, Les Liaisons dangereuses*—but not in the novels he was to write. Politics, after all, has its own dynamics, its own technique, as Stendhal was to show in detail in *Lucien Leuwen*, and those earlier writers concerned with the ontological and epistemological perplexities of the technique of fiction could not really afford to admit politics—or social history, or economics, or technology—on an equal footing in the fictional world. (By and large, when earlier fiction writers turned to political matters it was not in a truly novelistic vehicle but in the more schematic form of some satirical anatomy, like Voltaire's *Candide* or Fielding's *Jonathan Wild*.) This is not to say that the self-conscious novel is unable to tolerate any political materials, only that they must be made into grist for a novelistic mill with no ultimate extra-literary aims. To revert to Stendhal's comparison, the pistol shot may be orchestrated into the concert performance, if the impresario is daring enough; what cannot be allowed is that we attend to it as a pistol shot plain and simple from a world outside of and inimical to the concert of artistic means.

Perhaps an example will make this distinction clearer. The rebellion of 1745 visibly serves Fielding's ends in *Tom Jones*, but any other excuse to involve Tom with the army and have Sophia mistaken for a grand personage traveling incognito would surely do, for the only real exigency here is one of plot, not of a relation between individual character or destiny and the historical moment. The full title of the novel is, quite properly, *The History of Tom Jones, a Foundling*, the designation "foundling" in effect calling our attention to the author's management of the comic plot, to the literary design and the background of fictional convention out of which the book is made. On the other hand, one could not possibly use a subtitle like "A Chronicle of 1745" for *Tom Jones*, though Stendhal, by contrast, is perfectly justified in calling *The Red and the Black* "A Chronicle of the Nineteenth Century,"[2] or, more specifically, announcing *Armance* on the title page as "Some Scenes from a Paris Salon in 1827."

Examples of this sort could easily be multiplied. *Vanity Fair*, in its serial form, was subtitled "Pen and Pencil Sketches of English Society" a description that alluded not only to Thackeray's illustrations but also to the method and aims of his fiction. A generation later, *Middlemarch* carries an analogous subtitle, "A Study of Provincial Life." Now, a novel like *Tristram Shandy* gives us some vivid reflections of provincial life and characters in eighteenth-century England, but, in view of its purpose and procedures, it could not conceivably be called, let us say, "Sketches of a Yorkshire Parish," or "A Study of Provincial Life." By the third decade of the nineteenth century, the whole orientation of the novel had swung around to a new point. As a convenient landmark, one might cite the most paradigmatic of these "reportorial" titles and the most ambitious of realist enterprises in the great age of fiction, the whole group of Balzac's novels called *Etudes de moeurs au XIXe siècle*, a designation and a project that have no parallels in the preceding century.

What had happened to the novel in its transition to the nineteenth century? Yielding to common usage, and as a crude shorthand notation, one could say that realism came to be the central impulse of the novel, though the term is of course somewhat misleading, and not only

---

[2] After the first edition, he made this still more precise: "A Chronicle of 1830."

because of the philosophic difficulties involved. The very techniques of fictional self-consciousness, as we have seen, produce an experiential realism in Sterne, a metaphysical realism in Diderot, an epistemological realism in Cervantes, and (one might add) a moral-intellectual realism in Fielding. What changed, I would suggest, was not the degree of realism but its characteristic objects.

Now, the overriding subject of the novel in almost all its forms would seem to be the disparity between the structures of the imagination and things as they are, novelistic plot consisting in the multifarious effects of that disparity on the protagonist and the personages involved with him or (often) her. This is as true of *Emma, Middlemarch, Madame Bovary, Crime and Punishment, Anna Karenina*, as it is of *Don Quixote* and *Tristram Shandy*. Until the nineteenth century, however, the focus of novels exploring this tension tends to be on the operations of the imagination, on the literary and linguistic materials with which the imagination builds its ambiguous worlds, and therefore on the crisis of traditional literature reflected in the very emergence of the novel as a new genre. The nineteenth-century novel did not entirely abandon these concerns, but it is clear that the center had shifted, broadly speaking, from consciousness and how it shaped the world around it to the world around and how it impinged with its specific gravity, its full concreteness, on consciousness. One might note, symptomatically, how many nineteenth-century novels both in England and in France repeatedly address themselves, in proper capital letters, to Society or the Nineteenth Century, as though these were clearly discernible entities, distinct and scientifically describable in the forces they exerted on individual lives.

There is an obvious fascination in the nineteenth-century novel with the sheer mechanics of contemporary life—in politics, commerce, class relations, industry,

crime, education, entertainment, virtually every sphere.
One must not forget that in an age of rapidly expanding
mass audiences and serial publication, the novel was enormously important as a source of *information* in a way
it had not been before and would not be afterward, once
more rapidly accessible information media had developed.
To be sure, there are anticipations of these concerns with
contemporary processes and milieux in the circumstantial
realism of the eighteenth-century novel in England. One
recalls the concrete sense of the operations of the London
underworld in *Moll Flanders*, the minutely detailed vision
of upper-middle-class manners and values in *Clarissa*.
What is missing, however, in the circumstantial realism
of the eighteenth century is the presence of history as
a dynamic determinant. The underworld scenes of *Moll
Flanders*, though they embody specific practices of Defoe's
age, are not finally different in kind from the criminal
milieux depicted in the Elizabethan coney-catching pam-
phlets; in some cases they could even be interchanged with
the older material. The pressure of history as constant
and critical change is not felt in Defoe's conception of
his subject. On the other hand, in *The Red and the Black*,
as Erich Auerbach has so skillfully shown, the palpable
weight of a particular historical moment—the doldrums
of the Bourbon Restoration in the 1820s—makes itself felt
along the whole network of relations and social manners;[3]
and, similarly, in *Middlemarch* the period in England just
before the Reform Bill of 1832 is reflected not only in
explicit political discussions but in a whole complex con-
figuration of class attitudes, individual aspirations, and
the modes of wielding economic power.

The realist desire to register the minute oscillations and
effects of historical change leads novelists away from the
exploration of fiction as artifice for a variety of reasons

[3] *Mimesis: The Representation of Reality in Western Literature* (Princeton:
Princeton University Press, 1953), Ch. 18.

which I will try to make clearer as we go on. The imaginative involvement with history, in any case, is the main cause for an almost complete eclipse of the self-conscious novel during the nineteenth century; and so I think it may be helpful to consider first precisely why history came to play this new role during the period we are considering, and what writers wanted to do with the novel in responding to the historical moment.

The development of realism in the nineteenth-century novel means preeminently the development of the novel in France. It is quite appropriate that the best general study of the realist tradition, Harry Levin's *The Gates of Horn*, should concentrate entirely on the major French novelists from Stendhal to Proust. France's leading role in the creation of the great age of fiction calls for some reflection. Until the 1820s, it is clear that the vanguard of the new genre was in England, not in France. Sterne, Fielding, and, above all, Richardson, were commanding models for French novelists of the later eighteenth century, not merely sources to be drawn on as Fielding and Smollett had drawn on Marivaux and Lesage. The enormous vogue of Walter Scott in France, as elsewhere in Europe, during the second and third decades of the nineteenth century, continued the earlier pattern of influence. It was only in the 1830s, with the mature work of Balzac and Stendhal, that France clearly established its creative autonomy, in fact shaping a powerful new tradition of the novel that would become a common legacy of European and American literature through to the twentieth century. It has been suggested, by Ian Watt among others, that since the novel is the bourgeois genre par excellence, it could fully flourish in England only after a bourgeois revolution had taken place in 1688, in France only after the bourgeois revolution had occurred there exactly a century later. Though there may be an element of truth in this, it seems to me too facile as a way of connecting literary movements with political events and social change. One wonders, for example, how to explain the brilliant development of the novel in autocratic nineteenth-century Russia, where no bourgeois revolution had taken place, where, indeed, serfdom was still in force when Gogol, Turgenev, Dostoevski, and Tolstoi began their great enterprises.

The fact is that the Napoleonic era, with its long uneasy aftermath of dubious monarchies, abortive rebellions, and *coups d'état*, was at least as crucial in the coming-of-age of the novel in France as the French Revolution. Though the novelistic imagination was of course deeply affected by the visible transfer of power to a new social class, what moved it even more profoundly was a perception of the explosive force of historical change as such. This force was evident on an unprecedented scale throughout Europe during the nineteenth century, expressing itself through political revolution, radical shifts in demographic patterns, in the application and importance of technology, in the uses of labor and the organization of economic life. But nowhere was the explosive force of change so dramatically active as in France, with Paris, at the detonating center of historical transformation, manifestly the "Capital of the Nineteenth Century," in the memorable title Walter Benjamin devised for the book he did not live to write.

The Revolution of 1789 that had violently smashed a whole old order (in this quite unlike the Glorious Revolution of 1688) was quickly followed by the meteoric rise of Napoleon, then the expansionist wars of the *arriviste* emperor that almost overnight changed the face of Europe. Under the subsequent restoration of a discredited Bourbon monarchy without a solid base of power, the possessing classes in France were constantly haunted by the specter of imminent revolution, perhaps of a more radical sort than the one that had already occurred. (The provincial aristocrats in *Lucien Leuwen*, set in 1833-1834, fearfully speculate on how many more months Louis-Philippe can hold out against the coming revolution, even as they futilely scheme for the return of a legitimist monarch from abroad.) These fears of unimaginable upheaval seemed to receive temporary confirmation in the July Days of 1830, and more emphatically, in the workers' revolution of 1848 and the Commune of 1871, both savagely repressed. It is hardly surprising that Marx should have made the events of 1848-1851, and again of 1871, twin focuses for his perception of class-warfare and historical process. Instructively, even the planned transformation of the city scene in the first urban renewal takes place under the foreshadow of feared upheaval, Haussman's new Parisian boulevards being conceived—vainly—in the hope they would be too wide for the setting up of barricades in the coming insurrection. Under the fixity of any *ancien régime*, history might seem to stretch out as an unbroken continuum, fundamentally unchanging from age to age. The general sense of history as continuous, perilous change emerges after 1789 and appears to be mainly a Parisian invention.

Paris becomes the great crucible of social theory in the nineteenth century, even for those, like Marx and Engels, who reside elsewhere. It is, moreover, the place where the writing of history develops as an ambitious new activity aspiring to the comprehensive imaginative integration of the variegated experience of the past. The example of the nineteenth-century French historians is of the utmost relevance to the novel in France, because the essential innovation of the realist novelists was the attempt to write the history of contemporary society in their fiction, exploiting to this end the imaginative writer's freedom to invent aptly illustrative characters and actions. The realist novel was in a sense engendered by the Romantic historical novel, adopting from it a historical perspective to represent the contemporary world. Scott, the great innovator of the historical novel, came of age in Scotland toward the end of a period of murderous division within that country, in which a whole traditional way of life was irrevocably displaced, and so like his French followers he was in a specially sensitive position to feel the shocks of historical change through the whole frame of his social world. Edmund Wilson's deft summary of Michelet's enterprise as a historian could also properly characterize the various Chronicles of the Nineteenth Century, Studies of Manners in the Nineteenth Century, the Social and Natural History of a Family Under the Second Empire, which are the rubrics for the fictional projects of Stendhal, Balzac, Zola:

> Two principal problems confronted Michelet in writing history in such a way as to render the organic character of society, of that "humanity creating itself" of which he had caught the conception from Vico. One of these was the nerve-trying task ... of fusing disparate materials, of indicating the interrelations between diverse forms of human activity. The other was to recapture, as it were, the peculiar shape and color of history as it must have seemed to the men who lived it. ... [4]

Both these aims, the articulation of an interlinking structure and the evocation of a felt texture in the diverse components of the historical moment, repeatedly draw the novelist away from a contemplation of his medium as such, leading him instead to grapple energetically with the resistant world that is to be conveyed through the fictional medium. Of course, attention to the medium, as we have had abundant occasion to see, in no way excludes a probing concern with the world to which the medium responds. In the nineteenth century, however, under the urgent

---

[4] *To the Finland Station* (Garden City, N. Y.: Doubleday, 1953), p. 17. Harry Levin has noted the connection between novelists and historians, suggesting in fact that the goals of the modern historians were first realized in the historical novels of Scott and Chateaubriand (*The Gates of Horn*, New York: Oxford University Press, 1963), p. 27.

pressure of history, novelists were far less inclined to explore the problematics of their fictional instruments as they used them to engage historical reality. What I would like to stress is that the dynamic force of history is not just a challenge to nineteenth-century consciousness but a threat, and this menacing quality of contemporary history is brilliantly reflected, both formally and thematically, in the novelistic response to it. Revolutionary and counter-revolutionary violence of the most ruthless kind, bloody imperial warfare from Spain to Moscow, the deformation of human lives by the brutal developing phase of the Industrial Revolution, an unprecedented population explosion and a movement to the cities, converting the urban centers into vast anthills of filth and misery, the repeated reduction of human bonds to mere cash nexus in an expanding capitalistic society—all these had to be not merely portrayed but somehow *coped with* by the realist masters. I do not mean only that the novel was used for the moral or political critique of contemporary society, though that was surely one of its major new functions, but also that, psychologically, novel-writing was seized as a means of containing the mounting chaos of the contemporary world, recasting it in the molds of the imagination and thus transforming it, even as the deadly weight of its real menace was still felt in the finished fiction. If the novel, then, was in one aspect an embracing representation of contemporary society, it was also conceived as a vigorous competitor to the reality it was supposed to represent.

This peculiar direction taken by the realist novel may become clearer through example. Perhaps the most imperious of the new social realities with which the novel had to cope was the nineteenth-century metropolis. Paris, London, St. Petersburg are in a clearly justified way the subjects of Balzac, Dickens, and Dostoevski, as no city

is the subject of a novel in the eighteenth century or earlier.
Here is Balzac, describing the inhabitants of Paris in the
introductory section of *La Fille aux yeux d'or*:

> One of the spectacles in which the greatest dread is
> encountered is surely the general look of the Parisian
> population, a people horrible to see, pale, yellow, tawny
> ...faces twisted, contorted, ... not faces but rather masks:
> masks of weakness, masks of strength, of misery, joy,
> hypocrisy; all of them worn, all of them stamped with the
> ineradicable signs of panting greed. . . . Few words will suffice
> to justify physiologically the almost infernal hue of Parisian
> countenances, for it is not only in jest that Paris has been
> called an inferno. . . . There everything smokes, everything
> burns, everything blazes, boils, flares up, evaporates, goes
> out, rekindles, sparkles, crackles, and is consumed. [Pléiade
> edition of *La Comédie Humaine* 5:255]

The controlling metaphor of the urban hell is less a
means of interpreting the horrors of the modern city than
a way of transforming them. Balzac's infernal cityscape,
filled with crowds of distorted masks seen in flickering,
smoky light, looks forward to the spectral carnival scenes
in the paintings of James Ensor. Like those paintings, it
strikingly expresses the dehumanized existence of the
urban warrens, the freezing of flesh and blood into protec-
tive, deceptive façades by the harsh climate of a relentlessly acquisitive society which is composed of isolate
individuals. There is no attempt to cosmetize contemporary reality here, and yet its disparate elements have
somehow been gathered up into a poetic whole that has
its own principle of unity, its own grim beauty. Balzac,
of course, is the great poet of energy—energy and will,
indeed, were the recurrent fascinations of many novelists
in an age that had seen such dramatic assertions of those
qualities—and it is clear that what compels him in his
vision of Paris, for all its purportedly Dantesque gloom,
is the endless, restless energy of the metropolis. Every-

thing, to be sure, is finally consumed in the seething cauldron of the city, but the cauldron continues to seethe. The perceived energy of the city, moreover, has been transmuted into the asserted energy of artful language. The overflowing catalogues of examples, the extravagant use of anaphora (*masques* is repeated half a dozen times in quick succession in the French), the proliferation of associated verbs, the reiterated aim of the written word to encompass "everything" (*tout* occurs five times in a row) within its descriptive grasp—all these features of Balzac's rhetoric attest to a conquest of urban chaos by the novelist's verbal art, or rather, to the creation of a rival reality, profoundly linked to the reality without but superior to it as a manifestation of willed human control.

The process of imaginative shaping is even more spectacularly evident in Dickens's descriptions of the nineteenth-century city. Here is a portion of a much longer passage in *Little Dorrit* that purportedly conveys the look and feel of the Grosvenor Square district in the 1820s:

Wildernesses of corner houses, with barbarous old porticoes and appurtenances; horrors that came into existence under some wrong-headed person in some wrong-headed time, still demanding the blind admiration of all ensuing generations and determined to do so until they tumbled down, frowned upon the twilight. Parasite little tenements, with the cramp in their whole frame, from the dwarf hall-door on the giant model of His Grace's in the Square to the squeezed window of the boudoir commanding the dung-hills in the mews, made the evening doleful. Rickety dwellings of undoubted fashion, but of a capacity to hold nothing comfortably except a dismal smell, looked like the last result of the great mansions' breeding in-and-in; and, where their little supplementary bows and balconies were supported on thin iron columns, seemed to be scrofulously resting upon crutches. Here and there a hatchment, with the whole science of heraldry in it, loomed down upon the street, like an archbishop discoursing on vanity.

Dickens's modern critics have commented abundantly on his repeated displacement of animate life into inert objects and the corresponding assimilation of human beings into the dead world of things (like those masks in Balzac, or, to cite an example from *Little Dorrit*, like Mr. Pancks, whose speech, gestures, breathing are relentlessly translated into the mechanical activities of a tugboat). This weird displacement of animation does serve a "realistic" function of sorts because it reproduces the deformation of collective life, the reduction of individuals to instruments, in an acquisitive society that had scarcely begun to confront the grave problems of its own radical historical changes.

Nevertheless, the personification of the tumbledown houses around Grosvenor Square demonstrates how this technique goes beyond any mimetic function, however imaginatively probing, however addressed to spiritual conditions gone awry. The neighborhood described is dreary, dismal, disheartening, as one would expect any crowded district of a nineteenth-century metropolis to be, but the hideousness of the urban landscape is such a splendid occasion for the play of the writer's imagination that the effect of the passage is a paradoxical exuberance. After all, projecting the qualities of human agents into the realm of dead things is a way of possessing that alien realm, of subduing it, making it our familiar by turning it into a humanized object of infinite manipulability. As in Balzac, the proliferation of examples and related images—in the novel the description tumbles onward from the houses to shops, to footmen and butlers, to grooms and dogs—itself celebrates the generative power of the imagination in the very act of description. In an animating flourish of multiplied instances, the corner dwellings are wildernesses, the porticoes barbarous, the houses demanding, determined, frowning upon the twilight as though it were an affront. A kinesthetic apprehension of architecture is brilliantly

translated into physiological experience in the architectural structures themselves: a window is "squeezed"; tenements, like ailing elders, suffer "the cramp in their whole
frame." Dickens outdoes himself—the logic of the whole
technique is to outdo oneself—by vigorously elaborating
the dominant metaphor of disease and decrepitude in the
image of the houses "scrofulously resting upon crutches,"
their physical decay seen as some ghastly genetic deca-
dence, the result of excessive inbreeding among aristocratic
structures. Clearly, the awfulness of the scene is in no
way denied, but it is surely transfigured by the lavish
energy through which it is worked into a system of imagery
at once witty and fantastic.

The nineteenth-century novelists are, with rare exceptions (like Gogol, emulating Sterne), disinclined to play
with the fictive status of their fictions not only because
they are realists but equally because they are such intent
imaginists—writers caught up in the autonomous power
of their own fantasy world even as they strive to make
it a true image of the world of contemporary society. If
your purpose is to *outdo* a threatening or at least bewildering historical reality by remaking it imaginatively, the last
thing you want to remind yourself of is that everything
you write is, necessarily and ambiguously, artifice. This
is not to suggest that there is no love of artifice in the
nineteenth-century novel. One could scarcely imagine a
more elaborate scheme of narration-within-narration than
that of *Wuthering Heights*; and Dickens himself manifestly delighted in contrivances of plot and situation, and,
in his later work, in the possibilities of manipulating
different narrative voices. In a very different vein, Flaubert
could make the fashioning of perfectly wrought fictional
artifice into a private cult. The point about all this is that
the intensification of artifice does not necessarily imply
the questioning of the premises of the artifice as it is
employed, and that I would take to be an ultimate dividing

line between self-conscous and other kinds of novelists.
Dickens may have known perfectly well that he was
manipulating artifice when he wrote *Little Dorrit* or *Bleak
House*; but he allows the invented world to take on an
imperative authority, for his readers and for himself, and
he by no means intends to subject it to the continuous
ontological scrutiny that Sterne and Diderot focus on their
invented worlds.

The self-conscious novelists are always simultaneously
aware of the supreme power of the literary imagination
within its own sphere of creation and its painful or tragico-
mic powerlessness outside that sphere. The great nineteenth-century imaginists, on the other hand, are impelled
by a deep inner need to confuse the two realms. Balzac's
boast that he would achieve more with the pen than
Napoleon had achieved with the sword is not altogether
a rhetorical flourish. It is no accident that in this period,
for the first time, great fortunes could be realized through
novel-writing. Scott, of course, made and lost one, at-
tempting, interestingly, to recoup his losses by writing,
among other things, a biography of Napoleon. Dickens,
a "literary tycoon"—the phrase is F. W. Dupee's—in an
age of tycoons of industry, climbed through his writing
from that traumatic blacking factory of his boyhood to
the Gads Hill mansion he had long coveted, enthralling
untold thousands of readers as he enriched himself. The
novelist's power was in this fashion triply exercised: over
the mass audience he could make captive; through the
wealth and prestige he could if really successful achieve
by his writing; and over the world of imaginary beings
he conjured up not merely as the means to the first two
spheres of power but, above all, as supreme gratification,
excitement, and consolation in itself.

It is in this period that many major novelists begin to
talk openly about a hallucinated sense of the presence
of their imaginary characters, begin to record a feeling

of real loss or separation when they finish writing a book and thus take leave of the figures with whom they have been "living" over many months. To return for a moment to *Little Dorrit*, it is not just a trick of rhetoric that leads the author in his preface to claim that he, Charles Dickens, on a visit to the old Marshalsea building in real historical time—he specifies the date, May 6, 1857—was able to descry the room where Little Dorrit was born. At some crucial level of imaginative life, he needs to believe literally in the fantasy he has invented; and his readers' willingness to participate in this intensely serious half-belief is the ultimate secret of his power over them, as he himself seems to recognize, immediately going on to mention here the constantly growing number of his readers from one novel to the next.

Again, Balzac provides a neatly complementary example of this same nineteenth-century phenomenon. The French novelist devises a strategy for sustaining the imperative claim to life of his fantasies by writing a huge ensemble of overlapping novels in which the figures and actions invented in one are reinforced, in a sense confirmed, by their reappearance in other books. Balzac's *Comedy*, unlike Dante's, is not really a coherently interlocking system but rather like his own image of Paris—a cauldron boiling over and over. Marthe Robert has shrewdly seen that the Balzacian technique of the *retour de personnages* answers not so much a literary or formal need in the novels as a psychological need in the novelist. Though one may wonder whether the general project of Mme Robert's latest book, to define the novel generically in terms of the Freudian Family Romance, is not compromised by the very facility with which the definition is ultimately applicable to any fictional invention, she is finely perceptive in the way she sees the absoluteness, the peculiar self-insistence, of novelistic fabrication in the nineteenth century. Here is her comment on the Balzacian *retour* and what it suggests about the imperious imaginism of the great realist:

> He knows only that he needs it in order to prolong the novel well beyond the word *finis*. He needs it to fill space with a teeming population similar to that of a real society; to create families that have among them multiple bonds of kinship, feeling, interest, and as many conflicts as the human family can nourish. He needs the device so that he can cause crowds of people to be born and die as he joins the pathos of the sympathetic observer with nature's indifference to these daily dramas; so that he can catch up lives one by one in a network of events supposedly unforeseen and unpredictable; and finally, so that he can intermingle History with his stories [*ses histoires*] and thus play for the public the one role of omniscient, omnipotent, divine creator that can correspond to his immense thirst for domination.[5]

The thirst for domination through imagination is probably perceptible in its purest form in Balzac's enormous enterprise, but one can find it in nineteenth-century novelists as different in politics and sensibility as Scott, Melville, George Eliot, Tolstoi, Dostoevski, Zola. It has often been observed that the figure of Napoleon haunts the nineteenth-century novel, in France a vanished model of emulation, in Russia a specter to be exorcised, in England at times a devil to be reviled though also a figure secretly admired (Becky Sharp begins her career by defiantly calling out *Vive Bonaparte!*). But what is surely more significant not only in the course of the novel but also as a fact of European consciousness is that novel-writing itself, not just the characters within novels, became Napoleonic, a fact that applies as much to the emperor's sworn opponents as to his spiritual heirs. Earlier, I observed that

[5] *Roman des origines et origines du roman* (Paris: Grasset, 1972), p. 254.

the pressing fact of sheer historical change was a crucial determinant for the nineteenth-century novel. What must be added is that in the figure of Napoleon the idea presented itself that such change could be effected by one man, through a fierce assertion of will and the most cunning exercise of intelligence.

The flaming passage of Napoleon through European history destroyed old orders and called into question most received values. Here was a man who stood for absolutely nothing but himself, and who had managed for a while to make his will supreme, to set his impress on most of civilized Europe. The older quixotic novels tended to ask the question, What is literature that man should be mindful of it? After the Napoleonic upheaval, novelists seemed to be more directly pursued by the question, What is man?—for they had seen how one person could become a kind of god or a consuming blight, and in France especially they had seen how the same prominent figures could be first empassioned revolutionaries, then dedicated Bonapartists, and finally, when the occasion required, good monarchists once more. The literary question, then, was no longer of the ontological status of literature but of literature's more or less efficient function as a means. How was the novelist to represent the disturbing protean potential of the individual human being and at the same time realize or enact that potential through the exercise of the shaping power of fiction over an imagined, real-seeming world? Both challenged and threatened by the Napoleonic phenomenon, the novelist himself determines to set his impress on a world that he can reconstitute, combining or purposely confusing mimesis and poesis, imitation and making. Fictional invention for the self-conscious novelists of the pre-Napoleonic era is a process of intellection, simultaneously critical of its own operations and of the nonliterary objects toward which it is directed.

For the nineteenth-century novelists, fictional invention
often seems virtually a mode of action and as such cannot
afford the luxury of self-criticism.

Balzac and Dickens, in the examples we have seen and
throughout their work, *make* the metropolises over which
they can reign as absolute monarchs. The full distance
the novel has traveled may be measured by setting against
their manifold evocations of urban scenes the "description" of London Fielding gives us—there is nothing more
than this—when Tom Jones arrives in the city. Tom, too,
is looking for Grosvenor Square, which in the eighteenth
century was an unambiguously fashionable neighborhood,
but he is uncertain of the way, "So he rambled about
some time before he could even find his way to those happy
mansions where fortune segregates from the vulgar those
magnanimous heroes, the descendants of ancient Britons,
Saxons, or Danes, whose ancestors, being born in better
days, by sundry kinds of merit, have entailed riches and
honor on their posterity" (13:2).

The fundamental impulse in Dickens and Balzac is to
expand spatially, and so syntactically their writing often
tends to fall into large series of juxtaposed objects or
multiplied instances of the same general phenomenon,
using repetitive or parallel structures. Fielding, on the
other hand, is quite uninterested in the spatial expansion
of the represented scene. His own elaboration moves back
along a temporal axis into cultural history, and the syntactical form it takes is an intricate structure of subordin-
ation in which one senses the arch intelligence of the
narrator controlling the disparate members, manipulating
not only fictional objects but our judgment of men and
society, our awareness of the linguistic categories with
which we judge. The passages from Balzac and Dickens
are powerful conjurations; the one from Fielding is a
brilliant piece of rhetorical maneuvering quite willing to
be recognized as such. Fielding takes as given conditions

with which to work the existence of the city and of class divisions in society. They do not confront him as spheres of explosive change. He has no interest in invoking or recreating them in his fiction but instead is concerned with how literature and language lead us to think in certain ways about the social and moral facts of life, how these same means might be used to make us think in other ways. When Dickens refers to "the great mansions" of Grosvenor Square, the phrase is translucent, referring us straightforwardly to a known kind of building which Dickens will then metamorphose through the fantastic image of architectural inbreeding and degeneration. When Fielding mentions "those happy mansions," he at once invokes a literary context for the phrase, the New Testament, and consequently a distinct possibility of irony. "Magnanimous heroes," a designation that smacks of the eighteenth-century translations of Homer and Virgil, drives open the aperture of ironic perception, surely inviting some wry reflection on the actual brigands and brutal warriors who long ago invaded the island and thus made their posterity its aristocracy. By this point, virtually every significant phrase in the sentence opens up into an ironic doubleness of view. We wonder about that segregation of the wealthy from the vulgar by "fortune" (does the term mean "destiny," as it seems to at first, or only, tautologically, "wealth"?); about the characterization of the early period of conquest and plunder as "better days"; and, above all, about the aristocratic legacy of "merit" and "honor" as anything but flattering synonyms for riches. In Fielding, language mirrors itself mirroring reality; authorial intelligence operates confidently by playing with the many ways intelligence, through both its literary and social exercise, is commonly abused. The example I have chosen is one of the simpler ones in a novel that abounds in the most complex and inventive demonstrations of a basic perception: that literature, language, and the instruments of our social discriminations and moral judgments are all the products of convention and artifice, with truth of insight thus obtainable only through the critical exploration of convention, the shaking-up and realignment of artifices.

In nineteenth-century England, there are still some vestiges of Fielding's sense of the novel in Jane Austen, but the Waverly novels, in which Scott tries to conjure up a whole national history at a juncture of crucial transition, constitute a turning point. The next three or more generations of novelists, down to the Edwardians in England and the heirs of the French Naturalists in America, would variously attempt, in Balzac's polemic phrase, to "compete with the civic registry." With few exceptions, novelists no longer turned language back upon itself reflexively as an instrument of expression and conceptualization because all the resources of the written word had to be marshaled to making the imagined object as palpàble, as vivid, as emotionally demanding on those who experienced it, as possible. The quasi-documentary forms of the eighteenth-century novel, epistolary and autobiographic, had raised the possibility of the virtual reconstitution of reality in language (though not for critical observers like Fielding and Sterne). The history of the novel in the nineteenth century takes place under the sign of this Promethean enterprise, and the self-conscious novel is consequently driven underground, however much its vestiges may be traceable in the manifest love of artifice of some of the realists. The nature of this general shift to one pole of the novel's inner dialectic will become clearer if we have a closer look at three major novels of the mid-nineteenth century that approach, but in varying ways and degrees no more than approach, self-conscious subjects or self-conscious methods.

2. *"Lost Illusions" and the Assumptions of Realism*

At first glance, it might seem as though the central concern of Balzac's *Lost Illusions* should take us right back to that Barcelona printing shop where we observed Don Quixote quizzically contemplating the technological processes of which he himself was the product. After all, this is a novel about "two poets," a writer and a printer, who embody the split halves of Balzac's own professional identity, or, more generally, the two complementary activities through which all books come into being. The very first sentence of the novel is a notation about the technology of printing; before long we are given a whole disquisition on the history of printing and paper production; and the plot of Part 3 hinges on David Séchard's invention of a new process for making paper. In Part 2, moreover, Lucien de Rubempré's experiences as an aspiring writer in Paris involve an elaborate exposition of the politics of literature and book-reviewing in Restoration France, while his discussions with the astute young writer, Daniel D'Arthez, on his, Lucien's, historical novel constitute a concise poetics of the novel. Finally, both Lucien and David have been nurtured together on Romantic literature, and the blows of experience that make them feel the aching disparity between literary illusion and sordid fact clearly continue the familiar quixotic pattern of chivalric dreams colliding with unchivalrous windmills.

From all this, one might conclude that *Lost Illusions* reads like a novel by André Gide, but that is of course very far from the actual case. As preoccupied as the book is with all aspects of the business of making books, it conveys nothing of the self-conscious fiction's sense of novelistic reflexiveness. To see why this should be so, we might first go to the discourse on paper-making that David, in the most improbable of lover's speeches, delivers to his fiancée. Although Balzac informs us that for economy's sake he has summarized David's actual words to Eve, the resumé itself runs on for half a dozen pages, beginning with the invention of paper in ancient China, touching on its development in Asia Minor, Italy, modern England, and France, specifying the various raw materials used in its composition, the names and procedures of the important innovators in the manufacture of paper. All this is introduced with the following justification: "David gave her certain information about the manufacture of paper which will not be out of place in a work whose material existence is due as much to Paper as to the Press."[6] In the historical survey that follows, David indicates that literature is rapidly approaching a crisis because with the new mass market for books and periodicals and the demand for cheap paper, industry is still unable to produce a kind of paper that is both durable and inexpensive. "Shirts and books will not last, that's all there is to it. The solidness of products is disappearing everywhere" (p.119).

None of this leads to a self-conscious effect because there is no sense whatever of a paradox in the consideration of book production within a work that exists by virtue of those very technological procedures. Balzac has "information" (*des renseignements*) to convey. Indeed, at times the exhaustive report of the operations of the contemporary world seems almost an obsession with him, as when he takes us on an endless tour, appropriately marking the way stations with chapter headings, of one kind of Parisian bookseller after another, or when he details for page after page the legal maneuvers through which an innocent man may be imprisoned for debt. The point is that our attention is wholly directed to the information conveyed while the fictional conveyor is intended to be a transparent medium the status of which we are not really supposed to question. If the author momentarily reminds us that his work owes its material existence to paper and press, that is only a technical fact (material existence is not ontology) which does not modify the function of the novel as a transmitter

---

[6] *Illusions perdues*, ed. Antoine Adam (Paris: Garnier, 1961), p. 116.

of purportedly real actions comprising, as Balzac puts it in the 1837 preface to Part 1, "a complete description of society, seen in all its aspects, grasped in all its phases." The allusion in this case to the material condition of the novel as a printed book is merely a rhetorical excuse for inserting a survey of paper manufacture through the ages, but the survey itself is not different in kind from the circumstantial accounts of other technologies and institutional procedures that Balzac works into the *Human Comedy* to fill out his complete description of society in all its aspects.

We can instructively set these references to book production against Sterne's quick allusion to the same fact at the very beginning of Volume 6 in *Tristram Shandy*: "We'll not stop two moments, my dear Sir,—only, as we have got thro' these five volumes, (do, Sir, sit down on a set—they are better than nothing) let us just look back upon the country we have pass'd through.—" As elsewhere, Sterne is wonderfully apt in focusing the paradox of mere printed paper transformed into teeming reality by the imagination of the reader. The first five volumes of *Tristram Shandy*, in a swift dialectic movement, are an expansive country traveled through and experienced in time, then contract to a mere pile of books to be sat on ("better than nothing"), and, on the other side of the parenthesis, become a country once more. We are thus properly prepared for the exposition on the next page of Walter Shandy's outrageous notions of pedagogy, in which all possible propositions of thought are to be produced by conjugating every word in the dictionary backwards and forwards, language engendering all reality *ex nihilo*, out of the nothingness of its own formal constitution, as in the novel itself.

In Balzac, by contrast, we are not meant to wonder about the status of the reality conveyed in the fiction, and if we are apprised that the solidity of products is

disappearing, it is as a fact of commercial history, while
we are not invited to question the solidity of the world
constructed with such circumstantial care in the novel.
On the contrary, the incorporation of so much sheer
information in the novel reinforces the status of the
fictional personages as virtually real figures coping with
the real social, economic, and technological facts of contemporary France. When Balzac, in the disquisition on
printing, writes, "*Italics* were invented by the Aldes in
Venice, hence the name" (p.117), his illustrative use of
typography has precisely the opposite effect of the seemingly similar device in Sterne. In *Tristram Shandy* the
typographical tricks tease us into an awareness of the novel
as a printed artifact, make us ponder the limits or power
of language and its mechanical conventions for the conveyance of reality. The italicized *Italics* in Balzac, on the
other hand, are a transparently convenient pointer to the
referential object of discourse. Typography, book production, the conventions of narration, language itself, are all
assumed as effective means for bringing the reader precise
renseignements about the real word. In fact, without such
a confident assumption Balzac could not aspire to that
comprehensive portrayal of contemporary society of which
he speaks.

This novel about publishing and the career of a writer
illustrates with the greatest clarity how the realist must
avoid the serious paradoxes of the relationship between
fiction and reality, even when his material would seem
to invite them. Lucien, the young provincial who fancies
himself a writer of genius, is forced to recognize again and
again that literature in the nineteenth century has been
reduced to a mere commodity. As his cynical journalist
friend Lousteau tells him, for publishers a book is only
"capital to risk. The finer the book, the less likelihood
it has of being sold" (p. 311). What is peculiar about such
observations is that they do not at all lead us to wonder

about the book called *Lost Illusions* which we are reading. That, one assumes, is a "fine" book because it fulfills Daniel D'Arthez's program of accurately representing human passions in the context of contemporary manners and institutions—or perhaps the category of fineness is not even meant to be applied to it because it is simply there as the medium through which the truth about contemporary society is conveyed. Coming closer to the felt experience of Balzac's own writing, Lousteau warns Lucien of the frustrations facing a novelist:

> Yes, you will write instead of acting, you will sing instead of fighting, you will love, hate, and live in your books; but you will have saved your riches for your style, your gold and purple for your characters, and you will walk in rags through the streets of Paris, happy, in competing with the civic registry, to have produced a being called Adolphe, Corinne, Clarissa, or Manon. You will have ruined your life and your stomach to give life to this creation, and you will be libeled, betrayed, sold, consigned by journalists to the lagoons of oblivion, buried by your best friends. [pp. 276-277]

The intense living with imaginary personages, the competition with the civic registry, make us think at once of Balzac himself, though of course the fate of neglect and total misery diverges sharply from his. But there is nothing here that leads us to contemplate Lousteau and Lucien as members of the series, Adolphe, Corinne, Clarissa; they, on the contrary ask to be taken as "real" characters talking about fictional ones. The limits of Lousteau's calculating worldy perspective, moreover, are very nearly the limits of Balzac's, despite the novelist's moral disapproval of his character. That is, what might be an intriguing psychological or ontological paradox about living, loving, and hating in one's books instead of in reality is quickly converted by Lousteau, and by Balzac with him, into hard economic terms. The metaphorical riches, gold, and purple are edged toward a very literal application: by devoting all his inner resources to his writing, the novelist impoverishes himself in the plain sense of the word. In presenting through Lousteau this partial truth about the perils of the literary vocation in an aggressively commercial society, Balzac avoids the deepest, most suggestive contradiction of his own enterprise: the notion that enormous power and intensity, the ability to undergo an exhaustive variety of experiences, are achieved by the novelist in entering into his own fantasy world, implicitly renouncing direct engagement in the external world in his very boast of rivaling it with words.

We had occasion to note earlier in considering *Don Quixote* Marthe Robert's suggestive concept of *dédoublement*. One measure of the distance between Cervantes and Balzac is that in the case of the French novelist there is a perceptible doubling without dialectic. Cervantes, one recalls, splits off aspects of himself as writer into various fictional surrogates who interact with each other, qualify each other, generate still further dialectical pairings. Balzac, on the other hand, feeling no dialectical tension between himself as author and the fiction he makes, turns out a series of characters embodying aspects of himself, partial self-portraits seen as more or less adequate according to the degree they exercise the Balzacian—and Napoleonic—faculties of will and intelligence. (Stendhal in this regard offers an instructive contrast because he often seems to waver between using characters as conscious dialectic splits of himself and entering into them as fantasy surrogates.) The surrogates of the author, instead of interacting in pairs, are thus ranged along a hierarchical scale: the writer, instead of constantly reinventing and exposing himself as writer in the self-conscious manner, plays out various fantasies of himself that aspire upward to the greatest possible exercise of power. At the bottom of the scale, speaking for the most narrowly cynical self of the author, would be Lousteau, the hack journalist of modest abilities and limited aspirations. Lucien himself is a portrait of the artist still well below the real Balzac, having a flair for writing, a striking facility at adapting his work to the needs of the moment, but showing no real sign of genius, and above all deficient in resoluteness of will, allowing his determination to be undermined by every passing gratification. Daniel D'Arthez is the closest to a direct self-portrait, being a writer of fine intelligence, dedicated to his art, flawless in integrity, though the idealization of the portrait makes him the least interesting of Balzac's surrogates in the novel (one suspects, to Balzac as well as to the reader). At the top of the scale of surrogates, his entry, or *retour*, reserved for the last crucial turn of the plot, is a figure who is ostensibly no writer at all, the arch-criminal Vautrin, who accosts the despairing Lucien in the guise of a Spanish priest.

The reasons why this master of crime must be regarded as the novelist's most intimate and potent surrogate are not hard to find. He is the supreme will and the supreme intelligence in the novel, as he is in a larger sense in the whole world of the *Human Comedy*. He announces his long didactic discourse on the corrupt way of the world as a "secret history" which will expose the lies of official history, and that is substantially the general aim of Balzac's enterprise as a novelist. When Lucien expresses some surprise that the supposed Spaniard should be acquainted with Rastignac, Vautrin replies, rather mysteriously, "I know all of Paris," and in fact he seems to approximate within the framework of the fiction the omniscience of the fiction's author. (Lucien, of course, cannot know as the reader does that Vautrin is not only acquainted with Rastignac but has been for him, in *Le Père Goriot*, precise-

ly the same mentor in the higher cynicism that he is for
the young writer in this novel.) Vautrin, impeccable in
his impersonation of a Spanish priest, is a master of
disguise, acting out on the plane of fictional events the
novelist's own ability to play every possible role, to perform
all kinds of actions. If novel-writing is a Napoleonic activity for Balzac, Vautrin is the consummate Napoleonic man
in his novels. "Regard men, and especially women, as
nothing but instruments. ... For the sake of power do
everything [the Jew] does for the sake of money" (p. 711).
And Vautrin pointedly justifies this code of ruthless egoism
by a survey of French history from 1793 to the Restoration,
with special attention to the man who made himself
emperor, even quoting Napoleon's cynical maxims as a
practical guide.

What most clearly distinguishes Vautrin as the writer's
surrogate is that he chooses to exercise his enormous power
of action through other personages. In pulling Lucien back
from the brink of suicide, what he does in effect is to take
him over from Balzac, to become his author. Every man,
he tells the young writer, seeks an "accomplice in his
destiny," but as he goes on to explain just what he has
in mind for Lucien, it is clear that he regards him not
as an accomplice but a surrogate, through whom he will
enjoy all the intensity and variety of a vicarious existence:
"I will roll in your tilbury, my boy, I will enjoy your success
with women, I will say:—This handsome young man is
me, this Marquis de Rubempré, it is I who have created
him and placed him in the aristocratic world; his greatness
is my work, he is silent or speaks by my voice, he consults
me in everything" (p. 725).

What Lucien can give Vautrin, in other words, is precisely what all of the novel's characters, but most particularly Vautrin, can give Balzac—the experience of omnipotence. It is surely instructive that the paradigmatic

self-conscious novel, *Tristram Shandy*, turns in its cerebral circuit on a fantasy of impotence, while Balzac's novels, the realist enterprise par excellence, flesh out in a variety of characters, actions, and settings a fantasy of omnipotence. Balzac's relation to Vautrin is precisely the reverse of Sterne's to Tristram, or Cervantes' to Don Quixote. Tristram and the Don are, in very different ways, fictional projections of the faculty of imagination in their authors; acting out, or writing out, the impulses of the imagination isolated from the rest of the self, they show how circumscribed, how self-frustrating, how solipsistic, it can be, at the same time that they demonstrate its peculiar attractions and its elastic strength. Vautrin, on the other hand, is a projection of the faculty of will in his creator, and will, unlike imagination, does not readily suffer critical examination but seeks only to assert itself more fully. As an image of the novelist's inner life, Vautrin is not a dialectical self-confrontation but a wish-fulfillment, the fictional elaboration of a gratifying fantasy. I would contend moreover, that even when a protagonist is defeated or humiliated in a realist novel, like Lucien here or Emma in *Madame Bovary*, the case does not differ in kind. It is still some fantasy image of himself that the novelist needs to punish as well as to indulge, which is quite different from the dialectical self-confrontation of the quixotic novel, where the writer liberates a principle within himself, a basic aspect of his vocation as writer, to play out unhampered its ultimate possibilities, both good and bad, in a fictional world.

I observed before that fictional invention becomes a virtual mode of action in the realist novel. What this means in the exemplary instance of Balzac is that the novelist reconstitutes society in his fiction in order to act out his real hostility toward it, his fantasies of dominating it. The Napoleonic phenomenon and its aftermath of corruption, the simultaneous perception of dizzying upward mobility and the monopolization of power and prestige by the undeserving inspire a profound *ressentiment* in author and character alike, providing precisely the same motivation for the novel as for the revolutionary ideologies and the ruthless careerism of the age. "Why have I told you to become Society's equal?" Vautrin asks Lucien. "Because today, young man, Society has imperceptibly arrogated to itself so many of the individual's rights that he finds himself obliged to combat Society. There are no more laws, only manners, that is, affectations, always mere form" (pp. 717-718). The representation of society in the realist novel is also an assault on society, not merely social criticism but the translation into a complex series of imagined acts and personages of the writer's deepest social frustrations, rancor, impulses to rebel. The novelist's carefully mapped-out topographies of profession and class, his minute factual accounts of institutional processes, are there not just to inform, as Balzac consciously intends, but also to give the fictional illusion the massive, multitextured concreteness of social reality in order that the gratifications of fiction for the writer will come as close as possible to the gratifications of experience outside literary invention in the social world.

In a society where everything is mere seeming, pretense, contrived façades hiding an anarchy of values, the novelist both reproduces that moral chaos and triumphs over it by imposing upon it his own determined order. On one level, the illusions lost in Balzac's fiction faithfully repeat the pattern of the novel established by Cervantes. On another level, the nineteenth-century novelist reverses the direction of the quixotic model, being so intent in evoking the scenes and figures of his own Iron Age that they begin to perform for him the bizarre function of a new and private Golden Age, the fiction assuming, like the chivalric chimeras of the mad Don, the potency of stubborn fact.

3. *Wavering Perspectives in "Vanity Fair"*

Vanity Fair might at first appear to be the one signal instance in the Victorian period of a truly self-conscious novel. Thackeray's debt to Fielding is well known, and his emulation of that manifest manipulator of novelistic artifice leads him in a variety of ways to call explicit attention to the literary conventions with which he works. He begins, of course, by presenting himself in a little prologue entitled "Before the Curtain" as the manager of the performance, actually, as both the showman who controls the strings of the puppet characters and the artist who has cunningly fashioned each of the puppets. Once the curtain goes up, the showman will permit himself frequent asides to the audience. He will evoke a prototypical Jones sitting in his club reading this novel, marking disapproval of specific points in the margin. He will announce, then demonstrate, his freedom to step down from the platform and talk about the characters. He will allude to the dubious formulaic practices of popular novels, occasionally parodying them himself. He will exercise authorial omniscience, admitting that novelists do, after all, know everything, and in other ways will alert us to "the conduct of the tale"—the need to establish priorities among different groups of narrative materials, to backtrack in chronology, to simulate the passage of a certain span of time in the narration, and so forth. Finally, he will bring his main plot to its conclusion in a brilliant flurry of parodistic gestures where narrative statement and literary criticism intertwine:

> The vessel is in port. He has got the prize he has been trying for all his life. The bird has come in at last. There it is with its head on his shoulder, billing and cooing close

up to his heart, with soft outstretched fluttering wings. This is what he has asked for every day and hour for eighteen years. This is what he pined after. Here it is—the summit, the end—the last page of the third volume. Good-bye, colonel—God bless you, honest William!—Farewell, dear Amelia—Grow green again, tender little parasite, round the rugged old oak to which you cling! [Ch. 67]

The orchestration of maudlin mixed metaphors from the purple passages of bad fiction is perfectly controlled—from vessel to prize to cooing bird to the rugged old oak round which Amelia, devastatingly revealed at the last as a parasite, clings. The reality of the final union of Amelia and Dobbin is in a twinkling collapsed into the last page of the third volume, an event totally determined and circumscribed by the conventions of the popular novel and conveyed in the age's received format of publication. Appropriately, this self-conscious dénouement is followed by a typographical device, a solid line across the page, below which are half a dozen pages more to tie up loose narrative ends before the final *Vanitas Vanitatum* and the showman's shutting his box of puppets.

All of this, however, does not produce the general effect of a self-conscious novel because it is intermittent, inconsistent, repeatedly broken into by a very different conception of the fictional events and the narrator's relation to them. The discrepancy, from one point of view, could be stated as a matter of literary history: Thackeray is imaginatively excited by the kind of novel he discovered in Fielding but caught up rather more than he knows in his own age's prevalent assumptions about fiction, so that his use of Fieldingesque devices is bound to be discontinuous, incomplete.

The ultimate instance of Amelia as a tender little parasite is a case in point. There is only the sketchiest evidence before the conclusion that Thackeray has conceived her in parodistic terms as a conventional romantic heroine of a particularly selfish and mindless sort, as he seems to present her at the end. On the contrary, one is at times uncomfortably aware of the author himself sentimentally simpering over Amelia, imagining how sweet it would be for him to kiss her, holding her up as a perfect model of womanly integrity and selfless devotion. Admittedly, he tries to have it both ways by openly observing that certain fashionable readers may find Amelia dull and flat, but, with his moralistic bias in setting out his two heroines, he is scarcely ever willing fully to face up to Amelia's inevitable insipidness alongside the appeal of Becky with her "Napoleonic" energy. Amelia, in other words, is not enough a distanced fictional character, too much an idealized fantasy-figure for Thackeray, the image of the woman who is loving and loyal out of all proportion to the man's deserts, who can be nurturing mother or dependent daughter but never a threatening sexual free agent and an assertive free will like Becky. The sudden barrage of parodistic criticism leveled at Amelia in the dénouement is the expression of Thackeray's need to take vengeance on his own idealization, which at moments he is able to recognize for the empty, stultifying pastiche of literary and moral convention that it is. Thackeray's two attitudes toward his heroine are thus the opposite of Fielding's double attitude, for example, toward Squire Allworthy. In the case of Fielding, there is a clear, steady recognition of the price paid by the character in obtuseness and self-righteousness for being a paragon of virtue, and so the representation of Allworthy throughout the novel is dialectically double, at once affirmative and ironically qualified. In Thackeray, by contrast, there is a hiatus between the two attitudes, neither exerting any felt pressure on the other.

The inconsistencies in this Victorian adaptation of self-

conscious devices are clearest in Thackeray's treatment
of his narrating persona. The fact is that though the image
of the showman in motley is from time to time invoked
in the course of the narrative, the metaphor of the puppet
show is not really sustained. The characters that were
first introduced as mere puppets come to assume a life
independent of the narrator, who proves to be, for long
stretches of the novel, not the conductor of an artifice
but the faithful chronicler of true events. Thus, he can
tell us that Amelia wore a brown silk pelisse at her first
wedding because he has received direct information about
this and other details from Dobbin (22); he has examined
documentary evidence like Georgy's schoolbooks inscribed
in Amelia's delicate hand (46); he has been taken on a
tour of Lord Steyne's town house in Gaunt Square by
an "informant," little Tom Eaves (47). Finally, the pretense of a puppet show utterly vanishes when the narrator
enters the picture anecdotally as a British tourist in
Germany who actually met Colonel Dobbin and Amelia,
admired with some unnamed friends "that nice-looking
woman," and was present at the same performances of
Beethoven as Dobbin and his party. "It was on this very
tour that I, the present writer of a history of which every
word is true, had the pleasure to see them first, and to
make their acquaintance" (62). The assertion of the truth
of the story has none of the ironic duplicity of Cervantes'
invocation of that same notion upon the discovery of Cid
Hamete's notebooks; the "present writer" of a completely
true history does not interact with the artful manager
of the performance but is simply discontinuous with him.
The basic conception, in fact, of *Vanity Fair* would seem
to be of a true history of probable personages in contemporary (or nearly contemporary) society, with the puppet-
show vehicle serving as a justification for a certain heightening and stylization for both dramatic and didactic

purposes. Later, we will have a closer look at how that heightening and stylization operate.

The introduction of the author into a fictional town in Germany does not produce an instructively fictionalized version of the novelist's self, like Sterne's invention of Tristram, but, on the contrary, it insists on a substantive identity between the writer's real experience and that of the fictional characters. (The briefer anecdotal insets, where we see the narrator on top of a coach watching school children at play; strolling as a bachelor through Vauxhall; nostalgically recalling a coach trip made past Turnham Green, Brentford, Bagshot; have the same effect.) As we eventually learn, even the showman's costume is improvised finally not as a literary convention but as a moral-symbolic one, meant to indicate that this is a tale told by a jester in and for a world where we are all fools living weary lives signifying nothing: "O brother wearers of motley! Are there not moments when one grows sick of grinning and tumbling, and the jingling of cap and bells?" The brother wearers of motley are not fellow novelists but fellow men, all who live in Vanity Fair, and the little quaver that creeps into the narrator's voice betrays what is ultimately an extraliterary emotion, a feeling arising from William Makepeace Thackeray's sense of life unmediated by the fictional structure he has erected. This crossing of boundaries becomes clearer here as the narrator goes on: "This, dear friends and companions, is my amiable object—to walk with you through the Fair, to examine the shops and shows there; and that we should all come home after the flare, and the noise, and the gaiety, and be perfectly miserable in private" (19). That bleak cadence does have resonance but it is the wrong kind of resonance. The immediate fictional context in fact has been that zestfully fierce satire—the beady-eyed Mrs. Bute hovering possessively over the sickbed of Miss Crawley—in

which Thackeray is at his energetic best, and it does not
justify this sense of brooding misery, which would seem
to be the author's own. In the very act, then, of pointing
to his motley garb, he removes his artist's mask and takes
his place as a man among miserable men, one who happens
to be telling this true story.

If the self-conscious novelist crosses the border between
fiction and autobiographical experience knowingly, archly,
with pointed paradox, Thackeray does it inadvertently,
slipping backwards across the dividing line often in contravention of his own artistic purposes. This underlying
confusion in Thackeray has been precisely observed by
Dorothy Van Ghent:

> What we feel is that two orders of reality are clumsily
> getting in each other's way: the order of imaginative reality,
> where Becky lives, and the order of historical reality, where
> William Makepeace Thackeray lives. ... Whereas Thack-
> eray seems merely to be victimized or tricked by his adopted
> convention [of authorial asides] into a clumsy mishandling
> of perspectives, Fielding manipulates the same convention
> deliberately to produce displacements of perspective as an
> organic element of composition.[7]

There is no rule-of-thumb about how much or how little
of an author's actual life can be admitted into a fiction
without violating its integrity as an artifice. The contrast
between Thackeray and Fielding, which Dorothy Van
Ghent rightly introduces into the discussion, nicely illustrates this problem of "translation." The only information
we get about Thackeray's life in *Vanity Fair* is trivial bits
about places he has been, yet his presence, in attitude
and feeling, is often intrusive. Fielding, on the other hand,
is careful to begin *Tom Jones* by identifying the manager
of his more poised performance as a writer confronted with

---

[7] *The English Novel: Form and Function* (New York: Harper Brothers, 1953),
pp. 139-140.

a writer's problems ("An author ought to consider himself, not as a gentleman who gives a private or eleemosynary treat, but rather as one who keeps a public ordinary. . . .") The consistently defined figure that narrates *Tom Jones*, a voice projected by Henry Fielding but not confused with his nonliterary self, is appropriately both an author pondering authorial obligations, theorizing about fiction, and the arch ironist and literary gamesman who so adroitly maneuvers characters and readers alike.

By the time Fielding arrives at the invocation to Book 13, he can tell us quite autobiographically that the figure of Sophia is based on his late beloved wife, Charlotte, and he can express his real personal aspiration to be read by posterity "when the little parlour in which I sit at this instant shall be reduced to a worse furnished box," and do this without any violation of perspectives. The reference to "the little parlour in which I sit" has often been cited sentimentally out of context, but in fact it is totally surrounded by the narrator's characteristic self-mockery and his usual bantering concern with the conventions and practical business of literature. To be sure, the mention of Charlotte Fielding and the expressed hope to be read by future generations are "sincere," but the sincerity is, on one side, defined in terms of literary tradition and, on the other side, ironically set off by a sudden switch to the crass economic realities of the eighteenth-century writer's trade. That is, the image of the little parlour comes at the end of a mock-Miltonic invocation ("Come bright love of fame, inspire my glowing breast . . ."), over-abundant in mythological trappings and iambic cadences, which reminds us that it has always been the convention for the author *qua* author to hope vocally and rhythmically for undying fame. What immediately follows this ironic-serious prayer for literary immortality is the invocation of a "much plumper dame," the earthy goddess of material gain, whose sphere is not Maeonia or the banks of Hebrus

but Grub Street and the seamy mercantile haunts of
Amsterdam, who deals in convertible bank-bills to greedy
quacks, beaus, poets, romancers, and historians. Fielding's
keen perception of "this ill-yoked pair, this lean shadow
and this fat substance," is itself a token of his
ability to weave out of the materials of literary tradition and contemporary reality a single texture of self-conscious artifice in which even autobiographical details immediately become part of the pattern. In this regard his
position as a knowing innovator of the novel may have
been a positive advantage. For Thackeray, the fine poise
of self-reflexive fiction was difficult both because of his
Victorian notions of morally purposeful art and because
of his location in literary history. Living in the great age
of the novel, when fiction often aspired to be taken as
virtual fact, when the serialized novelist could imagine
exerting a direct, almost personal influence over his visibly
responsive audience, he was too inclined to let attitudes
unrelated to his fictional inventions impose themselves
within the fiction.

The often noted instance of the negative judgment
Thackeray passes on Becky illustrates in another way how
with all his talk about puppets and performance, he is
unwilling to give himself over to the inner logic of his
artifice as artifice. Becky, of course, is Thackeray's most
splendid invention, and I think it is clear that on some
level, of all his characters he identifies most intimately
with her rebellious energy and daring, as Balzac identifies
most fully with those same qualities in Vautrin. It is
notorious that Thackeray is unprepared to give Becky due
credit for her strengths and her genuine grievances. From
the start, he must not merely put her down—which in
some respects she obviously deserves—but he must mora-
listically demonize her. (Her thoroughly justified laughter
in the face of the awful Miss Pinkerton at the beginning
of the novel has to be characterized, excessively, as "de-

monical," and similar authorial insistences pursue her through the book.) Now, what is especially curious about the handling of Becky is that she is not just a fantasy projection of some secret self in the author but his unrecognized surrogate in regard to her mode of operation in the novel.

Becky is clearly the manager of the performance in the performance itself. It is not only that she manipulates the figures around her, arranging scenes for them by careful design, but also that she exercises the narrator's own specific skills. One of our earliest glimpses of her (2) is as a puppeteer, mimicking Miss Pinkerton with a doll which she makes move and talk for the amusement of the young artists who frequent her father's studio. The very fact that she is the daughter of an artist, which is intended to discredit her by giving her a bohemian background, provides another link with the vocation of the author. In a long letter to Amelia about life with the Pitt Crawleys (8), Becky displays a writer's adeptness at shrewd and lively satiric report which is quite like that of the novelist himself. Also like Thackeray, she has a gift for visual caricature, and in fact one of her supposed drawings (11) is included in the original edition of the novel. Finally, as an actress of considerable skill, she is fond of doing comic impersonations of other characters in the novel.

The remarkable thing about all this in a novel that is purportedly a manipulation of puppets and a stage performance is that nothing is made of it. The possibilities of playing with Becky's potential as the artificer within the artifice are intriguing, but precisely because "the famous little Becky Puppet," so "uncommonly . . . lively on the wire," is too real for Thackeray, he is uninterested in those possibilities. Becky moves for him on a moral rather than on an artistic plane: unconsciously, he is allured by the freedom and the resilient ingenuity of her ruthless egoism; consciously, he feels obliged to denounce her whenever she appears, to reduce the rebellious spirit to a petty Clytemnestra murdering for gain, and at the end to exhibit her as a shrunken devil with blunted horns.

Thackeray's self-consciousness is finally not as a novelist but as a moralist. It is entirely appropriate that he should take his title from Bunyan and edge his own fictional characters in the direction of allegory, giving them names like Bareacres, Slowbore, Lollypop, Crawley, Sharp, at times entirely dropping realistic surface texture for the clarity of the scheme and calling a rich man Dives, a sycophant Tom Toady, a profligate Thriftless. These gestures toward allegory, however, do not weaken Thackeray's general connection with the broad realistic orientation of the nineteenth-century novel. The attempt at a moral panorama of contemporary society in *Vanity Fair* is a distinctly British complement to Balzac's endeavor in writing a *Human Comedy*. Balzac, strongly influenced by the scientism of his age and place, tries to cope with unsettling social actualities by reconstituting them in a comprehensive description as a system of energies, a series of quasi-zoological phenomena. Thackeray, on the other hand, follows an English tradition of the prose writer as worldly moral arbiter that might be traced back as far as Addison and Steele. Confronted with a new mobile society of shifting appearances where rapacity, connivance, and pretense were common currency, with the Napoleonic upheaval in the background of his vision, he imposes a moralist's categories of classification and judgment on his contemporary materials as he represents them, and in this manner he makes the new fluid society imaginatively tractable. In any case, Thackeray and Balzac are equally committed to getting things straight about their societies through the medium of fiction, and each in his own way exhibits the delusion of grandeur characteristic of the nineteenth-century novelist: to ignore willfully the limits of fiction, to play the role of omniscient knower, absolute judge, omnicompetent arbiter of taste and morality, for a world supposedly shared by the novelist and his readers.

Perhaps a final example from *Vanity Fair* will make clearer how the concern with satiric judgment and moral design provides a motive for realistic representation and a means of organizing materials in a coherent, dramatically effective scheme. Here is a description of Becky and Lord Steyne at one of those questionable after-dinner parties she gives for the sake of her noble admirer:

> The great Lord of Steyne was standing by the fire sipping coffee. The fire crackled and blazed pleasantly. There was a score of candles sparkling round the mantlepiece, in all sorts of quaint sconces, of gilt and bronze and porcelain. They lighted up Rebecca's figure to admiration, as she sat on a sofa covered with a pattern of gaudy flowers. She was in a pink dress, that looked as fresh as a rose; her dazzling white arms and shoulders were half covered with a thin hazy scarf through which they sparkled; her hair hung in curls round her neck; one of her little feet peeped out from the fresh crisp folds of the silk: the prettiest little sandal in the finest silk stocking in the world.
> The candles lighted up Lord Steyne's shining bald head, which was fringed with red hair. He had thick bushy eyebrows, with little twinkling bloodshot eyes, surrounded by a thousand wrinkles. His jaw was underhung, and when he laughed, two white buck-teeth protruded themselves and glistened savagely in the midst of the grin. He had been dining with royal personages, and wore his garter and ribbon. A short man was his lordship, broad-chested, and bow-legged, but proud of the fineness of his foot and ankle, and always caressing his garter-knee. [37]

The writer's inherent ability to convey the objects of description authoritatively is never in question. The occasional irony—"The great Lord of Steyne" and the mincing mimickry of "the prettiest little foot," and so on—is aimed at the characters, not at the fictional process. One can see clearly here how the metaphor of stage performance is transferred to the technique of fiction not as a means of stressing fictiveness but of heightening satiric representation. Thus the whole scene, rendered with great visual sharpness, is "brilliantly illuminated with the Author's own candles," as Thackeray says in his preface, referring there particularly to his drawings. Becky, as always, is acting, carefully costumed and posed to look as fresh as a rose, to set off her white arms and shoulders, to display her pretty little foot; and so the scene itself is appropriately lit up as though it were being played out before footlights. The theater, however, is no more than a metaphor, a way of focusing vision on a world of role-playing, while the drawing room is meant to be vividly there for us in full verisimilar detail. Thackeray's method, however, does not accommodate much mimesis for the sake of mimesis. In this passage, only the sipping of coffee and the blazing fire at the beginning are present in their own right, as neutral details that help make the scene real to the imagination of the reader. Everything else falls into the satirist's moral design. The sofa Becky sits on must have a pattern of gaudy flowers; Lord Steyne has to be seen narcissistically caressing the emblem of his nobility; the candlelight that picks up his features reveals his physical grotesqueness, the wrinkles and bloodshot eyes of a debauched old age, and those buckteeth gleaming "savagely" like fangs. The very energy of insistence in this virtuoso piece shows how Thackeray's imagination is directed toward the fictional personages as moral agents quite like those of the real world, only heightened and emphasized for the purposes of narrative exhibition.

Intent on this process of representation and exposure,

he can allow little latitude to a problematic perception of his fiction as necessary artifice. The devices adopted from Fielding, then, must remain admiring gestures of deference to a kind of novel constructed according to very different notions of fiction and what it can intrinsically make of reality. If the metaphor of the showman would seem to reveal a certain diffidence on the part of the novelist in regard to his own role of public entertainer, the very invocation of a traditional spiritual guidebook like *Pilgrim's Progress* suggests that Thackeray, in his own moralizing and wavering way, eminently belongs to the century in which novelists aspired to write an imaginative *summa* of their age.

4. Fictional Confidence and "The Confidence-Man"

Melville's *The Confidence-Man* is one of the intriguing anomalies of nineteenth-century fiction. Published in 1857, within months of the appearance of *Little Dorrit* in England and *Madame Bovary* in France, it is neither a great expansive document of nineteenth-century imaginism, like Dickens's novel, nor does it like Flaubert's provide a point of departure for the chaste precision of the modern art-novel, but instead it peculiarly anticipates the postmodern phenomenon of *écriture blanche*, the literature that denies its own possibility of existence, pointing toward silence through cunning strategems of language. It was, of course, exactly into silence that Melville himself moved after *The Confidence-Man*, abandoning fiction entirely until the writing of *Billy Budd* some thirty years later, near the end of his life. He was impelled on this course away from fiction not only by the unfriendly reception his novels received but also by the intrinsic logic of the argument on the nature of fiction that is conducted in *The Confidence-Man*.

This last novel of Melville's is a masterpiece *manqué*, a book operating with considerable originality on split levels that make significant contact but are not fully coordinated. Melville in part wants to write a satiric panoramic novel in the grand nineteenth-century manner, giving us a crammed catalogue of mankind's teeming variety in the microcosm of the riverboat *Fidèle*. He also means to conduct a probing critique of the nature of fiction as his fiction unfolds, and to this end he closely imitates the prefatory chapters of *Joseph Andrews* and *Tom Jones* in three chapters (14, 33, 44) devoted to the poetics of the novel, placed, roughly, a third and two-thirds of the way through the novel, then just before the end. (The self-deprecating, teasing chapter headings are thoroughly in the manner of Fielding: "Worth The Consideration of Those to Whom it May Prove Worth Considering"; "Which May Pass for Whatever it May Prove to be Worth"; "In Which the Last Three Words of the Last Chapter Are Made the Text of a Discourse, Which Will Be Sure of Receiving More or Less Attention From Those Readers Who Do Not Skip It." The message of all three headings, interestingly, is a tautology, or a caustic disclaimer of meaning: what is said in the chapter, we are told, will be read by those who choose to read it.) There is no slippery inconsistency or unwitting confusion of modes here, as in Thackeray's emulation of Fielding. The exploration of the paradoxes of fictional invention is boldly pursued, and, indeed, proves to be rich in insights. The problem is rather that Melville does not have an adequate fictional technique for continuously integrating the imaginary personages and actions with the reflections on the nature of fiction.

The Confidence-Man comes closer to being an achieved self-conscious novel than any other major fictional work of its age because of the intellectual and spiritual intentness which Melville invested in the activity of novel-writing. His imagination touched by the peculiar biblical fervor of American Protestantism, Melville brings to a crisis that lingering Puritan suspicion of fictions one finds in many of the English and American masters of fiction. Other nineteenth-century novelists toyed with or indulged in the notion of the novelist as prophetic castigator and visionary guide, but Melville scrutinized the implications of that idea with absolute seriousness, and so more and more he came to ask himself, What is the nature of the truth that can be conveyed in a fiction? The general scheme he devised for *The Confidence-Man* is a brilliant invention, though I do not believe it is worked out to the degree that some of Melville's modern critics imply. The nineteenth century's shifting or upwardly mobile world of false appearances and pretense, seen in the British and French novel as a social phenomenon, is here elevated into a metaphysical absolute, a definition of the human condition. "What are you? What am I?" asks the Confidence-Man, in the last of his disguises, as the Cosmopolitan. "Nobody knows who anybody is. The data which life furnishes, towards forming a true estimate of any being, are as insufficient to that end as in geometry one side would be to determine the triangle" (36). We all inhabit, then, a world of elaborate fictions that we construct about our essentially unknowable fellow men and about ourselves as well. Reality is, as Melville calls it at the end of the book, a "Masquerade," and so the form of the novel is a masquerade in several acts, with the Confidence-Man, in his eight successive masks, the supreme maker of fictions about himself for the sake of exploiting that bewilderment of fictions which is human existence.

In discussing the realism of Balzac, I had occasion to suggest that the hallmark of the true self-conscious novelist is a keen perception of paradox in the relationship between fiction and reality. The sense of that paradox is deep and abiding in *The Confidence-Man*. If human reality is itself

a dizzying kaleidoscope of individually improvised fictions
that make real knowledge impossible, a novel is fiction
at a second remove, a manifest fabrication about fabrications. "If the acutest sage be often at his wits' ends to
understand living character, shall those who are not sages
expect to run and read character in those mere phantoms
which flit along a page, like shadows along a wall?" (14).
The likening of fictional characters to shadow-images
flitting along a wall, with its ultimate allusion to Plato's
Allegory of the Cave, is a comparison that will bear further
reflection. For the moment, however, we can observe that
Melville quickly goes on to pursue the antithetical other
side of his paradox. The reader, with expectations conditioned by shallow literary convention, may demand consistency in a fictional character, but human nature itself
is stubbornly inconsistent. The "great masters" of fiction,
by representing character in its essential contradictions,
exercise a godlike knowledge which they make accessible
to others, "in this way throwing open, sometimes to the
understanding even of school misses, the last complications
of that spirit which is affirmed by the Creator to be
fearfully and wonderfully made."

Later, in the second of his three theoretical chapters,
Melville carries the argument for the truth of fiction a
step farther, beginning with the observation of another
paradox: that we confess our willingness to drop real life
in the very act of picking up a fictional work, yet insist
on getting from fiction precisely what we were weary of
to begin with, reality. What follows is a beautiful statement about how fiction, in its freedom of uninhibited
invention, is able to give us a sharper reality, though I
think it is important to note that Melville never quite
says this is what fiction actually does, only that this is
the exorbitant requirement of readers which he must
somehow attempt to meet.

And as, in real life, the proprieties will not allow people to act out themselves with that unreserve permitted to the stage; so, in books of fiction, they look not only for more entertainment, but, at bottom, even for more reality, than real life itself can show. Thus, though they want novelty, they want nature, too; but nature unfettered, exhilarated, in effect transformed. . . . It is with fiction as with religion: it should present another world, and yet one to which we feel the tie.

The crucial question about *The Confidence-Man* is to what extent this sharply paradoxical conception of fiction and reality has been translated into the fictional world of the novel. R. W. B. Lewis, picking up a hint from Daniel J. Hoffman, notes a tendency in Melville's descriptive prose here to cancel out its own effects by piling on mutually contradictory attributes until we are left with airy specters where we thought we had vivid fictional evocations. As a result, "the first and most accomplished of the confidence men in the novel is the author," whose purpose is to produce in the reader "a sort of intellectual derangement, by arousing and deploying what Whitman called the terrible doubt of appearances."[8] This is shrewdly observed and seems quite accurate for a number of memorable passages in the book, like the description of the faithless wife Goneril that Lewis analyzes. For other parts of the novel, the generalization needs some modification. Here, for example, is Melville's rapid sketch of an authentic American skinflint in Chapter 15:

The miser, a lean old man, whose flesh seemed salted codfish, dry as combustibles; head, like one whittled by an idiot out of a knot; flat, bony mouth, nipped between buzzard nose and chin; expression, flitting between hunks and imbecile—now one, now the other—he made no response.

[8] R. W. B. Lewis, *Trials of the Word* (New Haven: Yale University Press, 1965), p. 65.

His eyes were closed, his cheek lay upon an old white
moleskin coat, rolled under his head like a wizened apple
upon a grimy snow-bank.

The uninhibited caricature is reminiscent of Dickens
and Smollett, but the effect of fantastication is more than
Dickensian because it is complicated by a Metaphysical
poet's zest for extravagant contradiction. The miser's flesh
is simultaneously salted codfish and dry inflammable stuff;
his head is like one carved by an idiot, someone who could
scarcely do any carving, out of a knot of wood, a material
with which carving is virtually impossible. Similes, often
bizarre or extravagant ones, play a very important role
in *The Confidence-Man*, and Melville seems quite aware,
like Fielding before him, that an obtrusive simile is one
of the most convenient ways for the literary artificer to
flaunt his artifice while using it to render his subject. The
buzzard nose and chin may be pure Smollett, but the head
resting on an old white coat (with a peculiar reverse twist
of syntax) like a wizened apple on a grimy snow-bank
illustrates *The Confidence-Man*'s strangely wild shuttling
between far-flung realms through figurative language.

What I would like to stress about this passage is that
the old miser does not disappear in a smokescreen of
contradictions, as Goneril does. Rather, he stands out as
a sharply realized figure, like any caricature in a Dickens
novel, while we are led at the same time to perceive the
necessary precariousness of his realization. He exists, one
might say, as a flashing back and forth between opposite
poles, an alternating current caught in the simultaneity
of the novelist's vision; as a near-impossibility translated
into concrete being by the persuasive ingenuity of a simile.
Even lexically he comes into focus by a leap between
opposites, alternating between the monosyllabic Anglo-
Saxon "hunks" and the Latinate dachtyl, "imbecile." The
key word in the description, located squarely at its center,
is "flitting," which is, instructively, the very verb Melville

chose in the preceding chapter to convey the phantom quality of paper-and-ink creatures in a flesh-and-blood world.

Paradoxes about fiction and reality are made to be turned round and round, and so it is quite appropriate that Melville should implicitly reverse in this passage the paradox of flitting phantoms enunciated in the previous chapter. Human existence in general, one infers, is a spectral flickering between contradictions, and as such it is by nature more susceptible to the novelist's ambiguous art than to our nonfictional perceptions. Fiction is at a double remove from reality, like the images on the cave wall in Plato's allegory, yet at the same time it provides our closest approach to reality's elusiveness. Projected shadow-images, magic lanterns, shifting theatrical illumination, are the guiding metaphors for Melville's conduct of his masquerade. In the chapter on original characters in fiction, just before the conclusion, he uses the image of a revolving Drummond light (that is, a limelight) to represent the operation of an original character: "raying away from itself all round it—everything is lit by it, everything starts up to it . . . , so that, in certain minds, there follows upon the adequate conception of such a character, an effect, in its way, akin to that which in Genesis attends upon the beginning of things." From the beginning of things, Melville moves us on in a brilliant montage effect to the end of things, starting the next, and final, chapter with a description of the peculiar solar lamp in the men's cabin that radiates light in dimming circles through a globe decorated with transparent images of a horned altar in flames and a robed man with a halo. In the muted apocalyptic intimation of the novel's ending, the solar lamp will go out, and with it the horned altar and the robed man, while the Confidence-Man leads someone away into darkness.

Now, Melville's imagery is so inventively apt that it

is easy by citing it to make his novel sound even better than it really is. The problem is that the whole magic-lantern mode of representation is alluded to and occasionally illustrated in brilliant ways but is not sustained throughout the novel. Thus, the focusing of phantoms through paradoxical similes occurs strikingly in certain brief passages but is not the continuous procedure of the novel as a whole. Despite Melville's acute perception of fictiveness and its dialectic nature, long stretches of the book, involving both authorial description and extended dialogue, seem like part of a much more conventionally realistic nineteenth-century novel. There are, to be sure, a couple of brief exchanges between characters about fiction and fictional personages, and some succinct reflections by the protagonist on storytelling as interpolated tales are told. Nevertheless, one begins the book and reads through thirteen full chapters with no more than an oblique hint that the author of these represented actions is steadily contemplating his narrative as a fictional object among other fictional objects, and so when the first theoretical chapter comes, there is a little jolt, an unprepared-for switch in perspective.

The explicit imitation of Fielding invites comparison and points up a formal deficiency, for the one thing this novel lacks is precisely what Fielding worked out so splendidly—a way of writing about the fictional events absolutely continuous with the theorizing, where in the narrative itself there is a seamless connection between narration and wide-ranging reflection, where at every moment the ostentatiously manipulated fictional materials are set in an elaborate grid of convention, genre, literary allusion, authorial intention. It would seem that Melville was too involved in the characteristic practices of the novel in his own age to break with them as decisively as his theoretical chapters implicitly require.

The other side of this novel's problem in finding an

adequate form for its insights is the kind of truth Melville imagines to be the proper object of fiction. Though he does talk about a truth of character and even refers to the category of "psychological novelists," his own novel reflects only the most limited interest either in psychology or in individual character. Generically, novels attempt to show how society and the individual—his values, his imagination, his temperament—interact, thrust against each other. *The Confidence-Man*, however, tends to represent individuals as examples of what men in general are like, without any novelistic concern for the predicament of the individual; and society here is only the conglomerate of these illustrative figures and their innumerable counterparts, not the nineteenth-century Society that is questioned, analyzed, puzzled over as a definite entity by Balzac, Dickens, Stendhal. It is worth noting that Melville chooses religion as his analogue for the other world akin to our own which fiction should give us, and that he compares the effect of the original character in a work of fiction to "that which in Genesis attends upon the beginning of things." The series of allusions to Satan in the figure of the Confidence-Man and the invocation of the Book of Revelations are also instructive in this connection, for what Melville really wants to represent is not particular destinies at a certain juncture in social history but the spiritual condition of mankind.

For this reason, there can be no sustained plot, only a series of illustrative vignettes, the novel reverting to the episodic form of the picaresque, but with a very different aim from that of the picaresque novel. More serious, the protagonist himself is less a realized character than a continuous performance, embodying the principle of protean deception and serving as the main mechanism in a revelatory scheme. The scheme is meant to run from spiritual alpha to omega, from Genesis to Apocalypse, but the principal actor achieves none of the power of the

original character that Melville describes in the image of
the Drummond light. On a purely technical level the
Confidence-Man maneuvers other characters into revealing their conniving motives or their gullibility, but he
himself hardly evinces that deep imaginative life which
makes a great fictional character a central source of
illumination pulling the whole world around it into vivid
being. One might put the difficulty in terms of an imitative
fallacy: Melville, having set the unknowability of human
nature as his subject—indeed, as the necessary subject of
fiction—creates a central character so unknowable, so
distanced from and uninvolving for the reader, that the
book reads more like an exciting plan for a great novel
than its realization.

In Thackeray, there are allegorical traits in the surface
texture of the novel, but the underlying conception of the
subject of the novel is realist in the central nineteenth-century manner. In *The Confidence-Man*, the surface texture is for the most part pungently realistic, despite
certain clues in allusions and names to an allegorical
scheme, while what is ultimately allegorical is the underlying conception of the subject. Thus the action is set
on a ship named Faith, where the barber at the very
beginning hangs out a sign, NO TRUST, where the passen-
gers, called pilgrims, are visited by a figure who in a double
irony emphatically, perhaps even sincerely, preaches confidence and plays on it. The theoretical chapters reflect
not only Melville's speculative shrewdness but also his
sense that what he had to do with the novel now was
to push fiction beyond its own limits, creating in the novel
a new Scripture that could follow the old in its inexorable
demonstration of a timeless truth about man's estate.

Melville remains, however, a novelist, not a religious
visionary, and in his very discussion of the immense
possibilities of fiction one senses a lurking apprehension
of the impossibility of the whole endeavor. The maker of

fictions, after all, knows he cannot escape his location deep within the recesses of the Platonic cave, intimating with the shadows of shadows the incandescent nature of the reality outside. If, in the words of the narrator at the very end, "Something further may follow of this Masquerade," it is not a sequel to the book that is promised but, on the contrary, a sequel in the long and devious charade of Creation that can no longer be imagined in a human book. There is something profoundly modern about Melville's ambivalent sense of his vocation, combining great excitement at the idea of what the novel might do with a growing vexation of spirit over the truths it will not yield. His true heirs in imagination are Conrad, reflecting through fiction on the illusion-masked abyss of emptiness over which everything human is built, including the fiction; Kafka, hopelessly committed to the writer's enterprise even as he commanded his writings to be burned for their lack of truth; and Beckett, who writes a literature about the end of literature, stubbornly hammering through words at a reality beyond the screen of language. This kind of experiment with the limits of fiction would be undertaken on a larger scale, without inhibitions, by a wide variety of novelists in the century after Melville's, when the crisis of confidence in fiction had become more general—at the very moment the novel was boldly renewing itself by smashing old forms, or recasting them in parody.

Chapter 5

The Modernist Revival of
Self-Conscious Fiction

> The novel must now prove that it can
> be something other than a mirror
> carried along a road, that it can be
> superior and a priori—which is to
> say, deduced, *composed*, a work of art.
>   André Gide, *Journal de la Brévine*

> In truth parody was here the proud
> expedient of a great gift threatened
> with sterility by a combination of
> skepticism, intellectual reserve, and
> a sense of the deadly extension of
> the kingdom of the banal.
>   Thomas Mann, *Doctor Faustus*

1. New Novels for New Men and Women

"On or about December 1910," Virginia Woolf announced in the most famous of her challenges to the practices of the nineteenth-century novel and its Edwardian heirs, "human nature changed." Her assertion has been specifically linked by critics with the first London exhibition of Post-Impressionist paintings organized at the time she mentions by Roger Fry and Desmond McCarthy. More generally, it has been associated with the signal innovations in psychology, philosophy, anthropology, physics, and most immediately, the shift in sexual morality, that began to make their potent presence widely felt in the first decade of this century. In any case, Virginia Woolf's choice of date seems particularly apt. She sets the supposed change in human nature a year after the programmatic beginning of the Age of the Avant Garde, that decade and a half of militant movements and counter-movements, manifestoes and plans of aesthetic rebellion, in which poets and artists from Barcelona to Moscow sought a radical redefinition of the very nature of their enterprises. December 1910 is three years before the publication of Biely's *St. Petersburg*, less than four years before the appearance in 1914 of Gide's *Les Caves du Vatican* and Unamuno's *Mist*, four years before Joyce begins to write *Ulysses*, two years before the publication of Mann's *Death in Venice*. The modernist revolution in fiction, of course, would not come to full fruition until what R. P. Blackmur has called the *anni mirabiles*, the 1920s, when the major innovative achievements of Joyce, Mann, Proust, Kafka, Faulkner, and of course Virginia Woolf herself, would all appear in a span of eight brief years; but the harbingers of the revolution were already abroad in the score or more of months after that symbolic date of December 1910.

One of several underlying patterns in this new constellation of creative forces is an artistically manifested self-consciousness about the processes of fiction-making the like of which had not been seen in the novel since the end of the eighteenth century. It would be too easy simply to say that novelists, fatigued and disillusioned after a century of strenuous engagement in history and society, turned back to an earlier pattern of exploring the fictiveness of fictions. Like any dialectical process, the history of the novel does not slip back to earlier stages but recapitulates and incorporates what it has previously undergone as it moves onward. Many, though not all, of the important self-conscious novels in the twentieth century are deeply concerned with a particular historical moment, with the very nature of historical process, even

with the future of Western civilization, as they deploy
their elaborate systems of mirrors to reflect novel and
novelist in the act of conjuring with reality. Though
Tristram Shandy may have been eagerly rediscovered by
the modernists (Virginia Woolf again bears witness in an
essay on Sterne), they had not altogether forgotten *The
Possessed* or *War and Peace*.

In trying to get a perspective on the nineteenth-century
novel, I offered as an instance of its intense imaginism
the novelistic reconstitution of the city in Dickens and
Balzac. Perhaps we might sharpen our sense of the transition of fiction into modernism by considering how novelists
begin to render urban experience in the first quarter of
the twentieth century. Three of the paradigmatic modernist masterpieces, after all, are ambitious novels that concentrate on a brief span of hours in the life of a metropolis—Biely's St. Petersburg, Joyce's Dublin, and the London
of *Mrs. Dalloway*. But, as we shall see, these novels are
"about" their respective cities in a different sense from
that in which *Bleak House* might be said to be about
London and its institutions or *Le Père Goriot* to be about
Paris and its worldly ways. Let us begin with a passage
from the Wandering Rocks section of *Ulysses*, the one
section in which Joyce offers an explicit panorama of life
in the Dublin streets. The stream of consciousness is
Bloom's:

> Cityful passing away, other cityful coming, passing away
> too: other coming on, passing on. Houses, lines of houses,
> streets, miles of pavements, piledup bricks, stones. Changing
> hands. This owner, that. Landlord never dies they say. Other
> steps into his shoes when he gets his notice to quit. They
> buy the place up with gold and still they have all the gold.
> Swindle in it somewhere. Piled up in cities, worn away age
> after age. Pyramids in sand. Built on bread and onions.
> Slaves. Chinese wall. Babylon. Big stones left. Round

towers. Rest rubble, sprawling suburbs, jerrybuilt, Kerwan's mushroom houses, built of breeze. Shelter for the night.
No one is anything.[1]

The contrast with Balzac's rendering of urban flux or Dickens's vision of a crazily crowded cityscape of architectural decay is startling. In the authorial voice of the nineteenth-century novels, one notices above all a confident mastery of the chaotic metropolis, a mastery reflected in the vigorously ordered, reiterative structures of rhetoric through which the scenes are reported. In Joyce, on the other hand, as attention turns inward to the movements of the protagonist's mind, what we become aware of is that the flux of the city scene and the great ebb and flow of life it implies are too vast and confusing really to be contained coherently by any single finite mind, and surely not by an average one like Bloom's. What figurative language Bloom uses—"mushroom houses, built of breeze," or "cityful," on the analogy of spoonful, boatful—has a vivid plebeian immediacy, but in order to suggest the rhythms of consciousness Joyce must renounce the sort of complex ordering of data available to a more syntactically elaborate, consistently developed use of metaphorical language by an overviewing narrator. Bloom, meditating on the transience of existence as he observes the city scene (he has just been thinking in a simultaneous flash of Mrs. Purefoy at the lying-in hospital and Paddy Dignam in his grave), offers us what amounts to a movingly expressive mental stammer, fragmenting the external world into a stacatto series of overlapping interior impressions. Passing away and coming and passing away again, the city is a continuous blur he cannot quite bring into focus. "They" are in mysterious control of things, buying and selling and always holding onto the wealth. Bloom vaguely suspects that there is a "Swindle in it somewhere," in all this process

[1] *Ulysses* (New York: Random House, 1961), p. 164.

of endless exchange, but the very nature of his language suggests he cannot fathom the process.

Earlier, I proposed that there was an underlying tendency in Dickens and Balzac to fill the imaginary space of the fictional scene by constant additive procedures. In Joyce's stream of consciousness, it is rather the defining limits of the space that are broken down, the associative movement of the mind repeatedly spilling over to other places and times—here, from Dublin, 1904, to ancient Egypt, Babylon, and the Great Wall of China. As a consequence, what is imparted to the reader instead of a solid-seeming illusion of reality is a phantasmagoric dissolution of external reality in the quick solvent of the mind: in this regard, Sterne is a real forerunner of the modernists.

Joyce, more than any other twentieth-century novelist, shares Sterne's exuberant reveling in the protean energy of the mind, but he resembles his own contemporaries and is different from Sterne in his ultimate sense of being as a precarious structure erected on a ground of nothingness. In Sterne consciousness constantly transforms reality, but there are no brooding metaphysical or metahistorical doubts about the stuff of reality. In Joyce, Faulkner, Proust, and Virginia Woolf, the stuff of reality, whether considered as personal history, cultural heritage, or metaphysical substratum, threatens to crumble into emptiness, and so the play of consciousness becomes a sustained act of desperate courage—a "violin in the void," in Nabokov's memorable phrase—creating form and substance where perhaps there would be nothing.

The formally modern character of our passage from *Ulysses* is obvious enough, but what is philosophically modern about the passage, embodied in the narrative form, is the sense not merely that all things are transient but that ultimately all things decay, fall apart. As in some recent American fiction in which the influence of modern physics has become conscious and direct, the implicit controlling concept here is entropy: systems of order continually tend to the greatest possible disorder and dispersal of energy. The historical direction of Bloom's reflections is from the crushing solidity of the pyramids to modern houses built of breeze, while the massive structures of fabulous antiquity are themselves reduced to large stones, rubble, perhaps even to the particles of sand in which the pyramids sit. "No one is anything," Bloom concludes starkly. Individual identity, all human projects, structures, cultures, are momentary configurations of seeming coherence pulled apart in the perpetual centrifuge of history and physical existence.

"The unity of any event," reflects Hermann Broch in the last part of his trilogy on historical disintegration, *The Sleepwalkers*, "and the integrity of the world are guaranteed merely by enigmatic, although visible, symbols, which are necessary because without them the visible world would fall asunder into unnameable, bodiless, dry layers of cold and transparent ash."[2] The emphasis on symbols as the bulwark against disintegration, an emphasis Broch would later develop in his major novel on art and the void, *The Death of Virgil*, bears directly on the central role of artifice in modernists like Joyce, Proust, Virginia Woolf.

The realism of *Ulysses* is highly paradoxical. In the interior monologue as it is employed by Joyce, we often have the illusion of immediate participation in the inner reality of the characters, as though there were no intervening authorial presence at all. That, I take it, is the intended effect in a passage like the one we have examined, however much a reader may detect elements of stylization,

[2] Broch, *The Sleepwalkers*, tr. Willa and Edwin Muir (New York: Grosset & Dunlap, 1964), p. 642.

of the creation of a new convention, upon reconsideration. Long sections of the novel, however, are written not in the stream of consciousness but in a variety of parodistic, rigorously formal techniques in which the presence of the artificer is extravagantly evident, and the careful rereader of *Ulysses* soon becomes adept at detecting the elaborate allusive tracery of the novel's archetectonic symbolism in the passages of interior monologue as well; so that even from the apparent immediacy of rendered experience the complex design of artifice emerges. The double edge of Joyce's purpose is perfectly expressed in Molly Bloom's concluding soliloquy, where in the midst of the unpunctuated, unparagraphed flow of language that directly gives us Molly's "real" inner world, she cries to the author who invented her: "Oh Jamesy let me up out of this."

The paradox is a necessary one for Joyce. Deeply affected by the immense avidness for reality of the nineteenth-century novel, he has a modern recognition not only that reality is always mediated by consciousness but that consciousness itself is an artificer in constantly making something of the formless flux of experience, inventing images and chains of connection to give it shape and substance. The prominent fault of Joyce's genius is a tendency toward the excessive elaboration of artifice, a tendency he would carry to Promethean ultimacy in *Finnegans Wake*, but in that regard he is only the most extreme example of an orientation shared by most of the classic modern writers. Where things fall apart, ontologically and historically, where everything is "worn away, age after age," there are moments when artifice will seem not a reflection on or transformation of reality but the only reality that one can count on, that one can humanly grasp. "No one is anything," unless artful consciousness makes him something, and even that identity is a moment of coherence suspended between twin eternities of dissolution.

Much the same dialectical tension between artful consciousness and nothingness that one finds in Joyce, but viewed, as it were, from the other end of the telescope, is evident in this rendering of a city scene near the beginning of Biely's *St. Petersburg*:

> The wet slippery prospect was intersected by another wet prospect at a ninety-degree angle; a policeman stood at the point of intersection.
>
> Precisely the same kind of houses rose here, and the same kind of gray human streams flowed by, and the same greenish-yellow fog hovered in the air.
>
> Parallel with the running prospect was another running prospect with the same row of boxes, the same system of numeration, and the same clouds.
>
> There is an infinity about the running prospects, and an infinity about the running intersecting shadows. Petersburg, as a whole, represents a sum to infinity of the prospect, elevated to the Nth degree.
>
> Beyond Petersburg, there is nothing.[3]

Unlike Joyce, Biely chooses to exercise the privilege of constantly shuttling back and forth between the experiencing consciousness of his protagonists and an authorial overview. The perception of the right-angle perspectives of Petersburg is triggered by the presence of Apollon Apollonovich Ableukhov, the aging czarist bureaucrat enamoured of symmetries and straight lines who contemplates the mist-shrouded city as he rolls along "confined within the dark cube of his carriage." The tension felt in much of the novel between geometrically ordering structures and the flowing contours of experience impressionistically perceived is particularly sharp here. The city seen through greenish-yellow fog is a blurred flux of "gray human streams," but the narrator, extrapolating a vision-

[3] Andrey Biely, *St. Petersburg*, tr. John Cournos (New York: Grove Press, 1959), pp. 12-13.

ary map from the bureaucratic consciousness of Ableukhov, envisages the planned prospects of Petersburg, a
designed city constructed by czarist edict, stretching out
to infinity in a rectilinear network, beyond which there
is nothing.

As in Joyce, the city can no longer be encompassed by
a finite imagination, but in Biely's novel it is seen in
alternating perspectives, either in quick flashes of haunting
fragmentary impressions with the ubiquitous fog to confuse details, or in that rectilinear design which betrays
the absurd futility of collective human consciousness at-
tempting to impose itself on the world's formlessness. Biely
participates in the general modernist impulse to develop
new narrative techniques in order to represent the subtle
movements of inner states, but what in part distinguishes
him is his acute awareness, explicitly embodied in the
novel, that consciousness itself is not an ultimate reality
but a possibly dubious operation performed on the stuff
of experience in endlessly different ways by different
minds. Thus he comments on Ableukhov: "The mind's
play of this recipient of many distinguished Orders was
conspicuous for strange, very strange, virtues: his box skull
was the repository of mental images that had their immediate impact upon this phantasmal world" (p. 21). The
perception of the artifice of consciousness, then, is an even
more directly guiding principle in Biely than in Joyce, and
more emphatically than in Joyce's Dublin, the images of
consciousness from which this Petersburg is evoked are
bedeviled by the apprehension that beyond them there
is nothing but gaping void. Framing these images of consciousness is the author's awareness, sometimes explicitly
obtruded (as at the end of the first chapter, pp. 37-38),
that the novel itself is an artifice erected by his own
consciousness. The English translation does not always
adequately represent these obtrusions.

As in Joyce, but again with more urgent emphasis, the

threat of the void is felt both ontologically and historically. When the collapse of history into nothingness is imagined as a sudden event, what one is confronted with is a variety of apocalypse. Joyce toys with apocalyptic motifs but confines the one real apocalyptic revelation of his novel to an act merely mimicking the end of things in the dream-world of the Nighttown scene, when Stephen smashes the chandelier with his ashplant, causing "time's livid final flame" to leap out, followed by "darkness, ruin of all space." The horizon of Biely's novel, on the other hand, is repeatedly darkened by the shadows of apocalyptic beasts. The action occurs during the Russo-Japanese War of 1905, with Russia itself shaken by the advance tremors of revolution. One of the young revolutionaries in the novel is constantly absorbed in reading the Book of Revelations, and Biely's own prose occasionally adopts the style of the biblical apocalypse as the narrator imagines a terrible destruction sweeping in from the East: "In those days all the peoples of the earth will scatter in panic. Voices shall be raised in horror, curses fill the air, unheard-of curses. A yellow horde of Asiatics, stirring from their age-long retreats, will redden the fields of Europe with an ocean of blood" (p. 72). In the epilogue, Biely combines this notion of apocalyptic destruction with the idea of the exhaustion and progressive disintegration of European culture. Ableukhov the younger, the novel's protagonist, has gone on a trip to Egypt after his abortive revolutionary activities, and, like Bloom, he contemplates the crumbling pyramids as an image of historical decay. As he looks, however, at the Great Sphinx, he adds to the idea of slow exhaustion a last sudden stage of apocalypse: "In the twentieth century, he foresaw Egypt: this decrepit head was the end of a culture. With this head all had died, nothing remained. There would be an explosion—everything would be obliterated" (p. 308).

The dalliance with the apocalypse of so many modernist

writers seems to me worth stressing in connection with
the resurgence of the self-conscious novel in the early
twentieth century because nothing reveals more clearly
how the relationship to history characteristic of the great
nineteenth-century realists had crucially changed. It is
almost as if the kernel of the modern novel were plant-
ed in the final apocalyptic charade of that intermittently self-conscious novel of mid-nineteenth-century America, *The Confidence-Man*. Realism had been impelled by
a general sense of being constantly at the riding edge of
critical historical change. By the time Virginia Woolf,
writing in 1924, retrospectively imagines a qualitative
alteration of human nature in December 1910, the hopes
and illusions of nineteenth-century liberalism had long
since been scattered to the savage winds of modern history,
and the tempo and cataclysmic scope of historical change
had achieved such startling magnitude that the concrete
imagination of history progressively unfolding in society
was hard to hold on to. History had become, in Stephen
Daedalus's famous phrase, a nightmare from which the
artist was trying to awake. When a writer observing history
sees apocalypse, his whole subject has radically changed.
The biblical prophets, like the nineteenth-century realists,
were essentially political; they were concerned with which
kings one might make treaties with, which should be
mistrusted, how questions of class relations and social
justice should be managed. By contrast, the apocalyptic
writer of Revelations, though responding to the felt pres-
sures of history, looks quite beyond it to a visionary world
of cosmic monsters, angels of destruction, things encoun-
tered only in the deep recesses of the imagination.[4]

I am not of course suggesting any sort of general equation between the apocalyptic imagination and fictional

---

[4] For an illuminating discussion of this general question, see Martin Buber's
essay, "Prophecy, Apocalyptic, and the Historical Hour," in *Pointing the Way*,
ed. Maurice Friedman (New York: Harper & Row, 1957).

self-consciousness. But when history seems to have become
intractable to the imagination, there is a certain tendency
for the writer—if he is not of an evangelical bent, like D.
H. Lawrence—to turn back toward his own creative activities, to affirm the integrity of his work against a background of historical chaos by directing attention to the
strategies of art through which the work has come into
being. This tendency is likely to make itself felt particularly when apocalyptic intimations are not accompanied
by any belief in a cosmic Manager of the apocalypse. In
that case, the writer is readily drawn to a contemplation
of how the mind, working through literary tradition, projects images of a Promised End, and how the mind can
also set up against the void images of order and perfection
in the here-and-now. This tendency at its most extreme
can result in sheer escapism, but it is not necessarily
escapist, for many writers have been able to concentrate
on an assessment of their own imaginative resources for
coping with reality without fleeing reality. A book like
Frank Kermode's *The Sense of an Ending*,[5] which reflects
on apocalypse as a model of how historical experience is
organized through fictions, in effect repeats on the level
of criticism what novelists and poets had consciously
executed on the level of imaginative invention since the
time of Joyce and Biely.

The consciousness of imagery, poetry, all the apparatus
of literary tradition, as means to a human coherence that
can be set over against the awaiting abyss is especially
central in the writing of Virginia Woolf. Though most of
the prominent surfaces of *Mrs. Dalloway* are brilliantly
sunlit, though Clarissa Dalloway is intensely absorbed in
being alive each moment, she is also pursued by the fear
of her own imminent mortality throughout the novel; and
the specter of bleak obliteration is externalized in the

---

[5] Kermode, *The Sense of an Ending* (New York: Oxford University Press,
1969).

suicide of Septimus Ward Smith, which calls to the heroine's mind an explicit image of the engulfing abyss as she imagines that "It was her punishment to see sink and disappear here a man, there a woman, in this profound darkness."[6] Indeed, the Shakespearian tag-line, "Fear no more the heat o' th' sun," that recurs as a refrain in the novel, is part of a song in *Cymbeline* that concludes with an image of living brightness dispersed in death's decay: "Golden lads and girls all must/ As chimney-sweepers, come to dust." Septimus Smith, moreover, that disturbing alter ego of Clarissa Dalloway, represents a shattering of order that is historical as well as personal since his derangement is the result of a trauma suffered in the Great War; and the seemingly peaceful London of the novel is also felt as a city standing on the still unquiet ground of recent cataclysm. Against this backround, what does Virginia Woolf make of her cityscapes? Here is a characteristic moment, rendered from the point of view of Peter Walsh:

> Like a woman who had slipped off her print dress and white apron to array herself in blue and pearls, the day changed, put off stuff, took gauze, changed to evening, and with the same sigh of exhilaration that a woman breathes, tumbling petticoats on the floor, it too shed dust, heat, colour; the traffic thinned; motor cars, tinkling, darting, succeeded the lumber of vans; and here and there among the thick foliage of the squares an intense light hung. I resign, the evening seemed to say, as it paled and faded above the battlements and prominences, moulded, pointed, of hotel, flat, and block of shops, I fade, she was beginning, I disappear, but London would have none of it, and rushed her bayonets into the sky, pinioned her, constrained her to partnership in her revelry. [p. 245]

Virginia Woolf, like Dickens, defines a vision of the city

---

[6] *Mrs. Dalloway* (New York: Harcourt Brace, 1953), p. 282.

by the patient elaboration of a unifying metaphor, but whereas in Dickens the urban scene itself *becomes* the metaphor, is absorbed into the writer's invention, transmuted into wonderful palpable substance in the alembic of the novelist's imagination, in the Woolf passage the metaphor is rather an artistically ordered means of describing how the consciousness of a particular observer represents the scene to itself. In the often-quoted passage of her 1919 essay on modern fiction, Virginia Woolf defines the "life" that the novelist must capture strictly in terms of consciousness—"a luminous halo, a semi-transparent envelope surrounding us from the beginning of consciousness to the end." The city exists only through the play of the character's consciousness upon it, is genuinely accessible to the novelist, who after all must also experience all things through a semi-transparent envelope, only in the rendering of consciousness. The obvious fact, however, that Virginia Woolf does not share Joyce's interest in suggesting the immediate texture and structure of consciousness has rather important consequences for the kind of "reality" she creates in her fiction. If consciousness is ultimately a kind of artifice for Joyce, it is always, necessarily, art for Virginia Woolf, and the difference is crucial. Even the metaphor of the luminous halo, one might note, is an image of consciousness not as flux or kinesis but as a circle perfected by art, taken from the tradition of iconography.

Critics have often observed that Virginia Woolf tends to build her interior monologues like lyric poems, endowing them with the formal symmetries and continuities, the polished verbal surface, the syntactical niceties, the sense of completion, of achieved poetry. All these qualities are evidenced in the passage we are considering, but one must add that this prose poem composed by the narrator to represent the consciousness of Peter Walsh at a particular moment calls explicit attention to its own status as poetry.

Turning on the elaborate comparison of the day to a woman changing to evening dress, the passage begins with the deliberate syntactical obtrusion of an extravagantly complicated simile, as though some Homeric bard with his extended similes—this one is urban pastoral—had been admitted within the semi-transparent envelope: "Like a woman who had slipped off her print dress and white apron to array herself in blue and pearls, the day changed. . . ." And on we go to the donning of gauze, the breath of exhilaration when petticoats tumble, and the woman's final futile attempt, after the assumption of formal attire, to withdraw from the evening's festivities. What might be stressed about all this is that a vividly dramatic event takes place solely on the metaphorical level, or at least the vehicle of the simile is endowed with such an abundance of life that the tenor to which it supposedly refers comes to seem quite secondary. I would suspect, in fact, that the imaginative energy Virginia Woolf lavished on the elaboration of the simile led her to give it even more life than she consciously knew. Thus the manifest image of military attack, London with its bayonetlike skyline charging against the hesitant evening, only barely conceals a latent sexual image of phallic assault—"rushed her bayonets into the sky, pinioned her, constrained her to partnership in her revelry"—which is, paradoxically but not surprisingly for Virginia Woolf, also an image of lesbian love, since both partners, the city and the evening, are designated "she."

One can infer from Virginia Woolf's own programmatic and critical statements on the novel that she did not conceive herself as breaking with the underlying assumptions of the realists, only with their technical procedures and with some of their notions about the materials through which reality was to be fictionally embodied. Like them, she aspired above all to represent "life" in her fiction. *Mrs. Dalloway, The Waves,* and *To the Lighthouse,* then, are not exactly novels of flaunted artifice in the sense that *Tom Jones* and *Invitation to a Beheading* are. In the passage we have been considering, though we are made keenly aware of the artful organization of the description, of its elaborate use of poetic techniques, the clear purpose of the techniques is to give back to us as vividly as possible a London familiar from our shared, extraliterary experience, as it would be plausibly seen at a particular moment by an observer such as Peter Walsh. The city, in other words, remains an imposing object of representation, and is not converted into the indifferent raw material of a patently autonomous fictional creation. We are led to a heightened awareness of the operations of artifice but not to a perception of the novel's world as an arbitrary structure built strictly on the decisions (or whims) of its creator.

What I should like to stress is that Virginia Woolf, like Joyce, Proust, and Faulkner, in balancing the claims of an acute consciousness of artifice and those of a psychological, social, even historical reality that still seems to her somehow transmittable through fiction, is preeminently a transitional figure. Indeed, much of the greatness of all these writers can be traced to their transitional character, precisely to the fact that they were simultaneously seeking to culminate, or outdo, the Promethean enterprise of the great nineteenth-century realists and to draw attention to the sustained intricacy of their own art as a self-justified act. Genius, of course, could bridge the seeming contradictions between these two aims. But for all the affirmation of artifice in the classic modern novelists, they retain a residue of belief in the large possibility of capturing reality in fiction, however much they may be troubled by a sense of things collapsing historically; and that sets off their work from the pervasive *philosophical* skepticism about fictions of, say, a Diderot.

The distinctive modernist achievement, then, is not an unambiguous expression of the new novelistic self-con-

sciousness but does provide a decisively important background for it. In the exemplary case of Virginia Woolf,
the writer's sensibility, her feeling for how art could
intervene between humanity and the essential chaos of
existence, her consequent insistence on giving consciousness an elaborated poetic shape, all lead her fiction
to a strange and moving borderland between art and life.
Ultimately, there is no reality but consciousness, and
consciousness is conceived as a tireless maker of poetic
constructs, an inventor of endless imaginary—or if you will,
fictional—events that order the data of experience, make
the world real. The implicit conclusion of this series, one
which Virginia Woolf herself pointedly never drew, is that,
finally, fiction is our reality. It is the kind of paradox,
of course, that Cervantes or Sterne would have grasped
at once. The very fact that one can detect its outlines
in the work of a novelist who was intent on an authentic
recasting of the realist heritage suggests that the novel
in general as it was transformed after December 1910 had
a new readiness to cultivate the inherent self-consciousness of the genre.

   That readiness comes to full expression in Miguel de
Unamuno's *Mist* (1914), a novel far less impressive as a
realized fiction than the three we have been considering
but one which has abiding interest as a critical statement
on the paradoxes of fiction and reality. The ontological
quandaries implicit in Joyce, Biely, and Woolf are made
perfectly explicit here; and the contrast between Unamuno's mode of fiction and that of the novels we have
so far considered in this chapter should make quite clear
the difference between a strictly self-conscious novel and
what I have proposed to regard as a mixed mode. *Mist*
begins with a prologue by Víctor Goti, the best friend of
the main character, Augusto Pérez. Goti admits to having
written the prologue after being importuned by Unamuno,
whom he sees apparently as his acquaintance and implicit-

ly as his inventor. Unamuno then appends to the prologue a two-page note, with his initials at the end, affirming his absolute proprietorship over Goti yet assigning to the character the entire responsibility for what is said in the prologue.

With this beginning, it is hardly surprising that Víctor and Augusto should devote a considerable part of their conversations to discussing the nature of fictional characters and their own possible resemblance to such characters. At more than one point, Augusto confesses to doubting his own existence—"I come to imagine that I am a dream, an entity of fiction."[7] Cervantes, directly mentioned several times (with allusions to Unamuno's well-known theories on *Don Quixote*), is very much in the background of the whole novel. The familiar Spanish Renaissance notion that *la vida es sueño*, life is a dream, is pushed here to its utmost metaphysical limits. The characters, who delude themselves into imagining they possess free will, are merely a dream of the author, who in turn, with his own illusions of autonomous existence, is merely a dream of God. Is what we think of as reality finally an infinite regress of dreams, or, alternatively, might the novelist's invention be more real than he himself is—the author, having imbued his fictional world with independent life, reduced to a reflected dream of that world? This is the position Augusto argues, taking his cue from an observation of Unamuno's on the relative reality of Don Quixote and Cervantes, when he comes to Unamuno's study in Salamanca in a futile attempt to argue the novelist out of killing him off. Unamuno puts his recalcitrant hero down with cool disdain: "My poor Augusto, you are only a product of my imagination and of the imagination of those readers who read this story which I have written of your fictitious adventures and misfortunes" (p. 294). To this seemingly

[7] *Mist*, tr. Warner Fite (New York: Knopf, 1928), p. 215.

unanswerable argument, the protagonist, fighting for his life on the level both of plot and of ontological discourse, rejoins with this canny reversal of logic: "May it not be, my dear Don Miguel, that it is you and not I who are the fictitious entity, the one who does not really exist, who is neither living nor dead? May it not be that you are nothing more than a pretext for bringing my story into the world?" (p. 295).

This casting of doubt on the reality of existence, fictional and nonfictional alike, leads Unamuno to raise certain radical questions about how fiction should be written, questions that might well be regarded as prolegomena for the self-conscious novel in the twentieth century. If there is no necessity that anything should be, including even God, then chance rules the world, necessity being "nothing but the highest form that chance takes in our mind" (p. 71), as Augusto tells his dog (!) Orfeo. "The world," then, Augusto pursues the same hypothesis earlier in the book, "is a kaleidoscope. It is man that puts logic into it. The supreme art is the art of chance" (p. 50).

If most of the classic modern writers respond to the perception of underlying disorder in the nature of things by splendid demonstrations of the patterning power of art, Unamuno suggests here that what art must do is embody randomness as an essential principle in its own operations. This idea has multiple, far-reaching ramifications. If randomness is to be introduced into the structure of the novel, if the invention of fictional character is to be an experiment in the possibilities of freedom, character as a consistent, fixed entity may be an obsolete convention. Unamuno is very close here to D. H. Lawrence's contemporaneous rejection of "the old stable *ego* of the character"; and Lawrence's new open form, in which protagonists end up talking about their lives as though they were novelists determining how to handle the fiction of their own experience, would be one possible realization of Unamuno's program.[8] The various twentieth-century experiments in creating a relativistic novel, from Ford Madox Ford's *The Good Soldier* (1915) to Lawrence Durrell's *Alexandria Quartet* (1957-1960), would be another mode of incorporating an element of indeterminacy into fiction, where the nature of character continually shifts with the position of the observer. Novels that offer deliberately indeterminate endings, or alternative endings, like *Invitation to a Beheading* and *The French Lieutenant's Woman* respectively, translate randomness into the very aspect of the novel where necessity had seemed most absolute—plot. The novels of Alain Robbe-Grillet represent a more extreme development of this last tendency because in them any particular fictional event is merely a hypothesis, a visualized construct that is repeatedly "retaken," modified, reassembled in varying combinations of its component elements. At this point, literature is but a step away from the aleatory art that has attracted certain contemporary composers and choreographers: creating art by the roll of the dice, literal or figurative, is indeed the ultimate implication of Augusto's pronouncement that "The supreme art is the art of chance."

The problem with Unamuno's novel—it is a recurrent trap for modern self-conscious novelists—is that nothing in its fictional realization is quite so interesting as the theorizing that goes on within it. The protagonist is involved in one attempted assertion of his freedom, when he confronts the author on the question of his own imminent death, but otherwise he seems consistent enough as a rather conventional character, finally not very interesting in the silliness of his oscillations between two women. What is nevertheless noteworthy about *Mist* is the strong

[8] This point has been shrewdly observed by Alan Friedman in *The Turn of the Novel* (New York: Oxford University Press, 1966), pp. 152-159.

sense it conveys that the twentieth-century novel can develop only by redefining itself against the perceived inauthenticities of the older tradition of the novel. Literary criticism is thus rehabilitated as an essential moment in the act of fictional invention, as it had been for Cervantes, Fielding, Sterne, and Diderot. The tendency of the earlier self-conscious novels to push epistemological paradoxes to their logical limits is again very much in evidence here. Thus, Augusto's dog, in his "Funeral Oration, By Way of an Epilogue," argues that all verbalization is fictionalization, hence falsification. From his canine viewpoint, Orfeo takes a wry view of man's craze to put everything into words: "As soon as he gives a thing a name he ceases to see the thing itself; he only hears the name that he gave it or sees it written. His language enables him to falsify, to invent what does not exist, and to confuse himself. For him everything in the world is merely a pretext for talking to other men or for talking to himself" (pp. 326-327).

From such radical skepticism about the relation between language and truth, there are two possible practical consequences. One may throw up one's hands in despair and abandon the enterprise of the novel in the recognition that all writing is lying and writing fiction is lying raised to the second power. The one obvious alternative is parody. Orfeo's strictures make lucid sense of the birth of the novel in parody with *Don Quixote*. The parodistic novel, exploding the absurdities of previous literary conventions as it unfolds, effects a kind of dialectical refinement and correction of lying, edging us toward the perception of certain truths about the manipulation of language, about character, about human nature, perhaps even about the kind of social world we inhabit. The solution of parody, to be sure, is neither entirely comfortable nor stable. Writers and readers tend to suspect that it is not a "primary"

mode of artistic creation, that in its obliquity it may beg
the basic questions of what truth it is that art can convey.
As the composer-hero of *Doctor Faustus* sadly observes
of parody, himself a master of it in his art, "It might be
fun, if it were not so melancholy in it aristocratic nihilism."
We will return to this brooding ultimate doubt about the
nature of parody, but for the moment we can note simply
that parody, whatever its inherent limitations, is able to
serve in a way no other mode can as an agency of renewal
and transformation of jejeune literary forms.

The necessity for such renewal and transformation came
to be increasingly felt in the early decades of our century,
and parody's immense utility as a means of refurbishing
old forms and giving fiction a new kind of vitality was
vividly demonstrated in a novel that appeared the same
year as *Mist*, André Gide's *Les Caves du Vatican*.[9] Gide
is a central figure in the development of modern fictional
self-consciousness, and this particular novel, in many ways
his most successful, is worth close attention as a significant
moment in our argument.

2. Gide and the Confidence Game of Fiction

By the time Gide came to compose this splendid satirical
farce, he himself had begun to chafe at the limitations
of working within what he conceived as a lesser variety
of creativity. In his *Journal* entry for June 30, 1914, shortly
after the appearance of *Les Caves du Vatican*, he recalled
a programmatic sentence from his suppressed preface to
the novel: "Tales and Farces [*Récits et Soties*], I have
written up till now nothing but ironic—or if one prefers,

[9] *Les Caves du Vatican* (Paris: Gallimard, 1922). The title has been variously
translated as *The Vatican Cellars*, *The Vatican Swindle*, and *Lafcadio's Adventures*, but since two of these lose the reference to a non-existent place and all
three must drop the pun on the Latin *cave*—"beware"—I have decided to use
the French title.

critical—books, of which the present is undoubtedly the last." There is an unintended retroactive irony in the statement, for Gide's playful, parodistic tale of swindlers and dupes, which he was careful to designate *sotie*, proved to be his liveliest, most sustained recreation of the novel form. By contrast, his one work of fiction that he would call a novel, *The Counterfeiters*, published eleven years later, is in the end a much more conventional book (in the pejorative sense), despite its very explicit mirroring device of a novelist within the novel writing a journal about how he might turn what he encounters into a novel called *The Counterfeiters*. Even critics more sympathetic to this particular book than I (Jean Hytier, for example) have sensed that it represents a not altogether happy mingling of narrative modes or aesthetic premises; and Edouard's journal here clearly illustrates that a central reflexive device in a novel does not in itself insure that the book will be a sustained self-conscious novel. The way the journal is handled, in fact, proves to be inadvertently self-defeating, because apart from Edouard's often-quoted observations on the aesthetics of the novel, his notebook is a rather ordinary first-person, quasi-documentary narrative that frequently seems a tedious interruption of the innovative novel which *The Counterfeiters* set out to be. The ultimate problem of this novel, I would suggest, is in Gide's relation to his imaginary personages. There is very little of the Cervantesque splitting off of the self into the mutually critical members of a dialectic of literary creation; and there is too much direct playing out of fantasy versions of the self. Edouard is of course not André Gide, but the distance between the two is often close enough to blur the realized outlines of the character. Thus, when Edouard becomes the sheltering father for his beautiful, beloved nephew Olivier, rescued from the brink of perdition, we are likely to sense an excessively facile, self-gratifying homosexual fantasy that the author has not subjected to the rigors of artistic criticism. Gide often seems to stand here in the same imaginative relationship to his characters as a nineteenth-century novelist without the nineteenth-century novelist's imaginative capacity for allowing the as-if autonomous lives of his fantasy figures to develop richly and variously. As a result, characters in *The Counterfeiters* seem either to drag on inconclusively or are put to an abrupt, melodramatically improbable end. More than anything else, it is Gide's failure to make his characters go anywhere after the exposition that leaves this an interesting but fundamentally flawed experiment.

The case is quite different with *Les Caves du Vatican*, which succeeds, I believe, on a scale beyond that which Gide himself orginally conceived. An entry in the *Journal* for May 7, 1912, when he was revising the manuscript of the novel, is especially instructive in this connection: "My characters, which at first I regarded only as puppets, are gradually filling with real blood, and I do not discharge my obligations toward them so easily as I had hoped." *Les Caves* is manifestly designed as a composite parody. There are wonderful ventriloquistic passages in which the narrator mimicks the tremulo of the pious novel of religious conversion, the factitious dash and fire of the popular novel of adventure, the effusions of the novel of sentimental romance, the pedantic circumstantiality of the family chronicle and the naturalist novel, the slow conversational musings about character and motive of the nineteenth-century realists. Lafcadio, the principal character, is equally a composite parody, a Young Man from the Provinces who concretely recalls Julien Sorel and Fabrice del Dongo as well as Raskolnikov, that other ill-fated perpetrator of a gratuitous murder (Gide's passion for both Stendhal and Dostoevski is well known), and who might also be regarded as an updated version of Rastignac, or,

being an attractive bastard who provides a moral measure
of others, a post-Nietzschean avatar of Tom Jones. Nevertheless, as the novel turns back again and again to reflect
the conventions of novel-writing, the characters, devised
as *fantouches*, parodistic puppets, act upon one another
in such a way that a dynamic new fictional reality begins
to emerge.

One might observe that whereas *The Counterfeiters*
abounds in parallels between characters and sets of characters, the action of *Les Caves* is generated by a genuine
doubling of character, the antithetical pairs interacting
dialectically, bringing each other out into complex life by
the ongoing mutual commentary they provide. The pervasive concern of the earlier novel is effectively what
Edouard in the later novel would announce but scarcely
demonstrate as the "deep subject" of his book—"the rivalry
between the real world and the representation we make
of it" (5:2). Which is only to say, of course, that *Les Caves
du Vatican* reverts, as most innovative novels have, to
the underlying problematic articulated in the quixotic
model of the genre. Since this is a novel about how the
literary imagination constructs reality, the parodistic set
pieces and the use of parody as a model for character are
not just playful self-indulgences but strictly functional
explorations through the exaggeration of convention into
what is hidden or revealed by convention. Similarly, Gide's
relationship to his personages is precisely that of a writer
exploring the status of character vis-à-vis author and—
much in the spirit of Unamuno's paradoxes—the status
of author vis-à-vis character.

In the novel's primary stage of doubling, then, the
author of *Les Caves* splits off his function as artist into
two opposing selves, the half-brothers Julius Baraglioul
and Lafcadio Wluiki, who belatedly discover their kinship
and for a time seem to exchange positions in their mutually
exclusive views of human nature and fictional character.

Julius is the conventional novelist with a vengeance, prudently pious, moralistic, bland and superficial in his knowledge of experience and his sense of mankind, cynically prepared to gloss over facts in his work and falsify what might not seem edifying if it will bring him closer to a seat in the French Academy. Lafcadio, the illegitimate brother, is an antiliterary Sancho to the worldly Quixote of Julius, the successful novelist. Although Lafcadio is fluently literate in half a dozen languages, he professes to reject literature as an authentic or interesting way of relating to experience, preferring to create the *romanesque* around him through artful action. The only two books he admits to having read to the end and enjoyed are *Robinson Crusoe* and *Aladdin*, the primary texts, respectively, for realism and fantasy in the Western tradition, but even toward these he evinces no piety: one of his first acts in the novel, a pointedly symbolic ritual for the young adventurer, is to tear to pieces and burn the few books he possesses, together with his photographs and the private notebook Julius has discovered.

It is appropriate that he and Julius should engage in discussions on the consistency of character and on what constitutes realistic psychology, with Lafcadio initially arguing on behalf of the quirky and the unexpected against the facile rationalistic neatness of Julius's views. What is interesting about Gide's presentation of this clash of theories is that the truth should prove to be not entirely with Lafcadio, who after committing murder as a purely gratuitous act finds himself pushed by events into behaving, despite all expectations, much like a murderer in a conventional novel of crime and punishment (here, as elsewhere, parody is an invaluable critical tool for Gide).

The quixotic doubling does not stop with Julius and Lafcadio. The pious novelist is bracketed on his opposite side, so to speak, with his brother-in-law Anthime Armand Dubois, the militant Mason and freethinker who, novelist-

like, plays god with his rats in their labyrinths, variously
blinding, maiming, castrating, lobotomizing them, in order
to study their responses. Anthime temporarily switches
positions with Julius, as Julius does with Lafcadio, becoming the most resigned of saintly Catholics when he thinks
the Virgin has miraculously cured his crippled leg—What
experimenter is playing with this rat? we are led to wonder
—and persisting in piety for a while as Julius flirts with
the heretical doctrine of the inconsistency of character.
Lafcadio on his part, the deceiver deceived of the novel,
is sandwiched in between another double, the ultimate
con man, and another antithesis, the ultimate fall guy,
of the book—Protos, the protean role player in this wild
crescendo of disguises, and Fleurissoire, the supreme naif,
in all senses taken in by the swindle, who has come on
a one-man crusade to rescue the Pope.

   Finally, the quixotic Fleurissoire himself is introduced
as part of an explicitly Cervantesque doubling, the pale-
haired, emaciated, ethereal figure paired with his friend
Blafaphas, who, as Sancho to the French provincial Quixote, is dark, squat, grubby, more calculating, and at least
a little more in touch with the physical things of this earth.
It is worth noting that in this twentieth-century version
of the Cervantesque novel, the figure most resembling Don
Quixote turns out to be a secondary character, destroyed
through the chance of a game played by the protagonist.
Of Fleurissoire we are informed that "the importance of
his mission dangerously overheated his brains. ... He
finally had his raison d'être. ... There are so few creatures
on earth who are able to discover their real usefulness"
(3:3). This precisely describes the chief motive of the
original Quixote in every respect, but in a world without
viable ideals where everything is conspicuously factitious,
the quixotic enterprise loses even its qualified claim to
heroism and can be no more than grotesque comedy,
doomed from the start in the patent absurdity of its

self-deception, and thus peripheral to the main novelistic action. The main action, in turn, is an inversion of the quixotic experiment in which the latter-day hero attempts to express his exceptional character not by living out a superannuated literary code, but by improvising his own self-validating code, setting himself above received values and preexistent models, whether social or literary. Gide, like Cervantes, can feel great sympathy for his hero's aspiration yet recognize that the character acts on an insufficient understanding of his own limitations and so is destined to painful pratfalls. In Gide's case, moreover, there is an ironic perception of how an anti-Quixote might unwittingly conform to established literary models even as he tries to become a perfectly spontaneous self.

It seems to me that the concept of game is the key one in this novel, and it is because of the to-and-fro connections between the games of art and the games of life that parody is not just an amusing interlude but an integral revelation of the novelistic world. Lafcadio, the artful man who has burned his books, is raised on an elaborate regimen of subtle games by the series of international "uncles" his mother provides him. (This training in deft gamesmanship clearly looks forward to two other fictional artists-in-action, Mann's Felix Krull and Nabokov's Van Veen.) Protos, the last of Lafcadio's gamesmen-instructors, will undertake an ambitious swindle as much, it would seem, for the love of the game as for the love of gain. Eventually, Lafcadio commits murder as part of a game he decides to play with himself, then rapidly discovers that the rules are far more complicated and have graver consequences than he had imagined. In this last regard, parodistic plot proves to be beautifully functional, for Lafcadio is caught in an incredible web of coincidences he could not have foreseen, the author behind him playing with the old novelistic convention of "conservation of character" where every personage introduced is put to use and somehow intersects in the plot. "The old boy is a regular crossroads," Lafcadio exclaims of Fleurissoire (5:3) when he discovers that the man he killed was not only carrying his half-brother Julius's circular ticket but was wearing the cufflinks Lafcadio himself had given to his former mistress, Carola. In effect, what the exclamation points to is the coy, disconcerting game art is playing with "life," or, if one prefers, the game that the artlike circumstances of life are playing with the botched art of Lafcadio's gratuitous act.

The main formal embodiment of the principle of game in the novel is the obtrusive, teasing, tongue-in-cheek narrator, ostentatious master of half-a-dozen parodied voices and manipulator of the whole elaborate play of coincidences and disguise. I would contend that Gide did much to solve the problem of the novel for himself, even as he set about to write a *sotie,* by adopting this oblique and playful relationship with his fictional material. Here he is, for example, describing Julius about to open Lafcadio's desk drawer to search through its contents:

> I would not want what follows to give a false impression of Julius's character. Julius was nothing if not discreet; he respected the cloak it pleased each man to draw over his private life; he held the decencies in great respect. But, in the face of his father's command, he had to lay aside his own preferences. He waited a moment more, listening attentively, then, hearing no one coming—against his inclination, against his principles, but with the delicate feeling of performing a duty—he pulled open the desk drawer, the key of which had not been turned. [2:2]

What Gide is doing here is obvious enough, but it may be worth commenting on what he gains by doing it this way. It would be easy enough for him to put down Julius with a directly satirical observation, as he occasionally does elsewhere—for example, at the beginning of this same chapter, when he notes that the popular novelist cherished "the flattering illusion that nothing human should remain alien to him." The ironic treatment of hypocrisy in this passage is strongly reminiscent of Fielding, one of Gide's favorite novelists. (Later, working on *The Counterfeiters*, Gide would reread *Tom Jones* and express the wish that he might dare to imitate Fielding's obtrusive self-conscious narrator more directly.) The obliquity of approach to the character accomplishes several ends. Most obviously, it draws around the character a circle of artistic play: the narrating "I" deliberately obtrudes itself at the beginning of the paragraph that is to relate a climactic moment of action, and makes a great display of its supposed desire not to give the wrong impression about Julius. We could hardly be made more clearly aware of the narrative as a manipulated procedure. The ostensible justification offered for Julius's action is of course an ironic mimickry, sliding into *style indirect libre*, of Julius's own rationalizations, virtually quoting the unspoken phrases Julius might use to explain himself: "he respected the cloak it pleased each man to draw over his private life"; "But in the face of his father's command, he had to lay aside his own preferences"; "against his principles, but with ·the delicate feeling of performing a duty." What should be noted is that, as with Fielding, this is not only an ironic exposure of the hypocrite but also a way of entering his inner world. One vividly feels how a middling man like Julius, perhaps a fool but hardly a scoundrel, seeks to preserve his habitual self-image of moral probity as he allows himself, from what is really a motive of base curiosity, to invade another man's privacy. If the main intended response is censure, there is also a possibility of the censure's being qualified by a degree of sympathetic identification, for we are all, finally, like this in our daily petty sins and our flimsy strategies of self-deception.

Watching Gide render Julius in this manner, one begins to see how by the logic of the technique the puppet fills with real blood, and consequently makes more demands on the writer because it asks to be taken seriously as a living creature aspiring to a concrete existence not wholly subsumed under the satiric design.

It is doubly important for Gide that his characters should come to life through such ironic obliquity and not otherwise, for it gives him a way out of the toils of effusive subjectivity on the one hand and banality on the other. Gide's early career was often affected, generally adversely, by the vogue of lyric confessionalism of *fin de siècle* writing, and the playfulness, the ironic perspectives, the consciousness of working with fictional conventions, made it possible for him here to create a credible world outside the private arena of a self struggling to achieve viable identity. At the same time, the turn toward parody made it easier for Gide, coming as he did after a great age of realism in the novel and all its popular debasements, to invent an engaging fiction that was essentially critical, commenting on "the deadly extension of the kingdom of the banal" as it reveled in the absurdities presented by the banal to the critical spirit. The parody-inventions in this novel are especially valuable means for the constitution of a critically fictive reality because most of them lead back in one way or another to the condition of artifice ambiguously shared by all fictional inventions and by the roles we make for ourselves within society.

Thus the story of the two friends, Amédée Fleurissoire and Gaston Blafaphas (3:2), is a study in the comic possibilities of schematization worthy of Sterne's Tale of Two Lovers. The narrator, following a novelistic precedent that goes back to the first chapter of *Don Quixote*, takes the greatest pains to remind us of the odd conventionality of naming names and the arbitrary relations literature and society tend to draw between name and role. Mimicking the earnest chronicler, "the writer of these lines" embarks, between parentheses, on a learned discourse concerning the currency of the name Blafaphas under a variety of orthographies in the French Pyrenees region. "But these philological observations," he apologizes, "could interest only a rather limited group of readers." Philology, however, remains the basis of reality in the relation between the two provincial friends and the woman they both love, after their respective fashions. The inseparable pair are designated *les Blafafoires,* grotesque nomenclature exhibiting a bizarre ability to combine and multiply. To fix this merging of monickers as a general principle, the narrator immediately informs us that the name of their business partner, Lévichon, is "amalgamated" (*agglutiné*) from the names of two local Jewish families, Lévy and Cohen. The unfortunately named Arnica Pétérat, courted by the two friends, is primarily dedicated to escaping by marriage from the malodorous associations of her last name and to somehow mitigating the "baroque" oddness of her given name. Offered, in perfect symmetry, the homage of these "parallel suitors," she conceives marriage as a purely verbal copulation of first and last names—in fact, her actual marriage with Amédée will remain unconsummated—and tries to decide between the two men by weighing which combination will be less atrocious, Arnica Blafaphas or Arnica Fleurissoire. Finally, it is an inadvertent modification by Amédé of her troublesome name that makes her favor him, when she imagines he has endowed her first name with rich romantic significance because he has given it an "Italian" accentuation on the middle syllable.

All this represents an ingenious reduction of the literary account of love and marriage to a set of purely verbal acts, unqualified by fleshly concerns or by the complexities of a realistic psychology. What brings a couple together is an adjustment of syllables and accents, a new combination of verbal constructs. From this one extreme reduction, which then ties back into the main plot through Fleurissoire's crusade, we are made keenly aware of the arbitrariness of all fictive characters, events, roles, and relations, those congeries of mere words assembled out of the stockpile of the writer's anagrammatic resources against a patterned background of literary convention.

In the last two books of the novel, Fleurissoire, whose ability to imitate the novelist's plastic power over names extends no further than a shift in the accent of Arnica, finds himself in a bewildering world where everyone seems to operate under an assumed name and a deceptive guise. Almost all the roles, in fact, are played by Protos, who is the perfect masquerader for this novel because he combines a consummate actor's skill with a sheer love of excessive gesture, so that his disguises repeatedly move beyond the utilitarian limits of deception to zestful farce. One recalls Protos as a tearful priest twisting his handkerchief distraughtly till it rips, Protos in his superb impersonation of a teetotaling, nearsighted professor who manages to get drunk on Lafcadio's wine, Protos playing roles within roles within roles, compounding disguises out of an actor's enthusiasm, as in the supreme moment of farce when he is pretending to be a priest pretending to be a lusty peasant before Fleurissoire's credulous eyes: "Cave [i.e., Protos], tumbling Assunta into his arms, nuzzled her; and when Fleurissoire, bending toward Cave, heartbroken, murmured—'How you must be suffering!'—Cave took his hand behind Assunta's back and pressed it wordlessly, his face averted, his gaze directed heavenward" (4:6).

If Fleurissoire finds that he cannot tell a true priest from a false one, a hotel from a whorehouse, the real pope from a sham, perhaps not even his brother-in-law Julius (who seems to have altered his views most distressingly) from an imposter, then reality itself begins to dissolve for him. Again and again, evocations of ontological vertigo—

the word *vertige* recurs—accompany Fleurissoire's perception of this world of masks. The brisk, solid-seeming reality,
precisely located in time and place, with which the novel
began now wavers into Unamunesque mists: "The light
morning mist and this profusion of brightness in which
every object melted [*s'évaporait*] and became unreal [*s'ir-
réalisait*] reinforced his dizziness; he walked on as though
in a dream, doubting the solidity of the ground, the walls,
the actual existence of the passers-by he met; doubting
above all his own presence in Rome" (4:7). Interestingly,
when the excited Julius imagines that in discovering the
principle of unmotivated action he has arrived at a turn-
ing-point in his life, he uses exactly the same vocabulary
of dissolving reality to describe his condition: "My head
is on fire and I feel a kind of dizziness through my whole
body, as though I were going to evaporate" (5:3).

The ultimate modernity of *Les Caves du Vatican* lies
in this sense of the instability of reality in general and
of personality in particular. There is a nice correspondence
here between the conventions by which we live and the
conventions by which we write. In both, we habitually
falsify to satisfy a love of consistency. As the temporarily
"converted" Julius tells Lafcadio, "We live counterfeit
lives rather than not conform to the self-portrait we
ourselves have drawn to begin with" (5:3). On examination,
the old stable ego of the traditional novel and of a defined
moral order is no longer tenable, and so the principle of
indeterminacy Unamuno discusses in connection with the
novel must be incorporated into characterization and plot.

Protos, disguised as a learned criminologist and consequently arguing the case on social rather than literary
grounds, proposes to Lafcadio that the difference between
an honest man and a rascal is no more than "a cessation
of continuity, a simple interruption of current" (5:5). What
used to be thought of, then, as moral character is a bundle
of necessarily unpredictable quantum leaps, and the same

would have to be true for realistic character in fiction. Gide is particularly shrewd in translating this notion into the concluding section of his novel because he makes his hero's indeterminacy consist both in his sudden and surprising conformation to literary models and in the intimated possibility of his again veering off from those models. Instructively, Lafcadio taken in by Protos's disguise experiences precisely the same kind of ontological vertigo as Fleurissoire, the man he murdered: "However terrible it might be, Lafcadio preferred a *reality* to this ridiculous nightmare in which he had been floundering for an hour" (5:5).

All this occurs two chapters before the end. In the last dozen pages of the novel, Gide will parody the conventional novelist's tying-up of ends in a breathtakingly swift, deftly managed series of dénouement procedures, while what he actually does is to flip his major characters through little quantum jumps to unforeseen new positions. Anthime converts back to Free Masonry; Julius reverts to his traditional notions of psychology in art and life; the imperturbable Protos (in the briefest syntactical aside) loses his temper and strangles Carola; the impregnably virtuous Genevieve comes to Lafcadio's room in the middle of the night to offer herself to him; and Lafcadio, the cool adventurer beyond good and evil, becomes a conscience-striken penitent. Parody is an invaluable resource in this final sequence, and the novel concludes with a parodistic *tour de force* that is worth special attention.

Throughout the concluding scene, Genevieve plays a sentimental Sonya to Lafcadio's improbable Raskolnikov. The clichés of an encounter between guilt-ridden lover and redeeming fair maiden are highlighted in both dialogue and description. Genevieve stands with her face in the shadows, her unbound hair falling loosely about her; tenderly, she reaches out to touch Lafcadio's burning forehead. "Have pity on me, my friend," she pleads. To which he responds, with a proper melodramatic groan: "Ah, why did I meet you so late? . . . Why do you speak to me so when I am no longer free and no longer worthy of loving you?"

What makes the parody here not only amusing but interesting as an experiment with fictional form is that it does more than expose the absurdity of a banal convention. The tremulous exchanges between the two young lovers are absurd enough, but perhaps, we are led to wonder, they may in some way correspond as much to the possible truth of human experience as Lafcadio's theoretical projection of a totally disengaged, amoral personality. The lovers' last scene is thus both a convention mocked in its creaking contrivances and a narrative hypothesis tried on for size. Fictional formulas, after all, are initially based on some direct perception of experience, however they stylize it, and despite their banality they might actually tell us something about how men and women could behave in given circumstances. One notes at the very end how parody elides into flaunted fictional self-consciousness, and how both are used to point to the provisionality of the fiction in question, the necessary indeterminacy of its principal character:

> But how could she tell him that she, too, until that day, had moved as though in a dream—a dream from which she escaped only momentarily at the hospital where, among the poor children, bandaging their actual wounds, she sometimes seemed at last to make contact with some sort of reality—a mediocre dream in which her parents moved beside her and she was surrounded by all the ridiculous conventions of their world, unable to take seriously their acts and opinions, their ambitions, their principles, or them as persons. Was it surprising that Lafcadio had not taken Fleurissoire seriously? . . . Could it be that they would part

like this? Love impels her, flings her toward him. Lafcadio
seizes her, holds her tight, covers her pale forehead with
kisses. ...

Here begins a new book.

O, palpable truth of desire! You drive the phantoms of
my imagination into the shadows.

We shall leave our two lovers at cockcrow, the hour when
color, warmth, and life are about to triumph at last over
the night. Lafcadio, above the sleeping Genevieve, lifts
himself up. It is not, however, the fair face of his beloved,
that moist forehead, those pearly eyelids, those warm parted
lips, those perfect breasts, those tired limbs—no, it is none
of all these that he looks at—but through the wide-open
window, at the dawn in which a garden tree trembles.

It will soon be time for Genevieve to leave him. Meanwhi-
le, he waits; leaning over her, he listens, through her gentle
breathing, to the vague murmur of the city already shaking
off its torpor. Far away, in the barracks, a bugle calls. What!
Is he going to renounce life? For the sake of Genevieve's
esteem—and he esteems her a bit less since she loves him
a bit more—does he still think of giving himself up?

The notion at the beginning of the passage of living
in a dream is, to begin with, a parodistic joke, alluding
to the hackneyed sentimental rhetoric of the novel of
popular romance. Moments earlier, the penitent Lafcadio
told Genevieve that he committed murder as though in
a dream, when in fact the narrator had presented the
killing as a perfectly lucid act following careful reflection
on the idea of an unmotivated crime, and resulting from
a private game of chance whose rules Lafcadio determines
and strictly obeys. Nevertheless, the rhetoric characters
use to falsify their own experience also firmly directs us
to the contradictory status of their lives between fiction
and reality, or, more properly, between one kind of fiction
and another. As we have seen, Fleurissoire, Julius, and
finally even Lafcadio found themselves floating in a

dreamlike world where reality proved to be a series of
masks, where in the end everything threatened to collapse
into illusion. Genevieve here reinforces the sense of difficulty in achieving reality either in life or in fiction by
reporting her existence in her parents' world of "ridiculous
conventions" as a mere dream. Ironically, now, when she
at last makes full contact with "reality" in her love for
Lafcadio, she acts out a whole set of timeworn literary
conventions even as she consciously abandons the social
conventions of the French Catholic upper class. Clasped
to the breast of her lover, who "covers her pale forehead
with kisses" which trail off into an ecstasy of suspension
points, Genevieve is allowed to enjoy the best of all possible
worlds in the worst of novelistic clichés.

Here, the narrator tells us, a new book would have to
begin. That is to say, all of this has been, to reverse
Diderot's phrase, nothing but a story: now that the puppets have been manipulated to the point of a conventional
happy ending, the curtain may be drawn, for what further
might happen between them would require a new scene
and a new plot. The interesting intrusion of an apostrophe
to the "palpable truth of desire" is purposefully ambiguous. "Desire" might refer to Lafcadio and Genevieve, the
"real" intensity of their consummated love escaping the
power of the writer's pen. Or, just as plausibly, that
palpable desire might be an immediate psychological reality within the writer, the felt libidinal energy out of which
he creates, and compared to which all the personages, all
the fictional constructs he has made, are shadowy projections, mere phantoms of the mind (*fantômes de mon
esprit*). Having thus exposed his artifice and brought us
back to its point of origin, Gide can go on in the two final
paragraphs to a concluding recapitulation of parodistic
motifs.

Dawn is breaking, as of course it should in an open
affirmative ending; life is about to "triumph at last over

the night"; and the happy lover is free to contemplate the sleeping body of his beloved in a conventional vertical catalogue of formulas for the representation of sensual beauty. (The resemblance to Don Quixote's version of Dulcinea is much to the point.) Lafcadio, however, switched by his author to still another track of parody, looks beyond the fair form of Genevieve to the city stirring to life, implicitly holding out to him an invitation and a challenge. Thus, he becomes the latest in the series of resolute young heroes of novels who, after the model of Rastignac at the end of *Le Père Goriot*, conclude by setting their faces toward the unimagined possibilities of the city and silently pledging, *A nous deux.*

The novel ends most aptly with two question marks. In accord with the new conception of character argued for within the book itself, Lafcadio's future remains an open question. The openness operates on two levels, that of the novelist as artificer and that of the character as a realized figure. For Lafcadio as a creature with a plausible psychology, the intoxication of penitence may well be fading after the fulfillment of desire, and the attraction of freedom could be renewing its force in unexpected ways. The shrewd turn of the little qualifying clause in the last sentence, where the narrator observes that Lafcadio may esteem Genevieve a bit less for loving him so much, introduces at the very end a new worldly psychology that breaks into the assumptions of pure passion and devotion of the "heroic" final scene. The current, to repeat Protos's metaphor, has been interrupted once more, and there is no telling where the character may move now. All this, of course, is equally a question of the author and his artifice: Lafcadio's open future might easily be described as a function of the literary models to which his author could choose to make him conform. By this point, we certainly have been reminded in a sufficient variety of ways that the character is, finally, both real-seeming and, even in his ideal of free selfhood, a composite study in the modification and direct imitation of established literary models.

There is, clearly, a central impulse of iconoclasm in the whole modernist movement. In consonance with that change in human nature polemically announced by Virginia Woolf, the artistic forms inherited from the nineteenth century had to be broken apart, violently refashioned, or in many instances simply discarded. Parody was bound to play an important role in this iconoclastic enterprise because of the very quality of "aristocratic nihilism" which Thomas Mann's Leverkühn detected in it. That is, parody, combining a coolly critical spirit with detached playfulness, was able to negate the immediate heritage of fictional forms by assuming it, keeping the worn conventions alive for the amusing display of their insipidness. The actual operation of parody, however, is still more complicated than this paradoxical formulation of it. The intellectual aristocrats of modernism also recognized a gross, endearing vitality in the vulgar forms they mocked, and thus parody was not merely a negation but a way of enlivening a self-consciously critical art form from below, as Joyce does through the prose of popular sentimental fiction in the Gertie McDowell section of *Ulysses*, or as Gide does in the concluding scene of *Les Caves du Vatican*. Parody is often thought of as a strictly secondary mode of art coming at the end of a period of achievement and decline, but there is ample enough evidence in literary history that parody often marks a beginning as well as an end. *Don Quixote*, in part a parody, inaugurates the novel; and it is at the inception of the genre in England, when the ink had scarcely dried on *Pamela*, the book that initiated a whole tradition of the English novel, that Fielding's successive parodies, *Shamela* and *Joseph Andrews*, launched a vigorous counter-tradition.

Les Caves du Vatican, a shrewdly imaginative response

to the decline into banality of the realist tradition, is implicit with beginnings as well as with the ends of old things. Critical and ironic, as Gide himself characterized it, its deployment of parody vividly demonstrates the bankruptcy of the traditional novel, at least in its popular forms. At the same time, Gide brings into being an engaging, and relatively complex, novelistic reality through the very shifting of parodistic perspectives, the playing with the mechanisms of the novel's artifice.

I do not, however, want to make excessive claims for the achievement of this book. One has only to compare it with its two chief nineteenth-century models, *Crime and Punishment* and *The Red and the Black*, to see that its strongly pronounced bias of parody, at times close to pastiche, precludes the kind of imaginative authority one associates with the greatest novels. For a self-conscious novel to achieve such authority—as I think *Don Quixote*, *Tom Jones*, *Tristram Shandy* clearly do—the novelist must probe the primary processes of the imagination itself more daringly, more relentlessly, than Gide does. That very probing will also lead the novel to be more spectacularly what Gide hoped it could be—not a Stendhalian mirror but superior, composed, a work of art. That is, finally, what both Joyce and Proust accomplish in very different ways, even though both maintain an underlying allegiance to the realist tradition of the nineteenth century in assuming the imagination ultimately as a vehicle for the conveyance of cultural and psychological facts outside its shaping. A generation later, Nabokov, no longer committed to the realist tradition—indeed, sometimes openly contemptuous of it—but duly impressed by the achievements of Joyce and Proust, will fulfill this program for the self-conscious novel with a new polemic insistence on the novel as a work of art and an a priori construct. In the four decades since the "years of wonder" of the modernist efflorescence,

ities and its relation to its antecedents; the self-consciousness of Nabokov presupposes a crammed history of
achievement and decline and renewal in the genre from
the eighteenth century to the modern masters. Nabokov's
intensified awareness, moreover, of artifice and literary
history has translated itself into an *oeuvre* of an abundance
and variety scarcely equaled among self-conscious novelists. In an age when most serious novelists, whatever their
orientation, produce a scant handful of titles in a lifetime,
Nabokov since 1926 has published seventeen novels, nine
in Russian and eight in English, to which one can add seven
Russian plays, several volumes of short stories and poems
in both languages, and *Speak, Memory*, one of his major
imaginative achievements, cast in the form of an autobiography. The extent and variety of Nabokov's *oeuvre* make
it particularly instructive for an understanding of the
self-conscious novel. All of his novels since the second one,
King, Queen, Knave (1928), are in one way or another
novels of flaunted artifice, but since they experiment with
different strategies and since they are not all equally
successful, they offer not only a whole spectrum of fictional
self-consciousness but also some monitory instances of the
traps, the inherent limitations, of this mode of fiction.

Nabokov's extraordinary inventiveness endows even his
flawed, or slighter, works with considerable interest for the
critical reader, but of his seventeen novels, I would be
inclined to argue for just four as sustained masterpieces
from beginning to end—*The Gift* and *Invitation to a Beheading*[1] of the Russian novels, and still more impressive,
Lolita and *Pale Fire* of the English ones. Early novels
like *King, Queen, Knave*; *The Eye*; *Laughter in the Dark*;
Despair, tend in various ways to press matters of design

---

[1] I have tried to define the achievement of *Invitation* in "Nabokov and the
Art of Politics," *Triquarterly* 17 (Winter 1970).

in a fashion that restrictively flattens the characters. The patterns of parody and obtruded artifice are cunningly devised but the constructed fictional world, however ingenious, is hardly allowed sufficient vitality to give the dialectic between fiction and "reality" the vigorous to-and-fro energy which it requires: a play of competing ontologies cannot fully engage us when one of the competitors, the invented world of the fiction, too often seems like intellectual contrivance. Or, to cite a somewhat different but related example, *The Real Life of Sebastian Knight* (1941), Nabokov's first English novel and the one rather perversely designated by Edmund Wilson as the author's best, is an intriguing introduction to the poetics of the self-conscious novel, but, like Unamuno's *Mist*, it is more interesting for its theory than for its realized fiction. A conundrum-novel, it gives the reader subtle pleasure in solving its puzzles of narrator and narration, subject and object, but its enticing descriptions of a "prismatic" novel and of parody as a springboard for the expression of the highest emotions would have to await *Lolita* (1955), *Pale Fire* (1962), and *Ada* (1969) for a forceful translation into fulfilled art.

If the self-conscious novel tends on one side to excessive cerebrality, to an ascetic avoidance of the pungent juices of ordinary fictional life, it tends on the other side to an unchecked playfulness that may become self-indulgent. Even a master like Joyce does not always draw the line between meaningful parody and schoolboyish verbal horseplay (one thinks of the hammering insistence on mock-heroic language in some passages of the Cyclops section, like the wedding of the trees, or the lengthy parodies of successive English styles through the ages in the Oxen of the Sun). Nabokov's characteristic indulgences are word-play and allusions, though he has made both of these beautifully functional in his most successful fictions. Even a powerfully original book, however, may in this regard be a mixed bag. Thus, *Bend Sinister* (1947) is a brilliant companion-piece to *Invitation to a Beheading* as an anti-utopian novel, and its central allusion to *Hamlet* has complex reverberations in the major concerns of the book; but its prose, though often wonderfully strange and sumptuous, at times strikes one as overwrought, gratuitously arcane, while the allusions to Mallarmé, Melville, and to various best-sellers of the 1940s seem too much a game the author is playing with himself. Again in *Ada* one finds a mixture of thematically justified allusions and gratuitous ones, of richly textured expressive prose and preciosity. The allusions to Marvell, Baudelaire, Chateaubriand, and Byron are imaginatively integrated with one another, suggestively reinforcing both each other and the fictional argument; but one wonders about the references to T. S. Eliot, John Updike, and a variety of lesser writers, about the quibbles with Freud, the constant trilingual punning, the baroque quality of some of the prose. It would be ungrateful to quarrel too much with a book that offers so many delights to the imagination, that is, after all, an extraordinary novelistic evocation of paradise regained. *Ada* is a novel where nice Art has virtually assumed the role of Nature boon pouring forth its inexhaustible riches, but precisely for that reason, the splendor of the achievement is marked with little spots of over-ripeness.

By contrast, Nabokov's control over his artistic means in both *Lolita* and *Pale Fire* seems quite flawless. In both, the repeated allusions to poets, to conventions of the novel, to all the trappings of literary tradition, beautifully fuse with the actual fictional predicaments of the protagonists, with the way they construe their worlds. The central characters themselves, even as we see them as artful designs in words, have a poignant intensity of life that surpasses any other characterizations in Nabokov; and their cadenced, at times extravagantly figurative language is always an expression of their nature and their plight, not a self-indulgence of the author. Both novels take up the basic quixotic theme of the tortuous, teasing relation between words and things, imagination and reality. The mental and sexual proclivities of Humbert Humbert and Charles Kinbote may make them among the most bizarre heirs of the Knight of La Mancha, but the lineage is clear, down to the assumption of a *nom de combat* and the attachment to a Dulcinea by each of these litera-ture-ridden lucid madmen.

Pale Fire, the more formally original of the two books, may be an apter culminating instance of self-consciousness in the novel because it focuses more directly on how the imagination both creates art and reflects it, and that ambiguous cyclical process of the production and reception of art is built into the novel's unique structure. For a detailed sense of how *Lolita* works as a self-conscious fiction, I could do no better than advise the reader to consult Alfred Appel's superb introductory essay to *The Annotated Lolita.*[2] The concluding sentence in Part One of that essay eloquently summarizes why in both these novels fictional self-consciousness—Appel calls it involu-tion—is able to move through the games of words and books to the urgent human predicaments equally shared by artists and ordinary mortals: "The ultimate detachment of an 'outside' view of a novel [i.e., seeing it as an artifact] inspires our wonder and enlarges our potential for compas-sion because, 'in the spiral unwinding of things' [a phrase from *Speak, Memory*], such compassion is extended to include the mind of an author whose deeply humanistic art affirms man's ability to confront and order chaos." Precisely how this amplitude of vision is worked out in *Pale Fire* will become clear through some attention to the details of the novel's intricate interlocking structure.

Let us recall briefly the peculiar general plan of *Pale*

---

[2] Vladimir Nabokov, *The Annotated Lolita*, edited, with preface, introduction, and notes by Alfred Appel, Jr. (New York: McGraw Hill, 1970).

Fire. It begins with a brief Foreword written by one Charles Kinbote, ostensibly to introduce a 999-line poem in rhyming couplets by the prominent American poet, John Francis Shade, a poem Kinbote has edited for publication after the poet's death. The text of the poem follows, and after it some 230 pages of notes by Kinbote, to which scholarly work the requisite Index is duly appended. One hardly has to read past the second note to realize that Kinbote's zany Commentary has precious little to do with the quiet meditative themes and the domestic academic settings that are the ostensible materials of the poem. In the Commentary, Kinbote, seeing himself as the real inspiration of the poem—indeed, as its covert subject— gradually emerges as King Charles the Beloved, hiding in exile after a revolution has taken place in the supposed European kingdom of Zembla, the magical homeland for which he constantly yearns. A victim of brilliant delusions, Kinbote, actually an émigré instructor at the small-town American university where John Shade teaches, would appear in fact to be neither Shade's intimate friend nor the king of anything, though he passionately, desperately, imagines himself to be both.

The wit and inventiveness of *Pale Fire* are so prominent in this plan that it is easy to "appreciate" the novel for the wrong reasons. On the most simplistic level, some readers have seen this as a satire on academe and a parody of the kind of exegetical erudition that Nabokov himself at the time of the book's composition was putting into his four-volume edition of *Eugene Onegin*. *Pale Fire* is of course both a satire and a parody, but to see it only as that is drastically to reduce its real scope. In quite another direction, I am afraid the novel has inspired its own Kinbotian commentators among Nabokov's critics. Exegetes of the novel, it seems to me, have tended to complicate it in gratuitous ways by publishing elaborate diagrams of its structure (which is, after all, clear enough in its main outlines), by devoting learned pages to wondering who—Nabokov, Shade, or Kinbote—is responsible for the epigraph, by exerting their own ingenuity to demonstrate dubious theses, like the one in which both the poem and the poet are argued to be Kinbote's inventions. This novel is not a Jamesian experiment in reliability of narrative point-of-view, and there is no reason to doubt the existence of the basic fictional data—the Poem and its author, on the one hand, and the mad Commentary and *its* perpetrator on the other, inverted left hand.

The besetting sin of criticism, in any case, has been merely to uncover intricate patterns of the novel's formal games and then to assume that intricacy itself is sufficient evidence of masterful imaginative achievement. One cannot discuss this book without attending to its extraordinary ingenuity, and in a moment I shall myself go on to consider some of the elaborate tracery of its design, but the essential question to be faced is what purpose the design really serves. *Pale Fire* is perhaps the most exquisitely fashioned variant of the "quixotic" novel in Marthe Robert's precise sense—a testing out through narrative invention of the double function of language as magical conjuration and radical probing, with an unblinking openness to all the moral and spiritual risks that each of those functions of language entails. It asks us, like *Don Quixote* itself, to ponder how the mind uses words to structure reality, to consider the deep trouble as well as the delights we make for ourselves through the stirring verbal realities we construct. But before trying to define any further these large issues that gradually emerge from the novel, we shall have to see how its principal mechanisms operate.

Self-conscious novels, because they are so aware of the arbitrariness of narrative conventions, tend to diverge in a variety of ways from the linear unitary structure of the usual traditional narrative; and as a result they exhibit a fondness for reproducing themselves *en abîme*, as Gide liked to say, working with Chinese-box constructions, or at least, repeatedly illuminating their devious narrative ways with small replicas of the innovative structure of the whole. This practice might be traced back as far as the doublings of narrative incident we noted in Cervantes, but its first full-scale use is easily observable in *Tristram Shandy*, where episodes like Slawkenbergius's Tale, the descent of the hot chestnut into Phutatorius's codpiece, the several variations on the story of Trim's amour with the fair Beguine, all reproduce the basic narrative operation of the whole novel: a great fuss and bother over misunderstandings permeated with hilarious double meanings hovering over a rude base of sexual fact.

This kind of self-replication is more pervasive in *Pale Fire* than in any other novel by Nabokov. The self-conscious activity of *dédoublement* and the self-conscious device of the mirror, both of which as we have seen began with Cervantes, and which are everywhere in Nabokov's fiction, achieve a kind of apotheosis here. Reflections, real and illusory, accurate and distorted, straightforward and magical, are absolutely ubiquitous. The title, in context in *Timon of Athens* (more of which later) refers to the moon's reflection of light from the sun. Kinbote, the supposed editor of John Shade's last poem, "Pale Fire," at once refers to it in the Foreword as a faceted crystal, and soon after strangely pauses over a vignette of the last John Shade watching a snowflake settle on his wristwatch and pensively declaring, "Crystal to crystal."[3] The poem itself begins with an elaborate—by now, duly celebrated—image of a deceptive reflection taken for reality, compounded by the optical illusion of objects within projected outside the reflecting translucence of glass:

[3] *Pale Fire* (New York: Putnam, 1962), p. 22.

I was the shadow of the waxwing slain
By the false azure in the windowpane;
I was the smudge of ashen fluff—and I
Lived on, flew on, in the reflected sky.
And from the inside, too, I'd duplicate
Myself, my lamp, an apple on a plate:
Uncurtaining the night, I'd let dark glass
Hang all the furniture above the grass. . . .

Zembla, the land of semblances that the megalomaniacal Kinbote invents to rule over in his Commentary, is a realm of mirrors. Rather like some fabulous world of science-fiction fabrication, it seems almost built of glass and reflecting surfaces. A skyscraper in its capital city is made of ultramarine glass. Most of its significant political events—strikes, conspiracies, explosions, revolutions—seem to take place in its glassworks. The names of its villains are anagrammatic mirror-reversals of the names of its heroes; most significantly, Jakob (or Yakob) Gradus, the Zemblan assassin chosen to track down King Charles, is an ex-glazier, and the anagrammatic mirror-reversal of Sudarg of Bokay, "a mirror maker of genius" (see Index). It is worth pondering the fact that the same elements which compose the super-thug of the novel, its paradigmatic anaesthetic man, need but to be read in the opposite direction to produce a master artist. Sudarg points toward another gifted worker in glass, a certain Rippleson—the name is suspiciously un-Zemblan—identified in the Index as "a famous glass maker who embodied the dapple-and-ringle play and other circular reflections on blue-green sea water in his extraordinary stained glass windows for the palace." The dapple-and-ringle play of circular reflections is precisely how *Pale Fire*—epigraph and Foreword and Poem, Commentary, and Index—is constructed, and so the mysterious artist Rippleson looks very much like a stand-in for Vladimir Nabokov.

Circular reflections and haunting realities entrapped in

the depths of mirrors figure significantly in the body of the poem. The often-quoted passage at the end of Canto Three (lines 806-829) gives a general description of this "plexed artistry," this narrative mirroring based on "some kind/ Of correlated pattern in the game," where the poet imagines the gods in "their involute/ Abode. . . ./ Playing a game of worlds" with mankind as the pieces on the mirror-patterned chessboard. Elsewhere in the poem, in more compressed visual imagery, Nabokov offers what amounts to a series of ideograms of the novel's structure. He has Shade describe an "iridule" (the word is Nabokov's invention)—an oval cloudlet that "Reflects the rainbow of a thunderstorm/ Which in a distant valley has been staged—/ For we are most artistically caged" (lines 112-114). A moment earlier, Shade had mentioned his Aunt Maud's "paperweight/ Of convex glass enclosing a lagoon" (lines 92-93), and a few lines further on he recalls "The miracle of a lemniscate left/ Upon wet sand by nonchalantly deft/ Bicycle tires" (lines 92-93). This seemingly precious piece of imagery is at first puzzling, and Kinbote of course quite misses the point in his commentary by citing a dictionary definition of lemniscate—"a unicursal bicircular quartic"—then dismissing the use of the term as an affectation. A lemniscate, however, is a continuous figure-eight curve, thus: ∞ ; and as such neatly diagrams the circular reflective relation of Commentary to Poem and Poem to Commentary. (The shape might also recall the wings of a butterfly, that inevitable Nabokovian "signature," which in fact appears again and again in the novel.) Even a rubberband on Shade's desk falls into the form of an ampersand (line 533), and a rubberband figured as an ampersand—&—is a lemniscate by another name, again the ideogram of the novel. The Commentary and Index play their own cryptographic games with these little emblems of the novel enunciated in the poem. There is even one instance where two ideograms are joined in a single figure, Iris Acht, the mistress of King Charles's grandfather, whose first name points back to the iridule and whose last name, "eight" in German, recalls the figure 8 of the lemniscate.

All this is clever enough, but like any cleverness exhibited at length, it would finally be tedious if it did not tie in as tightly as it does with the serious imaginative business of the novel, the inner life of the protagonists, the existential quandaries in which they are caught, the shimmering interplay of art and life generated by the events and the language of the narrative. Perhaps we can begin to move beyond the commonplaces of "explicating" the devices of *Pale Fire* and get closer to the distinctive poetic reality of the novel by focusing on one particularly suggestive mirror image. Fleur, a fetching young Zemblan woman, has been sent to the palace in an appropriate state of undress to lure the homosexual prince from his inverted ways.

> He awoke to find her standing with a comb in her hand before his—or rather, his grandfather's—cheval glass, a trip-tych of bottomless light, a really fantastic mirror, signed with a diamond by its maker, Sudarg of Bokay. She turned about before it: a secret device of reflection fathered an infinite number of nudes in its depths, garlands of girls in graceful and sorrowful groups, diminishing in the limpid distance, or breaking into individual nymphs, some of whom, she murmured, must resemble her ancestors when they were young—little peasant *garlien* combing their hair in shallow water as far as the eye could reach, and then the wistful mermaid from an old tale, and then nothing. [p. 111-112]

We have had occasion to examine evocative passages from *Ulysses* and *St. Petersburg* (two of Nabokov's favorite modern novels) which conclude by allowing the conjured-up mental moment to trail off into nothingness. As a post-modern writer, however, Nabokov is less interested in the immediacy of consciousness than in the art that creates consciousness and that, conversely, consciousness creates. The naked Fleur surrounded by the triptych of the cheval glass is a beautifully realized instance of the dapple-and-ringle play of circular reflections. The glass fashioned by Sudarg of Bokay, who as we have seen is just one remove from the fashioner of *Pale Fire*, gives back not a simple image but an infinite regress of multiplied images, and it is signed with a diamond by Sudarg—in a lemniscate &?—as Nabokov signs all his own works with butterflies. The mirror is "fantastic" not only in the colloquial sense of "extraordinary" but because it opens into a whole realm of fantasy, translating a simple naked girl into the mythological choreography of myriad dancing maidens, aptly caught in the alliterative music of the prose—"garlands of girls in graceful and sorrowful groups."

The relation here of the reflected image to time past is particularly noteworthy. Real mirror-images, of course, exist only at the moment of reflection, and so in a sense are cut off from the dimension of time. The figurative mirror of art, on the other hand, and especially of literary art, is deeply embedded in the multilayered experience of time. This is true first of all because art develops cumulatively and operates through repeated self-recapitulation, and the very medium of literary art, language, is the product of collective experience in time, suffused with the associations and recollections of times past and past literary uses. Any work of art, moreover, can exist only through an act of mediation in the consciousness of someone experiencing it, and consciousness, as the example of Joyce's technique must remind us, is essentially built up out of the infinite laminations of what the individual has seen, felt, read, fantasized in the past, however attuned he may be to the present moment. The mirror itself here is a legacy of the past, not properly King

Charles's but his grandfather's, the farcically named Thurgus the Turgid, who was, of course, the purple-nosed lover of Iris Acht, that hooded lady linked by appellation with circular reflections. Through the consciousness of Fleur, "murmuring" fantasies (the locution sounds like a parodistic reminiscence of Virginia Woolf) as she observes herself transfigured in multiple reflection, we are moved further back in time into a legendary past where pastoral ancestors preen themselves by still waters. Recessed within that memory is a more distant one of a wistful mermaid in an old tale; and at the end of this entrancing series one glimpses the empty ground where there is neither consciousness nor art nor anything but the eternal void that both must fill if we are not to be overwhelmed by the dedication of living things to death.

The "bottomless light" of the triptych, then, ultimately leads back to the mystery implicit in the title of the novel. The pale fire of art, in the usual view, reflects the sun of reality, but we also see it here become its own sun, turning its observers, like Kinbote vis-à-vis Shade, into light-thieving moons, uncannily providing from the recesses of the assembled artifact an undying source of magical illumination for all who come to study their reflection in its surfaces. Indeed, the very first occurrence of the phrase "pale fire" in the text of the novel (p. 15), where it is attached to the incinerator burning the rejected drafts of Shade's poem, which then ascend into the air as "wind-borne black butterflies," associates the term with the refining process by which art comes into being, consuming its own impurities—and that pale fire is no reflection at all.

In a novel constructed so that reflections continually reflect other reflections, a passage like the one we have been considering becomes still more complicated when it is seen in the rings of narrative context that surround it. Though it may be a hauntingly evocative, visually memorable moment, it is, after all, no more than "the dream of a reverie," part of the pure fabrication Charles Kinbote creates of a past he never experienced in fact, where he was king of Zembla, surrounded by futilely expectant female beauties and bevies of blooming boys. This whole fantasy, moreover, is the wildly distorted "reflection" of a poem in heroic couplets by John Shade which is in fact about other people, other places, other themes. At the outset of this study, in discussing *Don Quixote*, I suggested that the self-conscious novel tends to polarize the inherent tension between fiction and reality, then to make our perception shuttle between the poles. This procedure of polarization is given an ultimate acuteness of formulation in Kinbote's "twist[ing] and batter[ing] an *apparatus criticus* into the monstrous semblance of a novel" (p. 86). His tale of Zembla is manifestly a fiction twice removed from the reality in which the reader sits with the book in his hand, but in its vividness—witness Fleur at the mirror—in the way it manages to correspond through all its farcical gyrations to the truth of Kinbote's inner world and to the composite image of a possible European political history, it has a kind of authority, and does not allow us to dismiss it as "mere" fiction.

Nabokov is particularly shrewd in the way he focuses this polarized perception through a double awareness of language as historical fact and arbitrary construct. Zembla has its own language, a Germano-Slavic tongue (not unlike that of the imaginary country in *Bend Sinister*), and we are given frequent samples of the native lexicon, with even an occasional passage of verse quoted in the original Zemblan. The invention of a fictional language is a grand extension of the principle devised by Alonso Quixano when he fabricated a new name, Don Quixote, to confer reality upon his new role. There remains, moreover, some leeway of teasing ambiguity in the novel about the ultimate status of Zembla and its language. Are they purely the invention of the mad Kinbote, who is not really Kinbote but his anagrammatic double, V. Botkin, an American scholar of Russian descent? Or, alternatively, does Kinbote's madness extend merely to his delusion that he is the exiled king of Zembla, while the existence of the country and its language, now the creation of Nabokov, not Kinbote, is assumed to be "real" within the frame of the novel? The ambiguity is, I think, a fruitful one because it prevents us from drawing simplistic conclusions about the demarcations between truth and invention within an artistic fiction. When Kinbote, then, has Fleur murmur *garlien* in the original Zemblan, the introduction of the supposedly native word serves simultaneously to authenticate the remembered scene and to remind us of its status as sheer invention, of how an author behind Kinbote is giving free play to the pleasurable impulse of making fictions, at once word-building and world-building.

The double function of an artificial language is powerfully reinforced by Nabokov's numerous strategies for calling our attention, as most self-conscious novelists have done, to the fact that the reality of the fiction is assembled from words and letters. The Goldsworths, whose home Kinbote is renting, are perceived by their tenant as an "alphabetic family," having named their four daughters Alphina (that is, alpha), Betty (beta), Candida (is this a wry glance at Shaw?), and finally, quite simply, Dee. The books left behind in Mrs. G.'s bedroom run similarly from Amber to Zen (p. 83). Kinbote informs us of three conjoined lakes near the university town known as Omega, Ozero, and Zero, thus running us backwards from the ultimate end in the Greek alphabet to the point before beginnings in mathematical notation, with the Russian word for lake, *ozero*, in the middle. Ozero is also a double zero, 00, which, if the circles are tangent, is another version of a lemniscate.

Outside Kinbote's Appalachia, in both the poem and the projected world of Zembla, fictional reality exhibits a similar tendency to return to its alphabetic origins. The immediate line of succession in the Zemblan royal family is King *A*lphin (the masculine form of Alphina), Queen *B*lenda, King *C*harles (who is Charles II, a "successor" in role to Charles I, the deposed and executed king of England, but also Charles Xavier, that is, Charles X, the unknown one in this alphabet soup of a novel). In Shade's poem, skaters cross the frozen Lake Omega from Exe to Wye (line 490), and again in Kinbote's version of the Shade household, the mysterious alphabetical powers exert such dominance that Mrs. Shade even suffers from an alphabetically determined allergy, to artichokes, avocado pears, African acorns, and so forth (p. 230). Finally, all this patterning down of narrative materials into alphabetical schemata jibes perfectly with the prominent importance of anagrams in the novel. Anagrams, here joined with a transformational variant, word golf (q.v., Index), are a perennial passion of the scrabble-playing Nabokov; but here more than in any other of his novels they make fine thematic sense by demonstrating language's capacity for mirror-reversal, by showing how the universal elements of written language can be manipulated by the artificer through a constant chain of shifting patterns so that they make, or at least designate, different realities.

These reminders of the alphabetic constituents of the novel's reality are thematically complemented, on a higher level of complexity, by the reiterated imagery in which the things of this world turn into verse and literary convention, or, conversely, by which literature with its formal norms makes itself into a habitable world. John Shade invites his wife to enter with him into a secret geography of poetry and intellectual design, "Empires of rhyme, Indies of calculus" (line 602), and the first extended image of his poem after that initial reflection in and through the poet's window is of a *paysage littéraire*, of a landscape transmuted into literature:

> ... Whose spurred feet have crossed
> From left to right the blank page of the road?
> Reading from left to right in winter's code:
> A dot, an arrow pointing back; repeat:
> Dot, arrow pointing back. ... A pheasant's feet!
>
> [lines 20-24]

The image archly forces us to do a double take: we envisage a winter landscape—of course, conveyed to us in a poem by a fictional poet in a novel—at the same time that we see we are reading a printed page from left to right in which a series of conventional symbols encodes a meaning that we must decipher. All communication is a code, poetry being simply the most complex, integrated ordering of encoding elements. Kinbote's mad Commentary represents an extreme instance, at once moving and farcical, of the general difficulty of decoding such artful texts: he puts together Appalachia, waxwing, crystal land and gets ... Zembla, revolution, a stalking assassin. Shade, having begun his poem by transforming a landscape into printer's ink on a white page, concludes it, after the various musings on plexed artistry and games of worlds, by elevating the ordering idea of the writer's art, with some qualification, to a cosmic principle:

> I feel I understand
> Existence, or at least a minute part
> Of my existence, only through my art,
> In terms of combinational delight;
> And if my private universe scans right,

So does the verse of galaxies divine
Which I suspect is an iambic line.

[lines 970-976]

The poet's vision of an iambic cosmos is offered tenta-
tively, wistfully, by a man whose lifelong vocation has been
to achieve coherence through the formal symmetries of
language, but one begins to see concretely what Alfred
Appel means when he describes art in Nabokov as the
model of how we confront and order chaos. Shade is
pursued by the idea of death, the extinction of the self,
and he tries to imagine poetry as a vehicle of transcen-
dence. On the other side of the mirror, Kinbote is pursued
by his own derangement ("the frozen mud and horror in
my heart," [p. 258]), that is, a radical isolation of the self,
and his way out is the poem with which he thinks he
has "impregnated" Shade, his means of shaping the private
chaos and terror of his experience and entering through
art into the human community. A latter-day Quixote, he
aspires to become a hero of literature not by deed but
by talk alone. In point of fact, Kinbote's real poem is the
novel he builds out of Shade's poem in his Commentary,
interpretation turned creation. "I can do what only a true
artist can do," Kinbote justifiably boasts toward the end,
"pounce upon the forgotten butterfly of revelation, wean
myself abruptly from the habit of things, see the web of
the world, and the warp and the weft of the web" (p. 289).
The imagery of warp and weft takes us back to the
"link-and-bobolink," the "correlated pattern in the game"
(lines 812-813) of Shade's poem, at the same time that
it parodistically exaggerates in Kinbote, a mad version of
a Nabokovian artist, Nabokov's own fondness for alliterative effects. Kinbote immediately continues these alliterative flourishes in language that is expressively lurid,
marked by lambent iambs, in consonance with his own
sensibility and situation, as he recalls the theme of deci-
phering enunciated in Canto One of the poem and joins

an image of pale fire to the novel's emblematic association
of art with entomology. Clutching the poet's index cards,
"I found myself enriched with an indescribable amazement
as if informed that fire-flies were making decodable signals
on behalf of stranded spirits, or that a bat was writing
a legible tale of torture in the bruised and branded sky."
Clearly, Kinbote himself is the stranded spirit par excellence, but in his mental and social alienation he merely
embodies an extreme instance of the role of isolate in which
every human being is to some degree cast. The pattern-
making process of decoding art into art is an ultimate
necessity: without it the spirit is lost forever.

Pale Fire urges the idea of art as the sole way of coping
with chaos—Shade, coolly and ironically, Kinbote, desperately—but the idea is sharply qualified with a philosophical
realism by the steady awareness that any poetic invention
is, after all, a farrago of words, a delusional system, a form
of madness. The title of Shade's critical study of Pope,
Supremely Blest, refers us to a passage in the *Essay on
Man* (2:267-270) crucial to the plan of the novel, and
though the relevant lines have been duly brought forth
by previous critics of *Pale Fire*, beginning with Mary
McCarthy, they are particularly worth reflecting on in
the present connection:

> See the blind beggar dance, the cripple sing,
> The sot a hero, lunatic a king;
> The starving chemist in his golden views
> Supremely blest, the poet in his Muse.

The conjunction of lunatic king and poet is of course the
conjunction in the novel of those antithetical doubles,
Kinbote and Shade. There is, moreover, a thematic rather
than a structural revelation about the novel in Pope's
tartly satirical yoking, shrewdly reinforced by a rare en-
jambement, of the starving chemist (that is, alchemist)
and the poet. The alchemist deludes himself by thinking

he can effect a magical transformation of lead to gold (in the novel, Kinbote, no doubt with the art of Sudarg and Rippleson in mind, refers to writing as "blue magic"). The poet, for Nabokov's purposes at any rate, deludes himself by imagining he can transform the death-sodden mire of existence into a pellucid artifice of eternity. But perhaps, we are made to feel through both "Pale Fire" and its Commentary, the delusion is strictly necessary to make life livable; perhaps in some way it is not altogether a delusion.

Kinbote's *apparatus criticus* strongly confirms this double sense of poetry as delusion and ordering truth by repeatedly drawing attention to how real-seeming characters are laid out on a grid of literary coordinates, so that at moments those literary coordinates seem almost to constitute an autonomous reality. In a dream of King Charles—that is, the dream of a dream of a dream—the neglected queen is imagined assuming a variety of destinies, including that of becoming a character in a novel (p. 212). Sylvia O'Donnell, a fashionable and much-married supporter of the king, is said to be in the process of divorcing her latest mate "when last seen in this Index" (p. 311). Most centrally, Jakob Gradus, who in the perspective of Kinbote's novelistic omniscience becomes progressively more "real," down to an X-ray view of the partly digested French fries and ham sandwich roiling his insides, is constituted again and again wholly through the rhythms and rules of a poem where, of course, he never really appears:

> We shall accompany Gradus in constant thought, as he makes his way from distant dim Zembla to green Appalachia, through the entire length of the poem, following the road of its rhythm, riding past in a rhyme, skidding around the corner of a run-on, breathing with the caesura, swinging down to the foot of the page from line to line as from branch to branch, hiding between two words (see note to line 596), reappearing on the horizon of a new canto, steadily march-

ing nearer in iambic motion, crossing streets, moving up
with his valise on the escalator of the pentameter, stepping
off, boarding a new train of thought, entering the hall of
a hotel, putting out the bedlight, while Shade blots out
a word, and falling asleep as the poet lays down his pen
for the night. [p. 78]

This leaves the assassin Gradus—"tree" in Zemblan to
the poet's Shade—as a potent metrical illusion, now you
see him, now you don't, whose ambiguous existence projected onto the lines of a printed page by a madman forces
us to ponder the reality of fictional things. As a "fact"
within the novel, he is of course the product of sheer
delusion, what Kinbote's fantasies have made out of a
murderer named Jack Gray sentenced by Kinbote's land-
lord, Judge Goldsworth. And yet, the manifest fictionality
of Gradus's existence does nothing to diminish from the
progressive power of his presence in the novel; and set
between the two poets, one happily heterosexual and
lucidly witty, the other haplessly homosexual and darkly
melodramatic, the political assassin makes the most cogent
thematic and even historical sense. He is the consummate
embodiment of anti-imagination, asexual (he has tried to
castrate himself), impervious to the pleasures of the body
as of the spirit, the perfect political man of the modern
totalitarian state, a gross obedient goon with a gun in his
hand. One sees in his delineation the utter seriousness that
underlies the playfulness of Nabokov's fictional games.
The trauma of the murder of the writer's own father by
Russian fascists, compounded by his brother's death at
the hand of the Nazis, has haunted him throughout his
career, and he may play with assassinations and related
political themes but he does not toy with them.

In order to see more fully how *Pale Fire* opens up
perspectives on the luminous circularity of reflective relations between poetry and reality, it is important to observe

that not only is the novel built upon the reversed images of two different kinds of poet but that the two figures repeatedly allude to two antithetical English poets, and through them to the two opposite poles of English poetry. The poetic ascendancy of Shade's "Pale Fire" of course belongs to Alexander Pope. Shade is an academic specialist in Pope; he casts his poem in Popean couplets, divides it into four cantos like the *Essay on Man*, uses his verse, like the *Essay*, to discourse philosophically on man's estate, stretching his iambs, like Pope's, to the starry spaces, and speculating, like Pope, on a possible afterlife and its effects on the here-and-now (see, for example, *Essay on Man*, 4:173-180). Pope, too, published a poem with a hilariously addled commentary much longer than the original text, the *Dunciad Variorum*, and the theme of that poem, described in the 1728 preface as "the restoration of the reign of Chaos and Night," could easily characterize what happens politically and personally in the Commentary to John Shade's poem.

In any event, it is obvious that the texture of Shade's poem and its informing sensibility are far from Popean, despite the Popean prosody, but the disparity is quite to the point, for *Pale Fire* is in part about how literature reuses literature, assimilates it and makes something strange and new out of it. Thus the twentieth-century colloquial rhythms of "Pale Fire"—an eighteenth-century critic would have called them "nerveless"—constantly work against the formal emphases and tensions of the traditional couplet form, often producing an effect of studied gaucherie (though there may also be some awkwardness that is inadvertent). Some of the verbal clowning reminds one not of Pope but of his great Romantic admirer, the improvisatory Byron of *Don Juan*. There is real wit in the poem, but it is Nabokovian, not Popean, in its intense visuality and its flaunted ingenuity (for example, a blurry movie closeup rerun on TV is "a soft form dissolving in the prism/ Of corporate desire" [lines 456-457]). At its brilliant best, the poem, however philosophical, achieves a most un-Popean effect—poignancy. Vividly focusing the particulars of sensory experience taken from a familiar everyday world, and reveling in the gorgeousness of words, sounds, and imagery, it transmutes the heroic couplet into the distinctive handiwork of the writer who invented Adam Krug, Humbert Humbert, and Pnin:

> Nor can one help the exile, the old man
> Dying in a motel, with the loud fan
> Revolving in the torrid prairie night
> And, from the outside, bits of colored light
> Reaching his bed like dark hands from the past
> Offering gems; and death is coming fast.
> He suffocates and conjures in two tongues
> The nebulae dilating in his lungs.
>
> [lines 609-616]

What John Shade does to Pope is but a modest intimation of what Charles Kinbote does to John Shade. If Shade is a "Popean" poet (we have seen the necessity for the quotation marks), Kinbote, mulling over Shade's poem, becomes a "Shakespearian" one—in the old antithesis, Shakespeare as the untamed, enormously fecund genius over against the polished wit operating ingeniously within limited scope. A passage from Pope gives us the conjunction of the lunatic and the poet, but Shakespeare (in *Midsummer Night's Dream*) tells us that the poet, the madman, and the lover are one, and of course Kinbote is all three. His world bristles with reminders of the Bard, and even his name, transmogrified in the novel into the Elizabethan "bodkin," recalls the most famous of Shakespeare's soliloquies. Though the name Zembla is lifted from Pope, that dim distant country is thoroughly Shake-spearianized in Kinbote's presentation of it. As a young prince, Chales Xavier rents rooms in Corialanus Lane. His Scottish tutor, Mr. Campbell, is fond of reciting all of *Macbeth* by heart. Conmal, the prince's uncle, devotes half a century to the translation of Shakespeare's complete works. (It is Conmal's translation of *Timon of Athens* that Kinbote happens to have with him on his last retreat "like Timon in his cave" to a rural cabin.) Even the name Shakespeare is attributed to a Zemblan place name, Shalksbore, meaning "knave's farm." On the Appalachian side of things, Wordsmith (which is to say, "poet") Univer-sity boasts a famous avenue lined with all the trees mentioned in Shakespeare, and which Kinbote takes the trouble to enumerate. The account in Shade's poem of Hazel Shade's suicide leads the commentator in his note to line 463 into a Hamlet-like soliloquy on suicide. Both Ophelia and a bare botkin ("note the correct spelling," Kinbote tells us) are mentioned, while ironically, this self-designated Christian prince whose throne has been usurped comes out in defense of suicide, thus providing us one of several inverted reflections of Shakespeare.

Though the extravagances of Kinbote's paranoid mega-lomania lead to florid excesses in style, as we have seen and as we shall see, there nevertheless is something Shake-spearian about the poetry he makes out of his madness when one compares it to the poem by John Shade. Shade writes poetry out of his musings, a poetry always bound to his immediate personal experience, however large a metaphysical background he may set behind it. Kinbote, on the other hand, is able to create a whole world with a history, a politics, a class structure, a set of folk tradi-tions, and to people it with dramatically vivid figures. Soaring beyond the ordinariness of everyday things, his imagination delights in conjuring up traditional literary materials like exiled princes, palace intrigues, secret underground passageways, assassinations, beautiful noble ladies, and grotesque clowns. In this way the novel, with its "Popean" poem and its "Shakespearian" commentary, generates a genuinely binocular vision, showing forth in intricate interplay two kinds of poetry, two modes of imagination, that mark the opposite ends of the field within which literary creation is free to play.

Shakespeare, moreover, is repeatedly involved in the theme of translation that is one of the conceptual keys of the novel. Shakespeare, always the supreme poet of the Western tradition for Nabokov—see, for example, how he is spoken of and allusively used in *Bend Sinister*—offers in his richness the ultimate instance of the constant sea changes poetry suffers in the consciousness of the readers it needs in order to exist at all. Shade's advice to college students on the reading of Shakespeare, recorded by Kinbote in Boswellian fashion, intimates the consummate power of the master poet but offers no real practical guidance for the challenge of assimilating him: the student should "get drunk on the poetry of *Hamlet* or *Lear*, . . . read with his spine and not with his skull" (p. 155). (This is almost verbatim what Nabokov used to advise his Cornell students.) Shade, of course, has no idea that his own last poem will be subjected by Kinbote to a reading from the base of the spine and the floor of the psyche. King Charles's first experience of Shakespeare is through the mediation of Uncle Conmal's translations, and the most hilariously revealing comment on the accuracy of those translations comes in the last words of Conmal, whose English was self-taught—"*Comment dit-on 'mourir' en anglais?*" (p. 285).

Every literary work, even in a language one can read, must be inwardly "translated" by each of its readers, and all translations are, necessarily, mistranslations, differing

only in the direction and relative absurdity of their inaccuracies. Sybil Shade's French translations of Marvell and
Donne are stigmatized by the jealous Kinbote. He on his
part admits to having translated some of Shade's poetry
into Zemblan some twenty years previously, but if the
accuracy of the "translation" that his Commentary provides is any indication, one is happy to be spared these
juvenile gems. Communications between various members
of the Extremist secret service are a farce of mistranslations. A telephone conversation between Gradus and his
superiors, in which both sides have forgotten the code and
speak their own versions of broken English, offers a perfect
paradigm of the translation problem: "Each side, finally,
had forgotten the meaning of certain phrases pertaining
to the other's vocabulary so that in result, their tangled
and expensive talk combined charades with an obstacle
race in the dark" (p. 215). (This could be a perfect
characterization of *Tristram Shandy*'s world of miscom-
munication.) More laughably, a sentence written in "gov-
erness English" by Queen Disa to the king after the
revolution—"I want you to know that no matter how much
you hurt me, you cannot hurt my love"—is intercepted,
converted into crude Zemblan by a Hindu (!) Extremist,
and rendered back in English by Kinbote as: "I desire
you and love when you flog me" (p. 205). Oddly enough,
this howler is not altogether pointless, since there is surely
an element of masochism in Disa's futilely persistent love
for the neglectful King, so even an outrageous mistranslation (like Kinbote's Commentary) may turn up an un-
suspected face of the truth.

It should be observed that a translation from English
to Zemblan and back to English again is a circular reflection, which, as we have already seen through other images,
is what this novel is all about. The most pointed double
translation, of course, is the text from *Timon of Athens*

(4, 3:439-443) that supplies the title of the novel. The original lines, never actually quoted, sketch out a cosmic cycle of universal theft, everything working at a distance to borrow its light or force from something else, and completely transforming what it takes:

> The sun's a thief, and with his great attraction
> Robs the vast sea; the moon's an arrant thief,
> And her pale fire she snatches from the sun;
> The sea's a thief, whose liquid surge resolves
> The moon into salt tears.

Now, Kinbote quotes his own re-Englished version of Conmal's Zemblan translation of these lines, without, however, suspecting that they contain the phrase "pale fire." Since *Timon of Athens* in its Zemblan transmogrification is the only Shakespeare he has with him in his cabin, he aptly observes that his "luck would have been a statistical monster" (p. 285) if Shade's title had appeared in that particular play. The irony of Kinbote's ignorance on this, and many other, points reminds us of the crucial difference between poetry and statistics, of how much Kinbote is the creature, in a sense the prisoner, of Nabokov's combinational art. (The strategy for exposing the dependence of the seemingly autonomous creature on his creator is more subtle than Unamuno's having his doomed hero vainly confront him at his writing desk, but the underlying concept is the same.) The only lines Kinbote actually quotes anywhere in the novel from Conmal's *Timon* are, of course, just those that contain the title phrase, safely buried under the debris of translation and retranslation:

> The sun is a thief: she lures the sea
> And robs it. The moon is a thief:
> he steals his silvery light from the sun.
> The sea is a thief: it dissolves the moon.

[p. 80]

There is distortion but obviously no dapple-and-ringle play in this circular reflection. What it presents us with is a model of the lower limits of translation. Some literal sense of the imagery is preserved, though one might note that in the inverted reflection of the original, the genders of sun and moon are reversed; but this crude, flat-footed version destroys the dancing music of the verse, the emotional coloring of the language, the dramatized mystery of interplay among heavenly and earthly bodies—in short, the poetry of the passage. Furthermore, the sudden and arresting pulse of pathos in the conceit of the last two lines—"whose liquid surge resolves/ The moon into salt tears"—is lopped off by the ridiculous and abrupt "it dissolves the moon." The gauche mistranslation of this passage, then, serves as a counterpoint to the splendid mistranslation effected through the Commentary, where pathos is wonderfully twinned with absurdity, and the poetry of nostalgia for a lost world vivifies the fantasy images and imbues the prose with sumptuous life.

The life of the prose, to be precise, is extravagant, in perfect keeping with Kinbote's flamboyant nature and his sense of his own plight. The wild energy with which his language joins disparate realms and transforms things through metaphor is another measure of its "Shakespearian" quality. Here is Kinbote at the outset, in the Foreword, putting us on notice about the kind of sensibility with which we are to be confronted in this narrative: "Mr. and Mrs. Shade ... were having trouble with their old Packard in the slippery driveway where it emitted whines of agony but could not extricate one tortured rear wheel out of a concave inferno of ice" (p. 20). Anyone who has ever got a car caught in snow and heard the awful shriek of tires spinning in icy ruts will recognize the experience, but however sharply observed, the experience has been transposed by metaphor into the special key of Kinbote's inner world. In this extreme application of personification, everything has been stepped up—whines of agony, tortured wheels, an inferno of ice—into an externalized image of Kinbote's own writhing sense of entrapment. The imagination at work here is a powerful one, but, as it will proceed to do on a much larger scale in the Commentary, it insists on refashioning the outer world as an embodiment of its acute interior distress. The image of imprisonment in ice, moreover, is linked with the novel's emblematic images of being caught in crystal, buried in the depths of a mirror.

Such use of figurative language is complicated and enriched by a certain flickering critical awareness in Kinbote of how the choice of imagery transforms the object and constitutes a literary act. In describing, for example, the "actual" imprisonment of Charles Xavier, he adopts the following figure to represent the tired King's vision of his card-playing captors: "The King yawned, and the illumined card players shivered and dissolved in the prism of his tears" (p. 123). The metaphor has the studied quality of a conceit that characterizes a good deal of Kinbote's style, but the conceit very precisely focuses an understanding of how the refracting medium of perception frames, distorts, dramatically reshapes the objects perceived. Needless to say, the prism in the bleary eye of the beholder is continuous with the sundry crystals, rippled glasses, and iridules that provide models in miniature of how the novel as a whole works, something underscored by the fact that the source of illumination referred to here is a lantern around which lepidopterist Nabokov sets flapping a signatory moth.

As even these brief examples may suggest, Kinbote's prose delights in extravagance, but it is the extravagance of a wildly original observer who tries to place critical distance between his own perceptions and the exaggerated formulas of second-rate literature. The enlivening ironic intelligence, in other words, behind the novel as a whole works as a pale reflection in Kinbote, intermittently and most imperfectly, but sufficiently to provide little critical checks on the wonderful but outrageous excesses of his narrative. In describing Fleur, for example, he cites the view of her lover, Otar, who "said that when you walked behind her, the swing and play of those slim haunches was something intensely artistic, something Arab girls were taught in special schools by special Parisian panders who were afterwards strangled" (p. 108). Kinbote, however, is quick to put down this and related notions in the immediate context as "rather kitschy prattle." As generally happens with parody, he—and the reader with him—manages to have it both ways, reveling in the rich absurdity of pseudo-exotica and seeing the absurdity for what it is. One has only to compare a moment like this with the luridly illuminated scenes in Egyptian houses of child prostitution in Lawrence Durrell's *Justine* to see the difference between a novel where fictional self-consciousness is continuous and one where it is episodic. Durrell's *Quartet*, of course, is self-conscious in being a fiction about the writing of novels that experiments with different points of view and deploys several different novelists-within-the-novel. Nevertheless, it is hard to read long stretches of it except as highly colored set pieces or entertainments in which Durrell's own enjoyment of kitschy prattle tends to extinguish his critical consciousness of the problematic relationship between literature and reality.

In *Pale Fire*, by contrast, that authorial consciousness never falters, and Nabokov achieves a still more difficult thing by making parody work for him as he repeatedly goes beyond it. That is, Kinbote's prose includes a good many parodistic elements that aptly serve as means of inadvertent self-characterization, or self-incrimination; however, the writing here, unlike Gide's in *Les Caves du*

Vatican, is not in the least restricted to parody but creates a sumptuous poetry of its own, an original imaginative confection studded with parodistic plums. The shrewd double nature of Kinbote's prose is particularly palpable in those passage where he comes out most explicitly as a spokesman for the poetic imagination, as in the following reflection, triggered by thinking of the thug Gradus's dismally limited world:

> How much happier the wide-awake indolents, the mon-
> archs among men, the rich monstrous brains deriving in-
> tense enjoyment and rapturous pangs from the balustrade
> of a terrace at nightfall, from the lights and the lake below,
> from the distant mountain shapes melting into the dark
> apricot of the afterglow, from the black conifers outlined
> against the pale ink of the zenith, and from the garnet and
> green flounces of the water along the silent, sad, forbidden
> shoreline. Oh my sweet Boscobel! And the tender and
> terrible memories, and the shame, and the glory, and the
> maddening intimations, and the star that no party member
> can ever reach. [p. 232]

A good deal of this is surely meant to be taken quite seriously. Nabokov's work as far back as the thirties embodies a double perception of the artist as a monarch among men and, perhaps more prominently, as a vulner-able freak, and Kinbote-Charles is both. The whole Com-mentary is manifestly the work of a rich monstrous brain anxiously pursuing the memory of a cherished past through the verbal evocation of its concrete details. The precise painterly composition here of the remembered scene in line, color, and mass—the dark apricot horizon, the pale ink of the zenith, the black outline of the conifers, the green and garnet borders of the lake—is not the meandering of a madman but Nabokov's artful prose at its best. (No detail wasted, the pale ink brings us back to the motif of landscape as writing or drawing, while the garnet and green invoke the elaborate game of reds and greens played across the two parts of the novel.) Then, with the exclamation, "Oh my sweet Boscobel!" the passage swings into open parody, tripping on through those emptily rhetorical "ands" not only to a parody of bestseller *Kitsch*—"and the shame and the glory"—but also to a parody of one of Nabokov's favorite stylistic effects: the delicately beautiful alliteration of "apricot of the afterglow" and "garnet and green flounces" is crudely mimicked in the vapid cliché, "tender and terrible." Remarkably, Kinbote can be made to pirouette on parody and move a step beyond it to complete the initial statement about the poet and his experience. "Maddening intimations" is a phrase that straddles, almost seeming to belong to the string of bestseller clichés yet pointing past it to a complex sense of how the sensuous poetic imagination responds in recollection to the aching sweetness of what it has undergone. "The star that no party member can reach" then exhibits a kind of serious wit clearly beyond the immediately preceding series of banalities, and it marks a moment quite free of irony. For a brief but significant instant, the sense of life of Vladimir Nabokov, exiled novelist, makes full contact with that of the exiled King, this fantasy of a fantasy of the author's, and we glimpse the alignment between the fictionally refracted lost land of Zembla and a land on the real map, poignantly remembered but forever closed to one of its greatest living writers.[4]

We have seen how all such affirmations of faith in poetry and the superiority of the creative imagination are qualified by context—here, at the penultimate moment of the affirmation by the inset of parody. What gives *Pale Fire*

[4] Compare these lines in "An Evening of Russian Poetry": "Beyond the seas where I have lost a scepter/ I hear the neighing of dappled nouns,/ soft participles coming down the steps,/ treading on leaves, trailing their rustling gowns." Nabokov, *Poems and Problems* (New York: McGraw-Hill, 1970), pp. 159-160.

its fullness of statement about the ambiguous interlacing of imagination and reality, what makes it finally a major achievement in the tradition of the self-conscious novel, is that these dialectic qualifications are translated into the novel's most basic facts of character and plot. Charles Xavier, the tender-hearted homosexual King fleeing from Extremist blackguards, is a wonderful creation, however bizarre, and even when we "reconstruct" the novel and realize that he is the fantasy of Charles Kinbote, we are hardly prepared to give him up, to discount as mere fabrication the reality he and his native land have managed to assume: finally the King is more real as an imaginatively felt presence than Kinbote, who in turn is more real, by virtue of the narrative structure itself, than John Shade.

But the central paradox is pursued deep into the recessed interior of the novel. Kinbote as Charles Xavier is a "Shakespearian" poet realizing his dreams, which are made to seem bolder, more exciting and revealing, than the drab stuff of everyday waking reality. And yet, Charles (or Kinbote as Charles) is also the prisoner of his dreams, painfully incapable of acting in fact by his very addiction to acting in imagination. Kinbote's homosexuality, as several critics have observed, provides an "inverted" image of the heterosexual Shade, but I think we should not rule out some psychological interest in the phenomenon on the part of Nabokov, for all his forays against Freud. There is, after all, a prominent element of narcissism in the homosexual (certainly in *this* homosexual), who can love only one or another variation of his own reflected physical image. If Kinbote-Charles embodies what Coleridge called the "esemplastic" power of the poetic imagination, he also illustrates the painfully narcissistic side of the poet, unable to make contact at the most crucial moments with something outside of and different in kind from himself.

This whole aspect of the fantasied King is most vividly evident in the unconsummated relationship with his Queen. Her full name is Paradisa, but she is only Disa to him, the paradise from which his own nature excludes him. The interesting point made is that Charles is far from indifferent to Disa. He is sensitive enough to feel her frustrated love for him, and he would like to love her, actually does love her as a kind of repeated interior gesture, a wishful imagining. Whenever he is confronted, however, with her flesh-and-blood presence, the real fact of her otherness as woman, he hastily withdraws into his safe circle of pliant boys.

The most revealing moment in this process comes in his last meeting with her, at her Riviera villa, after his flight into exile. "He was, had always been," the King thinks back on his relationship with his wife, "casual and heartless. But the heart of his dreaming self, both before and after the rupture, made extraordinary amends" (p. 209). Nabokov, though at times troubled or intrigued by the idea of solipsism, is finally an antisolipsist, and here, as in Humbert's treatment of Lolita, he clearly sees that one's dreams, however beautiful, may make someone else their helpless victim if they are one's only chart to a human reality that is, after all, peopled by many souls, each with its own needs and prerogatives. Kinbote broadens the implications of the observed contradiction by immediately going on to talk of dreams as poetry: "These heart-rending dreams transformed the drab prose of his feelings for her into strong and strange poetry, subsiding undulations of which would flash and disturb him throughout the day, bringing back the pang and the richness—and then only the pang, and then only its glancing reflection—but not affecting at all his attitude toward the real Disa." The movement of undulations, flashing and diminishing reflections, returns us to the dapple-and-ringle play of Ripple-

son's mirrors and thus to the structure of the novel as
a whole, so the scope of the critical judgment expressed
reaches to the limits of *Pale Fire*'s world, where a "reality"
of strong and strange poetry is elaborately constructed
as a means of evading reality. The dialectic swing here
from thesis to antithesis is even translated into the
rhythms of the prose. As the sentence describes the king's
dreamworld of poetry, it catches us up poetically in a
pronounced rhythm that deftly imitates the process described—subsiding undulations and fading reflections.
Then, after the second dash, there is a break from the
mimetic music to a plain prose-rhythm which reveals the
unadorned truth beyond Charles's private poem, that none
of this passionate dreaming affected the King's attitude
toward the real Disa.

This contradiction between dream and reality is concen-
trated in what might be described as an anti-epiphany,
a moment of seeming revelation that proves to be a
moment of revealing delusion. The King, bidding his wife
a last farewell, holds her in his arms at her request, feeling
her as "a limp, shivering ragdoll." Then he begins to walk
off from the villa. On an impulse, he turns to look back
toward Disa, a "white figure with the listless grace of
ineffable grief" seen in the distance bending over a garden
table, "and suddenly a fragile bridge was suspended between waking indifference and dream-love." But the bridge
is more than tenuous, it is illusory: for the addiction to
dreams is not so easily broken, and he who regards life
from a distance, always through an interior prism, as the
King regards Disa, as Kinbote peering through windows
and blinds regards Shade, is apt to fall prey to optical
illusion. The bending figure moves, "and he saw it was
not at all she but poor Fleur de Fyler collecting the
documents left among the tea things" (p. 214).

The poignancy of this moment when the spell of the
dream breaks illustrates how a fiction focused on the

dynamic of fiction-making can address itself not merely to the paradoxes of the writer's craft but to the ambiguities of the human condition. *Pale Fire* is, I would contend, finally a philosophic novel in the same sense one can apply the term to Diderot and Sterne: its principal concern, moving through literature beyond literature, is with how each individual mind filters reality, recreates it, and with the moral quandaries generated by that problematic of epistemology. In the metaparodistic form of this novel, moreover, as of *Lolita*, Nabokov has overcome the weakness to which his earliest fiction—like *King, Queen, Knave* or *The Eye*—tends of producing characters who are too much *fantouches*, mere manipulated puppets. Of the cast of characters here, at least Kinbote, John Shade, Hazel Shade, and Disa have enough interiority, enough seeming autonomy as "living" figures, to engage us as more than ingenious fabrications, to reflect in the bizarrely cut facets of their existence the contradictions of our own.

In a way, *Pale Fire* is the most sober of Nabokov's involuted fictions. Both his novels on totalitarian states, *Invitation to a Beheading* and *Bend Sinister*, end by breaking through a hole in the fictional fabric from a world that has become a death trap to the artist's serene realm of freedom. In *Pale Fire*, on the other hand, the splendid edifice of poetic illusion is more seriously undercut by an exposure of the perils of involvement in such illusion, and the very end of the novel zigzags between artifice and reality and alternative artifice in a manner that allows no clear way out. "My notes and self are petering out," Kinbote tells us at the beginning of the third paragraph from the end, yet he and the terrors of his world are not simply cast aside as a used-up fictional hypothesis. He does, to be sure, intimate that he could become Vladimir Nabokov,[5] on the other side of the fictional fabric, or that

---

[5] See Chapter 1, pp. 17-18.

he might direct and act in another kind of fiction, a swashbuckling film to be called *Escape from Zembla*. He also offers a final hint of the "real" plot of *Pale Fire* by imagining he might devise a melodramatic play in which one lunatic (Jack Grey) pursuing another lunatic (Kinbote) accidentally kills a poet. But, most instructively, the concluding moment of the novel belongs to Gradus, or rather, to Kinbote's vision of "a bigger, more respectable, more competent Gradus," moving steadily across the map toward his victim with sudden death in his bulging pocket. The circuit of fictional illusion, just broken, is resumed at the very end as Kinbote's paranoia once more asserts itself: the last voice we hear is again, clearly and urgently, the voice of the hunted King. The fantasies of the fictional character Kinbote, however, also show a troubling correspondence to historical fact, weirdly refracted but also startlingly focused through the prism of art. *Pale Fire*, written after half a century of violent revolution, world war, totalitarian terror, and the genocidal slaughter of millions—an epidemic of barbarity profoundly shaking the personal life of the novelist—is very much a self-conscious novel of our times. Its display of the writer's blue magic of word-and-image play is a dazzling delight; its affirmation of the abiding beauty of life in the imagination is brilliantly enacted in the fiction; but after the last glitter of the prestidigitator's implements, it is the shadow of the assassin that falls on the final page.

There is, however, still one more dialectical turn in the paradoxical interplay between fiction and reality. Gradus's grim name occupies the very last moment of the main consecutive narrative, but it is the Index that actually completes the book, and that ends with the words, "*Zembla*, a distant northern land," taking us away from the stalking killer and the politics of terror back into the mists

among them, or to them from their common predecessors, often tend to waver and blur when closely examined. Some of these writers have tried their hand at shorter fictional forms, which, after the Borgesian model, one now calls "fictions" rather than "short stories"; but most of them, perhaps inevitably, have turned back to, or stayed with, the novel, attracted by its large and various capacity to convey a whole imaginatively constituted world. Scattered over three continents, they are an odd mixture of stubbornly private eccentrics, on the one hand, and promulgators of manifestoes, on the other; of powerfully evocative novelists or conductors of ingenious laboratory experiments in fiction; of exuberant comic artists and knowing guides to bleak dead ends of despair.

This mode of fiction is variously practiced by such diverse figures as Raymond Queneau, Samuel Beckett, Alain Robbe-Grillet, Michel Butor, Claude Mauriac in France; John Fowles in England; Robert Coover, John Barth, Thomas Pynchon, Donald Bartheleme, Kurt Vonnegut in this country; Borges and Julio Cortázar in Latin America; and, of course, Nabokov, perched on his height in Switzerland, working out of three literary cultures. The whole reflexive tendency in contemporary fiction has been reinforced by the prominence of self-conscious cinema since the early sixties in the work of directors like Fellini, Antonioni, Resnais, and Godard. Film, because it is a collaborative artistic enterprise involving a complicated chain of technical procedures, almost invites attention to its constitutive processes; and there is a clear logic in the involvement in film-making of several of the French New Novelists, or in the repeated recourse to cinematic composition by *montage* in a writer like Robert Coover. The close parallels between what is happening now in the two media suggest that the self-consciousness of both may reflect a heightened new stage of modern culture's general

commitment to knowing all that can be known about its
own components and dynamics. Our culture, a kind of
Faust at the mirror of Narcissus, is more and more driven
to uncover the roots of what it lives with most basically—
language and its origins, human sexuality, the workings
of the psyche, the inherited structures of the mind, the
underlying patterns of social organization, the sources of
value and belief, and, of course, the nature of art.

If this is the moment of the self-conscious novel, that
is decidedly a mixed blessing, as the spectacular une-
venness of innovative fiction today would indicate. The
growing insistence of self-awareness in our culture at large
has been both a liberating and a paralyzing force, and
that is equally true of its recent developments in artistic
expression. In this regard, criticism must be especially
wary. The kind of criticism that often has to be invoked
in discussing a traditional realistic novel is in the indicative
mode: yes, we know that a woman like Rosamund Vincy
would act in just that way, with just such a gesture, toward
her husband at a given moment in *Middlemarch* because
it *seems* right, because it corresponds to some subtle,
gradually acquired sense of human nature in our extra-
literary experience, and to this we can only point, signal-
ing an act of recognition we hope others will share. Most
self-conscious novels, on the other hand, lend themselves
splendidly to analytic criticism because they operate by
the constant redeployment of fiction's formal categories.
Is the critic interested in the narrative manipulation of
time, the arbitrariness of narrative beginnings, the writer's
awareness of literary conventions, the maneuvering of
language to produce multiple meanings, the expressive
possibilities of punctuation, paragraphing, typography? It
is all laid out for him across the printed pages of *Tristram
Shandy*, ready to be analytically described, with no apparent need for recourse to a touchstone of "rightness" outside
this and other literary texts. For this reason an astute

critic, impelled by his own professional concern with formal experiment, can easily make a piece of self-conscious fiction sound more profound, more finely resonant with implication, than it is in fact. None of Robbe-Grillet's novels really equals in fascination Roland Barthes's brilliant descriptions of them. Queneau's *Exercices de style* (1947) is an intriguing and at times immensely amusing book, but it is just what its title implies, a set of exercises, and to suggest, as George Steiner has done, that it constitutes a major landmark in twentieth-century literature, is to mislead readers in the interest of promoting literary future-shock.

The instance of *Exercices de style* is worth pausing over briefly because it represents one ultimate limit of the whole self-conscious mode. Queneau begins his book by reporting a banal anecdote of a young man with a long neck and a missing button on his coat who is jostled in a crowded bus. He tells this anecdote ninety-nine times, constantly changing the narrative viewpoint, the style, the literary conventions, going as far as the use of mathematical notation and anagrammatic scrambling of letters, in one direction, and the resort to heavy dialect and badly Anglicized French, in the other, even rendering the incident in alexandrines, in free verse, as a sonnet, as a playlet. All this is extremely ingenious, and, I would admit, more than ingenious, because as one reads the same simple episode over and over through all these acrobatic variations, one is forced to recognize both the stunning arbitrariness of any decision to tell a story in a particular way and the endless possibilities for creating fictional "facts" by telling a story differently.

The controlling perception, however, of *Exercices* is one that goes back to the generic beginnings of the novel, as I hope this study has shown; and to see how much more richly that insight can be extended into fictional space, one has only to think of Sterne, where a "Queneauesque"

passage like the deliberately schematic Tale of Two Lovers
(7:31), which we have examined, is woven into a thick
texture of amorous anecdotes that critically juxtaposes
literary convention with a sense of the erotic as a cogent
fact of human experience. Precisely what is missing from
Exercices de style is any serious sense—and playfulness
need not exclude seriousness—of human experience, which
is largely kept out of the book in order to preserve the
technical purity of the experiment. I do not mean to take
Queneau to task for what he clearly did not intend; I
mean only to emphasize that criticism need not make
excessive claims for this kind of writing. Queneau, of
course, has written full-scale novels of flaunted artifice,
both before and after *Exercices de style*, that do involve
a more complex sense of experience. One of the great
temptations, however, of the self-conscious novelist is to
content himself with technical experiment, trusting that
in these difficult times (but then the times are always
difficult) the only honesty, perhaps the only real profun-
dity, lies in technical experiment. This is the chief limiting
factor in most of Robbe-Grillet as well as in Coover's
collection of fictions, *Pricksongs and Descants*. In both,
one can admire the virtuosity with which narrative materials are ingeniously shuffled and reshuffled yet feel a
certain aridness; for the partial magic of the novelist's
art, however self-conscious, is considerably more than a
set of card tricks.

The other, complementary fault of the self-conscious
novel, also much in evidence among its contemporary
practitioners, is to give free rein to every impulse of
invention or fictional contrivance without distinguishing
what may serve some artistic function in the novel and
what is merely silly or self-indulgent. After all, if in an
old-fashioned novel you have to describe a petulant,
spoiled young woman like Rosamund Vincy, you are

obliged to make her as close a likeness as you can to observed examples of the type, and so some commonly perceived human reality provides a constant check on your inventiveness. If, on the other hand, you are writing a novel about a novelist who invents still another novelist who is the author of bizarrely far-fetched books, there is scarcely any piece of fabrication, however foolish or improbable, that you could not put into your novel if you set your mind to it. The Irish writer Flann O'Brien, in one of the earliest postmodern novels of flaunted artifice, *At Swim-Two-Birds* (1939), has devised just such a book. The second-remove novelist invented by the first-person narrator novelist gives birth to a full-grown man (that is, a new character), but while this writer fatigued with parturition is asleep, his characters rebel against him, resenting the roles he has assigned them. In the end, they subject him to the most hideous torture and maiming, recounted in detail for page after page—by writing chapters of a novel (within the novel-within-the-novel) in which he suffers these horrors. This scheme of recessed narratives also involves an amalgam of different kinds of fiction, starting with domestic realism in the frame story, and running through the gun-slinging Western and the novel of erotic sensationalism to fairy tales and Irish myth.

"A satisfactory novel," the young writer who is the narrator tries to explain to a friend at the outset, "should be a self-evident sham to which the reader could regulate at will the degree of his credulity."[1] At first glance, this might seem a perfect capsule definition of the self-conscious novel, but upon consideration the formulation makes it too easy for both the writer and the reader. If one thinks of the history of the self-conscious novel from its early masters down to Gide, to the parodistic or overtly

[1] O'Brien, *At Swim-Two-Birds* (New York: Pantheon, 1939), p. 33.

contrived sections in Joyce and the Nabokov of *Lolita*
and *Pale Fire*, "sham" becomes far too crude and demean-
ing as a synonym for artifice or imaginative contrivance.
The artifice, moreover, should not be flatly "self-evident"
but cunningly revealed, a hide-and-seek presence in the
novel, a stubbornly ambiguous substratum of the whole
fictional world. To imagine, then, the reader regulating
his credulity at will is to reverse the whole process of the
self-conscious novel, where it is the writer who tries to
regulate the reader's credulity, challenging him to active
participation in pondering the status of fictional things,
forcing him as he reads on to examine again and again
the validity of his ordinary discriminations between art
and life and how they interact.

Flann O'Brien, however, following the formula he attributes to his own protagonist, in fact produces a hodgepodge
of fictions where nothing seems particularly credible and
where everything finally becomes tedious through the
sheer proliferation of directionless narrative invention. *At
Swim-Two-Birds* is a celebration of fabulation in which
novelistic self-consciousness has gone slack because fiction
is everywhere and there is no longer any quixotic tension
between what is fictional and what is real. I am not aware
that it has influenced later books, but it has certainly
proved to be a novel ahead of its time, for its faults of
conception and execution provide a perfect paradigm for
those of much contemporary fiction, especially in this
country, where a new literary ideology of fabulation has
too often turned out to mean license, not liberty, for the
novelist. In reading many of the voguish new writers, one
is frequently tempted to invoke the words of the narrator
at the end of John Barth's story, "Title": "Oh God comma
I abhor self-consciousness."

Those inclined to argue that the novel today is in a
grave state of decay often draw evidence from the current

popularity of self-conscious fiction, which they tend to see as a dwarfed offspring of the modernist giants, turned away from life, dedicated to the onanistic gratifications of the artist pleasured by his own art. It would of course be foolish to claim that we are now in anything like that extraordinary period of innovative literary creativity of the 1920s when modernism was in flower, but the opposite inference, that narrative literature has reached some terminal stage of sterility, is by no means a necessary one from the facts of contemporary writing. I have dwelt upon the two chief temptations of the self-conscious novelist—arid exercise and indiscriminate invention—precisely because they should be recognized as dangers, not taken as the inevitable results whenever a writer determines artfully to expose the fictiveness of his fiction. In fact, the prominent flaunting of artifice has led to some of the most impressive successes in the contemporary novel as well as to some of its most evident lapses, and the successes are by no means restricted to elder statesmen like Beckett and Nabokov. (In America, one might mention Barth, who in different books has been an impressively original writer as well as an embarrassingly puerile one, or Coover, who has gone beyond manipulations of technique to a vividly imagined satire where fantasy and reality enrich one another.) The old question of the death of the novel, which seems as doggedly persistent as the novel itself, is in the air again, and I believe an understanding of the self-conscious tradition in the novel which stands behind many contemporary novelists may help set that hazy issue in clearer perspective.

One of the newly prominent American novelists, John Barth, has himself given a new twist to the death-of-the-novel argument in a widely read essay first published in 1967, "The Literature of Exhaustion."[2] Barth settles on

[2] *The Atlantic Monthly*, August 1967, pp. 29-34.

Borges, Beckett, and Nabokov as his exemplary figures
to expose the condition of narrative literature now, and
that condition as he describes it proves to be thoroughly
contradictory—apocalyptic and elegiac, at the end of an
ultimate cultural cul-de-sac yet somehow reaching toward
exciting new possibilities. The "exhaustion" of the title
is defined as "the used-upness of certain forms or exhaustion of certain possibilities," and the work of Borges is
taken to be the clearest model of this contemporary
literature of exhaustion. The Argentine writer "suggests
the view," according to Barth, "that intellectual and
literary history . . . has pretty well exhausted the possibilities of novelty. His *ficciones* are not only footnotes to
imaginary texts, but postscripts to the real corpus of
literature." The characterization of Borges' fiction is
memorable, and not without cogency, but Barth has
worked himself into a corner by following Borges in this
fashion, and he is constrained to use the last two paragraphs of his essay in a rapid maneuver to get out of the
trap. For even if reality has come to resemble for the writer
the library of a Borgesian fable where all the books that
can ever be written already exist, even if Borges' Pierre
Menard is an emblem of the modern writer's wry destiny,
"creating" the *Quixote* by laboriously reconstituting it
word for word in a version identical verbatim with Cervantes'—Barth himself nevertheless writes novels which he
hopes have some novelty, and he is not willing to dismiss
the literature of our age as a mere postscript to a completed
corpus.

   Now, two paragraphs are not much space to get out
of such a quandary, so Barth resorts to a kind of literary
intervention of divine grace: confronted with a labyrinthine reality of exhausted possibilities, the writer of genius
finally can rely on his genius to achieve the impossible,
to create a new literature when there is nothing left to
create. "It's the chosen remnant, the virtuoso, the Thesean

hero, who ... with the aid of *very special* gifts ... [can] go straight through the maze to the accomplishment of his work." (The italics are Barth's.) This strikes me as a peculiarly elitist and miraculist notion of literary continuity and renewal. Good writing has of course always required gifted writers. Now, however, Barth seems to be saying, we have come to such a pass that it is virtually impossible to write anything at all. Nevertheless, a few geniuses, having recognized that difficult task, will somehow manage to create.

Borges himself, as we shall see, is far from agreeing with this idea, but in any case the choice of Borges as the paradigmatic postmodernist is in one respect misleading precisely because Borges the prose-writer is an inventor of parables and paradoxes, not a novelist. That is, Borges of the *ficciones* is concerned with a series of metaphysical enigmas about identity, recurrence, and cyclicality, time, thought, and extension, and so it is a little dangerous to translate his haunting fables into allegories of the postmodern literary situation. Books, real and imaginary, and books about books, of course figure very prominently in Borges' fictions, but he is after all a remarkably bookish man, and the contents of a library are the aptest vehicle he could have chosen for writing about knowledge and its limits, the ambiguous relation between idea and existence, language and reality, and many of his other favorite philosophical puzzles. The fact that Borges is a fabulist, not a novelist, hardly suggests that the fable is all there remains for fiction to work with now. Were he a novelist, his prototypical protagonist would not be a meditative wraith wandering through the hexagonal mazes of the infinite Library of Babel, but a man or woman—one glimpses the possibility in his most recent stories—with a distinctive psychology living among other men and women, acting against a background of social values, personal and national history. Such a figure, it seems safe to assume, would have a rather different relationship to the written word, past and present, than does the inhabitant of the great Library or the assiduous Pierre Menard.

Borges, it should be noted, has argued trenchantly against the whole idea of exhausting artistic possibilities in a brief essay, "A Note on (toward) Bernard Shaw"[3]— which, not surprisingly, is hardly at all about Shaw. He begins with a list of fanciful notions from the thirteenth century to the twentieth of combinational reservoirs that would encompass all books, systems of ideas, or artworks. One of these, "the staggering fantasy" spun out by the nineteenth-century popularizer of science Kurd Lasswitz "of a universal library which would register all the variations of the twenty-odd orthographical symbols, in other words, all that is given to express in all languages," is nothing less than the scheme of Borges' "The Library of Babel." But, he immediately goes on to say, such writers, by reducing art and philosophy to "a kind of play with combinations," forget that a book is not a flat, fixed entity composed of combined letters making an unchanging design in language. Every book exists through a collaborative effort with the imagination of each of its readers—the controlling idea of *Pale Fire* is not a trivial one—and so it changes with its readers, with their life experience and their accrued reading experience. Literary tradition, in other words, does not and cannot exist as a mass of determined data in the memory bank of a computer. "Literature is not exhaustible, for the sufficient and simple reason that no single book is." The more books that are written, the more complicated with meaning are the books that exist before them, and the more possibilities there are for creating new works out of old books and new experience.

[3] Borges, *Labyrinths*, ed. Yates and Irby (New York: New Directions, 1964), pp. 213-216.

Nothing could demonstrate this more forcefully than the inherently allusive structure of the novel as a genre. *Don Quixote* becomes more than it initially was after its transmutation into the "Cervantick" *Tom Jones* and *Tristram Shandy,* after *The Red and the Black, Madame Bovary, Moby-Dick, Ulysses,* and *The Castle.* Each successive creation—to follow the implicit logic of Borges' plausible notion about a book's existence—does not foreclose future possibilities but rather opens up new vistas for creation out of the common literary tradition. A book is not an integer but "a relationship, an axis of innumerable relationships" which of course grow with the passage of historical time and literary history; and so "The Library of Babel" must be, after all, a metaphysician's nightmare, not a novelist's.

But let us return to the relation Barth proposes between Borges' own practice in his *ficciones* and the foreseeable possibilities of imaginative writing. Without begrudging Borges the general acclaim he has recently received, both in America and in France, I think one may resist the implication of Barth and others that he represents the future of fiction. Robert Coover, although he does not mention Borges by name, seems to have an idea of this sort in mind when he takes up where Barth's essay left off in his *Dedicatoria y Prólogo a don Miguel de Cervantes Saavedra,* the bilingual preface to his "Seven Exemplary Fictions."[4] Unlike Barth, Coover applies the notion of exhaustion not to literary forms but to a general contemporary sense of reality and to the whole legacy of cultural values today: "But *don* Miguel, the optimism, the innocence, the aura of possibility you have experienced have been largely drained away, and the universe is closing in on us again. Like you, we, too, seem to be standing at the end of one age and on the threshold of another. . . .

---

[4] Coover, *Pricksongs and Descants* (New York: E. P. Dutton, 1969), pp. 76-79.

We, too, suffer from a 'literature of exhaustion.'" A quiet version of apocalyptic thinking is very much in evidence here. We love to think we are on the threshold of a radically new era, but in fact the continuity of much of contemporary fiction with its literary antecedents is too substantive to be dismissed as mere vestigial reflex. Contemporary novelists resemble Cervantes (as Coover recognizes further on) because of the underlying operations of their imaginative enterprise, not because our historical moment parallels his in marking the beginning of a new age, while the proposed contrast between Cervantes and the contemporaries seems overdrawn. The least innocent of writers, Cervantes ironically undercuts the innocence and optimism of his hero, and through the strategies he devises for doing that he invents the novel. In any event, Coover goes on to argue from the supposed draining away of optimism in our age the conversion of the novelist to fabulist:

> We seem to have moved from an open-ended, anthropocentric, humanistic, naturalistic, even—to the extent that man may be thought of as making his own universe—optimistic starting point, to one that is closed, cosmic, eternal, supernatural (in its soberest sense), and pessimistic. The return to Being has returned us to Design, to microcosmic images of the macrocosm, to the creation of Beauty within the confines of cosmic or human necessity, to the use of the fabulous to probe beyond the phenomenological, beyond appearances, beyond randomly perceived events, beyond mere history.

Some judgments it may be wise on principle to decline making at all, and I see no way of knowing at this point in history whether we are in fact witnessing the death of the humanistic world view. To base an argument for a new form of fiction on such a sweepingly prophetic historical assertion must in the end compromise the persuasiveness of the literary argument. In any case, of Barth's three exemplars of the literature of exhaustion, only one, Borges, really corresponds to this description of Coover's. In regard to Beckett, all that strictly applies is the pessimism and the sense of a closed universe, and it is Nabokov who once tartly observed that "cosmic" is but a slippery 's' away from "comic." Both Beckett and Nabokov are by intention, in their radically different ways, comic rather than cosmic writers; both are novelists rather than fabulists in their concern with the naturalistic textures of experience, whatever various structures they make of them. Both resemble Cervantes in deriving Design not from an image of eternal Being but, on the contrary, from a sense of the contradictions between traditional literary practice and their immediate perception of human reality.

The most questionable of Coover's claims, however, is that the writer of fiction is now moving "beyond mere history." Borges the fabulist does just that, but unless the novel is really dead, the one thing it ultimately cannot dispense with is history. The pressing actuality of historical time, or of an individual lifetime, or of both, is the stuff of all good novels, including self-conscious ones, the perennial subject that the medium of the novel—a sequential narrative use of unmetrical language extended at length in time—seems almost to require. Cervantes initiates the genre by using parody and the translation of literary criticism into narrative invention to juxtapose a literary dream of a Golden Age with real historical time. On the plane of individual experience, Sterne in his ultimate self-conscious novel makes time so much his subject that the printed text becomes a maze of intersecting, mutually modifying times—the time of writing and the time of reading, the actual duration of an event, time as a literary construct, time as an ambiguous artifact of memory or consciousness.

Perhaps the most reliable index to whether a piece of self-conscious fiction is closed off from life is whether it tends to diminish the actuality of personal and historical time. Queneau's *exercices* are only exercises precisely because time does not really exist in them; it is only a necessary hypothesis to move the skinny young man from the beginning of the anecdote to the end. Robbe-Grillet's cinematic use of the present indicative, together with his constant shuffling of versions of each narrative incident in order to destroy all sense of causal sequence and of time, is a technical *tour de force* precisely because it goes so strenuously against the grain of the medium, which is, after all, prose fiction, not film. As a result the virtuosity of his achievement is inseparable from its marked limitations. The same could be said of the composition by *montage* in Coover's shorter fiction, or, on a cruder level of technical skill and imagination, of Bartheleme's satirical collages. It is instructive, however, that Coover should now be working on a novel involved with public events in the Eisenhower years, a book he describes as "an historical romance," and to judge by a published section, his reentry into history, cannily seen through the revealing distortions of fantasy, can produce energetically engaging fiction.

In the case of Robbe-Grillet, the one really striking success among his novels is the book in which his ubiquitous technique of suppressing temporal progression has a powerful psychological justification. *Jealousy* is a compelling novel precisely because its imprisonment in a present indicative that circles back on itself again and again is the perfect narrative mode for a man whose consuming obsession has robbed him of any time in which things can unfold. The jealous husband, always the excluded observer peering at his wife and her supposed lover from oblique angles through a hatchwork of screens and obstacles, can only go over and over the same scanty data, reordering them and surrounding them with conjecture, describing them with a seemingly scientific objectivity that is actually quite maniacal. Consequently, what is often felt elsewhere in Robbe-Grillet as an anomalous mannerism is here firmly grounded in the novel's peculiar facts of character and fictional situation.

Queneau's *Exercices de style*, as I intimated earlier, is a limited experiment that explores the most extreme possibilities of an underlying practice of his novels while deliberately omitting what is ultimately most essential to them—the potent force of time, analogous to the time of real experience, that sweeps along the imaginary personages and events. Over against *Exercices* one might usefully set a novel like *Le Chiendent* (1933), Queneau's remarkable fictional farce in the self-conscious mode. At the center of this grand display of verbal highjinks, parodistic ploys, hilarious stylizations, and satiric illuminations, stands a death, that of Ernestine the serving-girl, which, for all its abruptness, improbability, and absurdity, has large reverberations in the novel. "When a tree burns," says Ernestine, dying on her wedding-night, "nothin's left but smoke and ashes. No more tree. That's like me. Nothin left but rot, while the li'l voice that talks in your head when you're all alone, nothin's left of it. When mine stops, it ain't gonna talk again nowhere else."[5]

The last section of *Le Chiendent* takes off on a zanily fantastic extrapolation from destructive modern history. At the very end, three of the protagonists, among the handful of survivors of a long bitter war between the French and the Etruscans (!), meet again and openly share the awareness that all their actions have been relentlessly

[5] Queneau, *Le Chiendent* (Paris, Gallimard, 1933), p. 206.

tracked down and recorded in a book—the one we have
been reading and are about to finish. Not pleased with
all they have done, they wonder whether it might be
possible to erase—*raturer*—or rather "literase"—*littéra-
turer*—certain episodes. But, no, the thing cannot be done:
as one of them observes, even in these literary circumstances, "time is time, the past is the past." Then, in a
final paragraph, Queneau dissolves his joined characters
into separate and unconnected entities, concluding with
a single silhouette, not yet a realized character, one among
thousands of possible alternatives—which was precisely the
image of the novelist-artificer's arbitrary choice in the
making of fictions that began the whole novel. And yet
the arbitrary invention is one that has been elaborated
in order to reveal something about the real world. The
whole farce is in fact a sustained metaphysical meditation
on the dizzying paradoxes of being and nonbeing, in life
and in fiction; and that meditation culminates in these
last two pages, where the characters are finally shuffled
back into the shadowy preworld of fictional beginnings
but are not allowed the more-than-human luxury of re-
versing, altering, or erasing the particular experiences they
have lived out in the time allotted to them.

It may seem a bit odd to insist on a connection with
historical or personal time in a kind of novel devised to
mirror its own operations, but the contradiction, I think,
disappears upon close consideration. Language, as we have
had occasion to observe in connection with Nabokov, is
of all art media the one most thoroughly and subtly
steeped in memory, both public and private. It is not easy
to use language variously and richly for the length of a
novel, out of a self-conscious awareness of its function as
the medium of the fictional artifice, without in some way
confronting the burden of a collective or individual past
that language carries. Language through its layer upon
layer of associations opens up complex vistas of time, and

these tend to reveal—ultimately for cultures, imminently for individuals—loss, decline, and extinction. The continuous acrobatic display of artifice in a self-conscious novel is an enlivening demonstration of human order against a background of chaos and darkness, and it is the tension between artifice and that which annihilates artifice that gives the finest self-conscious novels their urgency in the midst of play. Tristram Shandy's wild flight from death across the pages of Volume 7 in Sterne's novel provides the clearest paradigm for this general situation. In the two major novelists of our own century who magisterially combine the realist and self-conscious traditions of the novel, Joyce and Proust, it is again death and the decline of culture into ultimate incoherence that powerfully impel the writers to the supreme affirmation of art. The void looms beyond Bloom's Dublin and Marcel's Paris, as it does beyond Biely's St. Petersburg, Virginia Woolf's London, and the invented lost realms of Nabokov; and that is why art is indispensable.

Perhaps this may make every novel with self-conscious aspects sound like a version of Sartre's *Nausea*, but that is only because Sartre provides an emphatically defined, programmatic formulation of the general pattern. What I would like to stress is that even a novel worlds away from any intimation of existentialist views may tap this tension between the coherence of the artifice and the death and disorder implicit in real time outside the artifice. The tension is present even in Fielding, with his fine old eighteenth-century confidence in the possibilities of coherent order and his meticulous preservation of the purity of the comic world. An example may be helpful here. In Book 5, Chapter 12, of *Tom Jones*, after a bloody brawl in which Tom has laid Blifil low only to be vigorously battered by the redoubtable Thwackum, the narrator, surveying the bruised combatants, takes off on one of his so-called essayistic excursuses:

Here we cannot suppress a pious wish, that all quarrels were to be decided by those weapons only with which Nature, knowing what is proper for us, hath supplied us; and that cold iron was to be used in digging no bowels but those of the earth. Then would war, the pastime of monarchs, be almost inoffensive, and battles between great armies might be fought at the particular desire of several ladies of quality; who, together with the kings themselves, might be actual spectators of the conflict. Then might the field be this moment well strewed with human carcasses, and the next, the dead men, or infinitely the greatest part of them, might get up, like Mr. Bayes's troops, and march off either at the sound of a drum or fiddle, as should be previously agreed on.

The narrator spins out this fanciful hypothesis for another paragraph, then brings himself up short: "But such reformations are rather to be wished than hoped for: I shall content myself, therefore, with this short hint, and return to my narrative." What is all this doing in the middle of *Tom Jones*? To dismiss it as mere casual banter or extraneous digression is to ignore the integrity of Fielding's art and of his vision of life. The passage is a virtuoso aria set in the optative mode. It turns from *The History of Tom Jones* to history proper, but with a series of careful indications of a condition contrary to fact. It begins and ends with an explicit stress on "wish," and all the verbs are subjunctive or conditional. The emphasis through anaphora on "then" ("Then would war . . ."; "Then might the field be . . .") points to an era that exists not now or soon but in the imagination alone. This condition is underlined by likening the weaponless battles to those of a popular Restoration farce, *The Rehearsal* ("Mr. Bayes's troops"), and by proposing that war should be conducted like theatrical convention, by previously agreed-upon signals.

Within the comic frame of *Tom Jones*'s fictional world, we know very well that no fate much worse than a bloodied nose will be allowed to befall any of the personages who matter. Fielding, by proposing for the space of two paragraphs that this frame be extended into real historical time, is doing something more than make a suggestion for "reformation," as he pretends, or a satirical comment on historical man's irrationality, as is evident. What the excursion into optative history points up is that the whole comic world of the fiction is beautifully arranged, sanely humane in its essential playfulness—and ultimately unreal. The age-old impulse of the storyteller bespeaks a basic human need to imagine out of history a fictional order of fulfillment, but when the narrative is a novel and not a fairy tale, one is also made aware of the terrible persistance of history as a murderous realm of chaos constantly challenging or violating the wholeness that art can imagine. By the time we arrive at the narrator's explicit signal for the end of the excursus, "I shall content myself . . . with this short hint, and return to my narrative," we see with renewed clarity all that stands outside the artful narrative, inimical to it.

I have chosen from many possible texts, old and new, an example from Fielding in order to emphasize certain underlying continuities of concern between the novelists of our own age and the early masters. A clearer recognition of such continuities, which more often than one would suspect manifest themselves even on the level of fictional technique, might make us less inclined to see ourselves at the decisive end of an era, our writers footnoting with fables a literary corpus that has used up all the possibilities of primary creation. Looking over the actual production of living novelists in both hemispheres, I find it hard to believe that it is inherently more difficult to write a good novel now than in earlier periods. The realist mode of

fiction that attained such splendid achievements in the
nineteenth century may by now largely have run its course
(though that, too, might be a presumptuous conclusion),
but the self-conscious novelistic dialectic between art and
reality initiated by Cervantes seems abundantly alive with
new possibilities of expression, perhaps even more than
ever before as the self-consciousness of our whole culture
becomes progressively more pronounced. To write a good
self-conscious novel today one does not have to be a unique
"Thesean hero" finding a way out of some impossible
labyrinth, but simply an intelligent writer with a serious
sense both of the integrity of his craft and of the inevitably
problematic relationship between fiction and life.

A case in point is Claude Mauriac's *The Marquise Went
Out at Five* (1961), one of the most interesting novels to
come out of the fervor of fictional experiment in France
during the past fifteen or so years. Mauriac's book might
be especially instructive as a concluding example because
in both its design and its execution it ties up many of
the major themes we have been considering, and because
Mauriac, a gifted writer but surely no Borgesian wonder-
worker defying the limits of nature, achieves what he does
not through impossible genius but simply by an imaginative and keenly critical management of the self-conscious
mode.

The Marquise Went Out is the third of four interlocking
novels aptly called *Le Dialogue intérieur*. The title of the
novel is taken from Breton's "First Surrealist Manifesto,"
the relevant passage appearing as the epigraph. Breton
quotes Valéry on the imbecilic beginnings of most novels.
Valéry would never permit himself, he once told Breton,
to write a sentence like, "The Marquise went out at five."
We then turn the page of Mauriac's novel and of course
find it begins, "*La Marquise sortit à cinq heures.* The
Marquise went out at five." At first, in the kaleidoscopic

shifting of interior monologues—perhaps a hundred different characters become posts of observation—with no indication of transitions, the reader has difficulty orienting himself; but gradually a fictional novelist, Bertrand Carnéjoux, emerges distinctly as the principal point of reference. As Carnéjoux stands at his window looking down over the Carrefour de Bucis where all the events of the novel take place, one begins to suspect that all the interior lives exposed in the book are finally what he, the writer as distanced observer, projects onto the figures he sees. He is the fictional writer acting out his author's own literary impulse, in a contemporary version of the old quixotic pattern, by making a novel out of the world he inhabits:

> ... Express the double brilliance, orangish red bright yellow, of the bouquets, no, they're potted plants. Add to these two patches of bright color the movement transporting them, not fast but jolting, and the black mass of that old lady carrying her nasturtiums—they are nasturtiums, I think. I'm no different as an author from all the authors who ever existed since men first began to write. Using other devices, but analogous ones. Making use just as fallaciously, as arbitrarily, of the world I claim—quite insanely—to possess. At best I've tried to explain and justify the increasing presence, considered ridiculous by some people, of writer-heroes in the works of writers. ...[6]

The sense of the writer's predicament as a perennial, not peculiarly modern, difficulty is notable: all serious novelists must confront the arbitrariness, the necessary falsification, of the worlds they invent through words. In his critical writings, Mauriac has coined the term *alittérature* to describe this intrinsic problematic of literature. All literary creation worthy of the name, now and in

[6] Mauriac, *The Marquise Went Out at Five*, tr. Richard Howard (New York: George Braziller, 1962), p. 69.

previous ages, is seen as a reaction against the inevitable falsity of antecedent literature, a restless devising of strategies to escape being "just" literature. I think the idea is more historically accurate than the notion of a contemporary literature of exhaustion, and *The Marquise Went Out at Five* is a persuasive demonstration of its efficacy as a rationale for the continual renewal of literature.

By the conclusion of the novel, Carnéjoux, the novelist as self-observing observer, imperceptibly gives way to the author of *The Marquise Went Out at Five.* The evoked world of fiction, revealed as fiction, shrivels up, and, as at the end of many of Nabokov's novels, the fabricator of the fiction himself stands in its place. Mauriac now describes precisely what he has given us: "A novelist animated by a novelist whom I (myself a novelist) have put into a novel in which, however, nothing was invented, a labyrinth of mirrors capturing some of life's sensations, feelings and thoughts" (p. 310). Cervantes' emblematic image of the mirror—it is of course also Nabokov's favorite—is complicated in Borgesian fashion by a labyrinth not because the old quixotic probing of reality through fiction has changed in nature, only because our sense of the complexity of the enterprise has been many times multiplied by both historical and literary experience. (One might observe that as early as 1913 Andrey Biely was using the image of the labyrinth of mirrors in *St. Petersburg.*) Mauriac, it should be noted, does not in the end make the facile gesture of some contemporary novelists who simply shrug off their own fictions as, after all, mere fictions: he avows the artifice but affirms it as a means of mirroring "life's sensations, feelings and thoughts," fiction seen perhaps as the only way to get at a whole range of real human experience.

After a paragraph of reflections on the Parisian square that has been the scene of the novel, Mauriac goes on

to summarize and make even more explicit this baring
of artifice as the basic procedure of his book: "Thus the
novel has in its penultimate pages gradually faded away,
and disappeared, without masks or make-believe, giving
way to the novelist who, if he has put himself directly
into his book, has at the end purified it of its last traces
of fiction by granting it a truth in which literal exactitude
was preferred to literature" (p. 311). The literal exactitude
is of course necessarily a pretense, still another novelistic
gesture (as Cervantes first shrewdly saw in his play with
supposed documents), literature passing itself off as *alittérature* in order not to seem "literature" in the pejorative
sense. In any case, the edifice of fiction that engaged our
thoughts and emotions for a good many hours has been
swept away, and the novel can conclude in the very next
sentence by setting on its head that beginning borrowed
from Valéry by way of Breton: "The Marquise did not
go out at five. ..." Much earlier, we learned that the
marquise of the initial sentence was no marquise at all,
and now the predicate as well as the subject is torn from
its apparent exactitude and cast into the shadowy realm
of fabrications.

All this might be mere cleverness if the novel did not
have the impelling sense it does of the urgency, the
philosophical seriousness, of its enterprise. What drives
Bertrand Carnéjoux, and behind him Claude Mauriac, is
an acute perception of two concentric abysses beneath the
artifice of the novel—history and death. *The Marquise
Went Out*, set between five and six on one warm afternoon
in a few thousand square feet of the Carrefour de Bucis,
attempts to exhaust the human experience intersecting
that carefully delimited time and place. But as Carnéjoux
and his inventor realize, such an undertaking is "doomed
to failure" because "the unity of actual time ... [is]
surrounded, penetrated, absorbed ... by the infinite pullu-

lation of innumerable past moments" (p. 270). Though
Mauriac explicitly compares the achronological method
of composition here through a long series of separate
"takes" with the methods of a film maker, the effect is
precisely the opposite of cinematic composition in Robbe-
Grillet because Mauriac accepts and works with the essentially time-soaked nature of language as a medium of art.

Each of the interior monologues gives us glimpses of
a deep tunnel into a private past, while Carnéjoux, overviewing the scene, weaves into the texture of the novel
substantial quotations from actual historical documents
of life in the Carrefour de Bucis from the middle of the
thirteenth century to the post-World-War-II era. The
documents reveal what in the poesy of a blurb one might
call a "vivid panorama" of Parisian existence from medieval artisans to activists of the Revolution to the literary
dinners of the Goncourt brothers. What is actually revealed, though, is the raw realm of chaos on the other
side of Fielding's ironic observations about history—a long
catalogue of rape, murder, torture, theft, perversion, bru-
tality. Contemplating these documents, Carnéjoux is simultaneously aware of the senselessness of history and
of the incomprehensible brevity of all human life. As he
writes, he is rapidly, irrevocably, rushing toward the point
where he will be no more than a few scratches on the
historical record, like Mestre Giles the tile maker and
Richart the baker, listed as residents of the Rue de Bussy
in the *Tax-Book of Paris for the Year 1292.* At the end,
the author draws particular attention to this perception:
"Bertrand Carnéjoux records in his novel, and I record
in the ,novel in which I have given life and speech to
Bertrand Carnéjoux, that impossibility of conceiving what
seems so natural in others, what one has spent one's life
fearing, knowing oneself ineluctably threatened by it in
the beings one loves and in oneself: death" (p. 309).

Some readers may feel that Mauriac is too explicitly direct in the way he reveals these fundamental matters of motive and design in the making of his novel, but the fiction itself bears out in concrete detail what otherwise might seem portentous assertion. A writer, about to vanish like every human being born, has only words to grasp with at some sort of tenuous, dubious permanence. Words console, words are the most wonderful of human evasions; but the writer, using them as truly as a writer of fiction can—which is to say, with a consciousness of how their enchantment transmutes reality into fiction—comes to perceive profoundly what words help us to evade. The seriousness and the ultimate realism of the novel that mirrors itself could have no more vivid demonstration.

Perhaps the most basic paradox of this mode of fiction which functions through the display of paradoxes is that as a kind of novel concentrating on art and the artist it should prove to be, even in many of its characteristically comic embodiments, a long meditation on death. Myth, folktale, fable, and romance, all the archaic forms of storytelling from which the novel was a radical historical break, overleap or sidestep death as an immediate presence in the timeless cyclicality of divine lives or in the teleological arc from "once upon a time" to "lived happily ever after." The great realist novels of the nineteenth century, though they may be filled with scenes of disease and dying, are in another sense also an implicit evasion of death because, as the paradigmatic instance of Balzac makes clear, behind the vast effort to represent in fiction a whole society, the spawning of novel after novel with crowds of personages overflowing from one book to the next, was a dream of omnipotence, the novelist creating a fantasy world so solid-seeming that he could rule over it like a god.

When the writer, on the other hand, places himself or

some consciously perceived surrogate within the fiction's field of probing consideration, his own mortality is more likely to be an implicit or even explicit subject of the novel. It was Diderot who observed that one should tell stories because then time passes swiftly and the story of life comes to an end unnoticed. The novel as a genre begins when Don Quixote, approaching the grand climacteric or fiftieth year, which was old age in his time, realizes that his existence has amounted to nothing and proceeds before it is too late to make his life correspond to a book. The knight's peculiarly literary quest is a revealing functional analogue to that of the novelist, the literary man who invented him, and so Cervantes is not merely mocking chivalric romances through the Don's adventures but contemplating, in the most oblique and searching way, the unthinkable prospect posed by his own imminent end.

I suspect that death in the novel might be a more useful focus for serious discussion of the genre than the death of the novel. What I have in mind is of course not the novelistic rendering of deathbed scenes but how the novel manages to put us in touch with the imponderable implications of human mortality through the very celebration of life implicit in the building of vivid and various fictions. This is the ultimate turn of the Copernican revolution in the making of fictions that Cervantes effected. The impulse of fabulation, which men had typically used to create an imaginary time beautifully insulated from the impinging presence of their own individual deaths, was turned back on itself, held up to a mirror of criticism as it reflected reality in its inevitably distortive glass. As a result it became possible, if not for the first time then surely for the first time on this scale of narrative amplitude and richness, to delight in the lifelike excitements of invented personages and adventures, and simultaneously to be reminded of that other world of ours, ruled by chance and given over to death. The mirror held to the mirror of art held to nature, in Cervantes and in his countless progeny, proved to be not merely an ingenious trick but a necessary operation for a skeptical culture nevertheless addicted, as all cultures have been, to the pleasures and discoveries of fabulation. Ongoing literary history is always modifying our vision of earlier stages of literary development, and the course of the novel from Joyce to Nabokov and beyond may to some degree require a shift of perspective upon what happened in the novel during the three centuries before our own. Today, as varieties of novelistic self-consciousness proliferate, the mode of fiction first defined when a certain aging hidalgo set out to imitate his books appears far from exhausted. On the contrary, in the hands of gifted writers it comes to seem increasingly our most precisely fashioned instrument for joining imagined acts and figures with real things.

Index